BARBECUE! BIBLE

BEST RIBS EVER

100 KILLER RECIPES
Including
SLAWS, BAKED BEANS & FINGER-LICKIN' SAUCES

STEVEN RAICHLEN

WORKMAN PUBLISHING
NEW YORK

Schaumburg Township District Library
130 South Roselle Road
Schaumburg, IL 60193

P9-BYK-845

641.76
RAICHLEN, S

3 1257 01936 0238

Copyright © 2006, 2012 by Steven Raichlen

Photographs © 2006, 2012 by Susan Goldman

Barbecue! Bible® is a registered trademark of
Steven Raichlen and Workman Publishing Co., Inc.

This book references websites that may be of interest to
the reader. Every effort has been made to ensure that the
information about these websites is correct and
up-to-date as of press time.

All rights reserved.
No portion of this book may be reproduced—
mechanically, electronically, or by any other means,
including photocopying—without written permission of
the publisher. Published simultaneously in Canada by
Thomas Allen & Son Limited.

Library of Congress Cataloging-in-Publication Data is available.
ISBN 978-0-7611-6894-2

Cover design: Raquel Jaramillo
Book design: Lisa Hollander
Cover and book photographs: Susan Goldman
Author photograph: Sylvia Pedras
Cover skewer: EuToch/istockphoto

Workman books are available at special discounts when
purchased in bulk for premiums and sales promotions as
well as for fund-raising or educational use. Special editions or
book excerpts can also be created to specification. For details,
contact the Special Sales Director at the address below or send
an e-mail to specialmarkets@workman.com.

Workman Publishing Company, Inc.
225 Varick Street
New York, NY 10014-4381
www.workman.com
www.barbecuebible.com

Printed in the U.S.A.
First printing, April 2012
10 9 8 7 6 5 4 3 2 1

DEDICATION

TO BARBARA, WHO WARMS MY BONES

■ ■ ■ ■

ACKNOWLEDGMENTS

his may be a small book, but it involved the help of a huge cast of characters. It gives me great pleasure to thank some of the many individuals who helped make it possible:

From Workman Publishing: Editor extraordinaire Suzanne Rafer; copy editor Barbara "Hawk-eye" Mateer; production editor Irene Demchyshyn; art directors Raquel Jaramillo and Lisa Hollander; photographer Susan Goldman; typesetter Barbara Peragine; publicist Selina Meere; marketing maven Jessica Wiener; sales wizard Walter Weintz; editorial assistant Erin Klabunde; and of course, all my other friends at Workman, including Bob Miller, Jenny Mandel, Pat Upton, and David Schiller; plus, the one and only Peter Workman.

Thanks, too, to the photogenic cast of Workman rib eaters, who were happy to "ham" it up for the camera.

From The Greenbrier, where the recipes for this book were tested: Rod Stoner, Peter Timmins, Sue Moats, Maria Battaglia, and Ken Clasen. Also Ethan Hileman, Ken Hess, Dave Thomas, James Crookshanks, Brenda Goins, Kathy Bailey, Dee Given, Bill Zimmerman, Raymond Ramos, Gunnard Cunningham, Lynn Swann, and Steve Halliday.

Pit masters and mistresses: KC Masterpiece creator, Rich Davis; Dinosaur Bar-B-Q founder, John Stage; BB's Lawnside founder, Lindsay Shannon; Joffre DiSabatino and George Holder from Porkosaurus; Dianna Fick, Philip Fick, Sandy and Danny Crabtree, and Mel and

Janet Holle; and other pit masters unnamed here who so generously shared their knowledge.

Thanks also goes to Heidi Friedlander, Linda and Fred Griffith, and Sanford Herskovitz, aka "Mister Brisket."

On the home team: Super kids Betsy and Jake; BBQ University producer Charlie Pinsky; manufacturing genius Chuck Adams; and legal eagle Mark Fischer and Leslie Arnold. A huge thanks to my ruthlessly efficient and completely indispensable assistant, Nancy Loseke, who did research, tested recipes, proofed these pages, and generally kept me on the straight and narrow.

And, above all, my lovely wife, Barbara, whose wisdom, good sense, and love inform everything I do.

CONTENTS

Hands down, this is America's favorite rib, here
cooked to glorious perfection. From the deliciously
simple First-Timer's Ribs to the Maple-Glazed Ribs of
Quebec to Chinatown Ribs, Buccaneer Baby Backs,
Peanut Butter Ribs, and Porkosaurus Memphis in May
Championship Ribs—these are ribs at their finest.

There's much more to pork ribs than
baby backs. Fire up the grill and test
out Jamaican Jerk Spareribs, Milk
and Honey Spareribs, BB's Rib
Tips, and Country-Style Ribs
with Chilean Pepper Sauce.

THE POPULAR CHOICE

The rib is surely the most perfect morsel of meat known to man. Most of the world's great food cultures back me on this. The Chinese have their lacquered sugar and soy spareribs. Argentineans prefer *tira de asado,* simply seasoned, crustily grilled, crosscut beef ribs. Koreans favor *kalbi kui,* slicing short ribs paper-thin, grilling them over charcoal, and serving them wrapped in lettuce leaves with a high-voltage array of *panchan* (pickled vegetables) and spicy condiments. Italians slow-cook pork spareribs with the age-old Mediterranean trinity of rosemary, garlic, and wine. Even lesser-known food cultures have their rib specialties, from Norway's *pinnekjøtt*—salted lamb ribs served with mashed rutabagas—to Brazil, where they marinate baby backs and expertly cook them on a rotisserie.

This doesn't begin to address the multiplicity of ribs enjoyed in the United States. If ribs are an article of faith in much of the world, in America they've evolved into a full-blown "religion." There are "sects" (adherents of spareribs, baby back ribs, or beef ribs, for example). There are "dogmas," including the best way to cook ribs, from smoking to indirect grilling to direct grilling. There are even "heresies," such as boiling, braising, or microwaving ribs before putting them on the grill (for an overview of the great rib debates, see page 59). But there *are* two points on which just about every American barbecue buff can agree: No self-respecting cookout is complete without some sort of rib. And when it comes to flavor and the pure, unadulterated enjoyment of eating barbecue, ribs are hard to beat.

What accounts for the rib's near universal popularity? I think there are a number of factors. First, meat that's next to the bone tends to be the best marbled and the most flavorful, and no other cut offers a higher proportion of bone to meat. Second, the rib bones give the meat structure, presenting a broad surface to smoke and fire and keeping the meat from shriveling up on the grill. Third, there's the sheer versatility of ribs, from the ubiquitous pork and beef to the more rarified lamb, veal, and bison. Fourth, ribs can be cooked using myriad methods, including smoking, indirect grilling, direct grilling, braising, stewing, and spit roasting. Many pit masters employ multiple methods, braising the ribs first, for example, then sizzling them on the grill to brown them. And portion sizes vary widely, ranging from the delicate single- or double-bone portions served by *robatayaki* (mixed grill) masters in Japan to the plate-burying slabs we've come to expect from pit masters in the United States.

Finally, ribs are just unabashedly fun to eat, evoking the memory of our cave-dwelling ancestors roasting meats over open fires and devouring them with no more finery than their bare hands. (Admit it: Part of the perennial pleasure of ribs is that you get to eat them with your fingers.) A rack of ribs—fragrant with spice, dark with smoke, glistening with fat and sauce—is the very embodiment of the spirit of barbecue.

WHY I WROTE THIS BOOK

This book has been "simmering" on my metaphorical back burner almost since the day I started writing about barbecue. But it really came into focus a few years ago when we ran a Lip-Smackin' Rib Recipe Contest on the www.barbecuebible.com website. I expected dozens, maybe hundreds of responses. We received literally thousands. I anticipated the predictable pork and beef ribs. We got recipes for lamb ribs, veal ribs, even venison ribs. I thought I'd see the usual barbecue rub and/or red sauce ribs in the style of Memphis or Kansas City. There were recipes seasoned with everything from Dr Pepper soda to coffee, black tea, green tea, chai tea, cherry juice, and . . . gasp! . . . Hershey's chocolate sauce.

The sheer number of entries and the ingenuity of the recipes led me to realize two things: Americans in general (and the www.barbecuebible.com community in particular) are even more obsessed with ribs than I knew. And, when it comes to mixing up rubs and concocting basting and barbecue sauces for ribs, no ingredient is off-limits, no flavor combination is too outlandish.

But, despite the popularity of these meaty staves, a surprising number of people are intimidated by the prospect of cooking ribs. (Granted, there *is* a lot of confusion surrounding ribs—how to season them, cook them, and serve them.) Whenever I teach a session of Barbecue University, I conduct an informal poll to see what dishes my students would most like to learn to make. Topping the list are how to grill fish and steak, and above all, how to grill the perfect ribs.

So, what will you find in this book? A complete crash course on the art of grilling and smoking ribs, including how to recognize the different cuts (and what to look for when buying them). A review of the various cooking methods, plus how and when to use each. And, of course, how to make rubs, the various spice pastes, marinades, mop and finishing sauces, basting mixtures and glazes, and all manner of barbecue sauces—and what they're best for.

■ ■ ■ ■ ■

RIBS 101

This may seem like a small book on a single topic, but it covers a big and complex subject. You might think that a rib is a rib is a rib—throw enough spice and wood smoke in its general direction, and you'll wind up with respectable bones. The fact is that, while cooking ribs is not complicated, there's an enormous amount of technique, tradition, lore, and yes, science behind preparing the perfect bones. In this chapter you'll learn about the various types of ribs and about rib anatomy. You'll become acquainted with the different methods for cooking ribs and how to use a variety of grills and smokers, not to mention useful grilling accessories, tools, and fuels. You'll get to know what constitutes a perfectly cooked rib (hint: it's *not* fall-off-the-bone tender). You'll learn such indispensable techniques as trimming ribs and recognizing when they're done. And throughout this book you'll find "rib tips"— ingenious rib cooking and serving advice from the pros.

AN ANATOMY LESSON: KNOW YOUR RIBS

All ribs are equal in their delectability, but not all ribs are alike. First, there's the species. Best known, and perhaps best loved, in North America (not to mention China) are pork ribs. But dine out in Argentina or Korea and you'll soon see that beef ribs are king. Lamb ribs may seem strange, or downright exotic, in Kansas City or Memphis, but they're common culinary currency throughout the Mediterranean, Middle and Near East, Central Asia, and India.

These "big three" meats dominate the world's barbecue scene, but a growing number of pit masters are serving bison (buffalo) ribs and veal ribs. A few years ago, one American chef and restaurateur, Rick Moonen, actually served fish ribs—the meaty bones of a giant Amazonian fish called the tambaqui. (Don't laugh; there's a developing commercial market for them in the United Kingdom.)

Even within a single animal, different cuts of ribs have remarkably different textures and flavors. The pork baby back rib is tender and well marbled—ideal for direct grilling or spit roasting. Spareribs are tougher, meatier, and more flavorful; they need a slower, gentler cooking method like indirect grilling or smoking. The rib tip is mostly connective tissue and cartilage, but gentle smoking transforms it into barbecue that has made at least one Kansas City rib emporium famous (you can read about it on page 156). The country-style rib is all about the meat; it cooks and tastes more like a pork chop than a rib.

Here are some common—and not so common— ribs that are available in the marketplace. As you work your way through this book and ascend the ladder of barbecue enlightenment, you'll want to sample each one.

To help orient you as to where on the animal a particular rib is located, imagine the cross section of the animal's rib cage to be the face of a clock, with the spine at 12 o'clock. In each case, the "time" I've given indicates where on both sides of the animal that particular cut of ribs comes from.

PORK RIBS

For many pit masters (especially those from the American South) the sun rises and sets on pork ribs. With good reason! Pork ribs are widely available, mercifully affordable, easy to cook, and richly flavored. Their taste is robust and versatile enough to stand up to all manner of rubs, glazes, and mop and barbecue sauces. At the same time, they have enough innate flavor to be delicious seasoned with nothing more than salt and pepper. Although they come from the same animal, not all pork ribs are alike. Here are the players.

TOP LOIN RIBS (FREQUENTLY CALLED BABY BACK RIBS)

If pork is the preferred meat of barbecue in many parts of the country, top loin ribs (most often referred to as baby backs) are America's favorite ribs. The reason is simple: They're the most tender, succulent, and generously marbled ribs on the hog. The top loin starts just below the backbone and extends down 4 to 5 inches (on our porcine clock face from 1 to 3 o'clock on one side and from 9 to 11 o'clock on the other). In general, the meat closest to the backbone is the most choice and tender—hence the expression "eating high off the hog." A full rack of top loin ribs consists of at least eight ribs and can have up to fourteen (most have twelve). Weighing between 2 and $2\frac{1}{2}$ pounds, a rack will normally feed two people. Another advantage of top loin ribs is that the racks are rectangular—the ribs are all more or less the same length, so you eat well no matter which end you're served.

How to cook top loin baby back ribs: By direct grilling, indirect grilling, smoking, grill-top braising, spit roasting—in short, any way you cook any rib.

"TRUE" BABY BACK RIBS

Although the term *baby back* is used widely to refer to top loin ribs, it means something different to rib purists. For them it refers to a small ($\frac{3}{4}$ to $1\frac{1}{4}$ pound), well-trimmed rack cut from the upper rib cage of a young hog. Sometimes, you see "true" baby backs at upscale butcher shops; Denmark is a major exporter. These racks are so small, you should allow one whole rack per person.

How to cook "true" baby back ribs: The way you would cook top loin ribs. They're especially good for direct grilling.

SPARERIBS

Continue down along the sides of the hog and you come to a section of ribs that are bigger, fattier, and tougher than top loins: spareribs. (On our porcine clock face, the spareribs extend from 3 to 6 o'clock and from 6 to 9 o'clock.) Bigger, fatter, and tougher may seem like drawbacks, but these qualities actually make spareribs more flavorful than top loins. That's why spareribs are frequently the bones of choice for skilled pit masters. A full rack of spareribs usually has thirteen ribs and, untrimmed, weighs 5 to 6 pounds, containing both the curved ribs from the side of the hog and a cartilaginous section located toward the belly and called the rib tips or brisket bone (see facing page). There's a flap of tough meat on the inside called the skirt or flap or brisket; it's almost always removed before cooking. The point, the small triangular end piece, is also usually cut off. A trimmed rack of spareribs typically weighs 3 to 4 pounds and will feed three or four people.

The bones at the shoulder end of a rack of spareribs can be as much as two to three inches longer than those at the loin end. This gives rise to the Kansas City expressions "long ends" and "short ends." Long ends tend to be a little tougher and meatier, short ends are slightly fattier and more tender. Both have their partisans.

How to cook spareribs: Because they're considerably tougher and fattier than top loin (baby back) ribs, spareribs are best cooked using the indirect method or smoked.

ST. LOUIS–CUT RIBS

Combine the compact size, rectangular shape, and relative tenderness of a rack of baby backs with the rich flavor of spareribs, and you get the cut we like to serve at Barbecue University: the St. Louis cut. This handsome rack (it really *is* handsome) is cut from the flattest part of the spareribs (approximately 3 to 5 o'clock and 7 to 9 o'clock using our clock face guide). It has the long, slender shape of a rack of baby backs. The rib tips, skirt, and point are always removed. St. Louis–cut ribs weigh 2 to 2½ pounds or more per rack and will comfortably feed two or three.

RIB TIPS

Rib tips (or brisket bone) are the cartilaginous lower part of a sparerib, often discarded on account of their abundant connective tissue and scant meat. But judiciously apply a rub and smoke the rib tips low and slow to soften the tough cartilage, as they do at BB's Lawnside in Kansas City (see page 156), and they become a dish worthy of reverse snobbery. (Frugal and savvy barbecuers sometimes freeze the tips to save for pork stock, or they throw them into a pot of baked beans.) On our porcine clock face, rib tips would roughly correspond to 5 to 6 o'clock and 6 to 7 o'clock. Rib tips vary in weight from 6 to 16 ounces, depending on what's been trimmed and where it's been trimmed from. Figure on one pound per person.

How to cook rib tips: Low and slow in a smoker or on a charcoal grill; that's what it takes to make the connective tissue edible—even delicious.

Note: In some circles the term *rib tip* is used to describe the point, the triangular end of a rack of spareribs. This point typically measures 3 to 4 inches across and has small bones or riblike strips of cartilage. You can cook the point as you would conventional rib tips.

PORK RIBLETS

This is a new cut that turns up at some mass-market restaurant chains, such as Applebee's. It applies to top loin ribs cut lengthwise on a meat saw into 1- to 2-inch-wide strips. As far as I know, this kind of riblets is not widely available at the retail level, although you could certainly ask your butcher to cut some for you.

How to cook riblets: Any way you would cook top loin ribs, with the exception of spit roasting; they're too slender to thread on a spit. But some butchers call the point—the triangular section of meat at the end of a rack of spareribs or baby backs—riblets. This sort of riblets can have bones or be boneless. Cook these riblets just like you would rib tips. Figure on ¾ to 1 pound of riblets per person.

COUNTRY-STYLE RIBS

The country-style rib is actually a sort of long, skinny pork chop cut from the upper shoulder, or blade, end of the loin. If left whole, it has three to six bones. Usually, however, country-style ribs are cut apart before being sold and are often deboned. Country-style ribs are meaty and generally weigh about a third of a pound each; two ribs will serve one person amply. Fastidious diners take note: This is one rib you'll want to eat with a knife and fork.

How to cook country-style ribs: Country-style ribs taste best grilled directly over the fire, like pork chops. You can also use the indirect method.

BEEF RIBS

Cattle also have ribs, of course—thirteen pairs, to be exact. These meaty staves can bring out the carnivore—and caveman—in just about all of us. Beef ribs combine the rich meaty flavor of steer with the bone-gnawing pleasure of pork ribs. Although some cuts possess an abundance of tough connective tissue, all can be rendered delicious by a savvy application of indirect heat and wood smoke.

BEEF LONG RIBS

Beef long ribs—also called beef spareribs, back ribs, or Texas ribs—are the racks that remain when the butcher bones a prime rib to make a tied rib roast or boneless rib eye steaks. A full rack will consist of seven bones (ribs six through twelve), with the bones varying in length from 6 to 8 inches. (On a bovine clock face, the long ribs would correspond to 1 to 3 o'clock and 9 to 11 o'clock.)

Generally, beef long ribs are not very meaty. Butchers have an economic incentive to trim as much meat as possible from the bones, as prime rib and related cuts sell for much higher prices than ribs. However, you can purchase a whole bone-in rib roast and request that the butcher debone it, leaving a generous portion of meat on the rib rack. A typical rack of beef back ribs weighs $2\frac{1}{2}$ to 3 pounds and will feed two or three people. Meatier racks may feed four.

How to cook beef long ribs: Because they come from the prime rib, beef long ribs are relatively tender. I like to cook them at the higher temperature range of indirect grilling or smoke roast them, but you can also smoke them low and slow.

INDIVIDUAL BEEF LONG RIBS

Cut from the chuck (front) end of the animal's rib cage, individual beef ribs (sometimes poetically called "dinosaur bones") have considerably more meat left on them than those cut to form a rack from the prime rib area farther down the back. (On the bovine clock face, the ribs would line up at 1 to 3 o'clock and 9 to 11 o'clock.) Of course, since they are cut from the chuck end, they're a bit tougher, as they come from active muscle. Cooked right, this is no problem. The meaty single ribs are less common than racks; you may need to order them ahead from your butcher. One of these staves is almost a meal in itself, tipping the scale at 9 to 12 ounces.

How to cook individual beef long ribs: Individual beef long ribs give you plenty to gnaw on, but as the meat *is* a bit tough, you'll need to cook them slowly using the indirect method and at a low temperature on a charcoal grill or a smoker.

BEEF SHORT RIBS

This is a catchall category that includes ribs from the chuck end and from the middle rib (the plate section) of a steer's lower rib cage. On a bovine clock face, the short ribs would be between 3 and 4 o'clock and 8 to 9 o'clock. Their rich flavor—not to mention relatively modest price—has endeared them to chefs high and low (you'll sometimes find them featured on the menus of tony New York restaurants like Per Se and Café Gray). Bone-in short ribs are roughly 2-inch-long pieces of rib bone topped by a thick layer of flavorful, well-marbled, but tough meat (you can also buy them boneless). They are sold both as individual bones and in strips of three or four ribs. Short ribs are often sold by the pound. Depending on the length of the bone and the amount of meat on it, a single short rib can weigh 4 to 7 ounces; figure on ¾ to 1 pound per person.

How to cook short ribs: Pit masters and chefs have devised multiple strategies for making these tough but tasty ribs palatable. The short list includes tenderizing short ribs by smoking, stewing, braising, and even by cutting the meat off the bone in paper-thin sheets to be grilled directly over a charcoal fire (that's the technique used to make one of Korea's national dishes, *kalbi kui,* see page 191). I often wrap short ribs in aluminum foil during the grilling process for a modified braise; the steam and juices that are trapped in the foil penetrate and soften the connective tissue.

CROSSCUT BEEF RIBS

A traditional Argentinean cut, crosscut beef ribs have started to appear in meat markets in Miami and other

American cities with large Latino communities. Called *tira de asado* in Spanish, they're made by cutting short ribs crosswise with a meat saw into long, plate-overhanging strips that are $1/4$ to $1/2$ inch wide (for a recipe see page 199). The "official" name of this cut in the United States is beef flanken–style ribs; on our bovine clock face, they'd line up between 2 to 4 o'clock and 8 and 10 o'clock. You may find crosscut beef ribs labeled flanken. These can be as wide as 2 inches; to make *tira de asado* make sure the ribs you buy are no more than $1/2$ inch wide. One serving is about 12 ounces.

How to cook crosscut beef ribs: Grill them using the direct method, just as you would grill a steak.

LAMB RIBS

L amb ribs aren't what you'd call commonplace in the United States. I first tasted them in the 1980s at an infamous Boston rib joint called Hoodoo Barbecue (more on page 238). But lamb ribs are widely enjoyed in Europe, North Africa, Australia, and New Zealand, where they're grilled directly over the fire or roasted on a spit. Lamb breast ribs are as popular in Australia as pork baby backs are in the United States.

When it comes to the various cuts of lamb ribs, the nomenclature is somewhat fuzzy. All lamb rib cuts come from the breast, a roughly 6-pound section of the lower rib cage loaded with meat, fat, and connective tissue. Hormel Foods' glossary divides lamb ribs into three categories: spareribs, Denver ribs, and riblets. Lamb spareribs, large slabs of ribs with more bone and fat than meat, are sometimes seen in butcher shops. On an ovine clock face, the spareribs would correspond to 4 to 5 o'clock and 7 to 8 o'clock. They're best cooked by an indirect method, such as indirect grilling, smoke roasting, or smoking.

DENVER RIBS

L amb spareribs that have been trimmed of most of the fat and connective tissue are frequently referred to as

Denver ribs (you may also see the trimmed ribs sold as lamb breast). A rack of Denver ribs usually consists of seven or eight ribs. Typically, they weigh around a pound, although some are as small as 10 ounces and others are as large as a pound and a half. A rack of Denver ribs will serve one person.

How to cook Denver ribs: Thanks to their tenderness, Denver ribs can be cooked by any method—direct grilling, indirect grilling, smoke roasting, smoking, spit roasting, or even braising with a little liquid in an aluminum foil–covered roasting pan away from direct heat.

LAMB RIBLETS

Lamb riblets are individual rib bones cut from a rack of spareribs. Typically there are five riblets to a pound; you can count on five or six riblets as a serving.

How to cook lamb riblets: Lamb riblets tend to be somewhat tougher than Denver ribs, but they can be cooked using the same methods.

VEAL RIBS

When most people think of veal and bones, they picture veal chops, but calves possess ribs, just as steers do. Veal ribs aren't nearly as widely available as beef ribs, but persistence will reward you some of the sweetest, tenderest meat and bones on the planet. You may get lucky and find them at your local supermarket. Or on page 305, you'll find Mail-Order Sources.

VEAL LONG RIBS

Combine the sweet, delicate flavor of veal with the tenderness of pork baby backs and you get one of the most appealing racks on the barbecue trail: veal ribs. A veal rack can range from six to twelve bones and weigh $1\frac{1}{4}$ to $1\frac{1}{2}$ pounds. (They are located between 1 and 4 o'clock and

8 and 11 o'clock on a bovine clock face.) But like beef long bones, veal long ribs are difficult to find in the retail marketplace because they usually come attached to higher-priced chops or rib roasts. (As with beef ribs, you can buy a whole bone-in roast from the butcher and ask that it be deboned, leaving more meat than is customary on the bones.) One rack of veal ribs serves one or two people.

How to cook veal long ribs: Indirect grilling, smoke roasting, smoking, and spit roasting are all good methods for cooking veal long ribs. They're certainly tender enough to be grilled directly.

VEAL SHORT RIBS

Veal short ribs are also relatively elusive in the marketplace. I suspect restaurant chefs have a corner on the market, as they are appearing on more and more menus. Cut from the chuck, veal short ribs are meaty and much more tender than short ribs of fully grown cattle. Each weighs about a quarter of a pound. Two ribs will make a serving—three for more robust appetites.

How to cook veal short ribs: Veal short ribs are theoretically tender enough to grill using the direct method but are best, I think, when slowly indirect grilled or smoke roasted over low heat. Braising is an option, too.

VEAL BREAST RIBLETS

Most consumers want their veal breasts boned, making the veal breast ribs relatively easy to find, particularly if you order them in advance. (On the clock face, they are between 4 and 5 o'clock and 7 and 8 o'clock.) Veal riblets are small and come in racks of about nine ribs; sometimes they are cut into single rib pieces. Figure on at least four to six ribs per person.

How to cook veal breast riblets: Low and slow using the indirect method, smoke roasting, smoking, or braising—you want the fat to break down and the connective tissue to soften, rendering veal breast riblets delectable.

BISON RIBS

Bison (aka buffalo) was the red meat of choice in North America for 10,000 years or so prior to the arrival of the first European settlers. Within three hundred years, this regal beast was hunted almost to extinction. Leaner and a bit sweeter than beef, bison has begun to return to the range and the barbecue pit. (CNN founder Ted Turner owns the world's largest private bison herd, approximately 40,000 heads.) Of course, it's unlikely you'll find bison ribs, either long or short, in the meat section of your local supermarket— at least not yet. But you can purchase them through specialty butchers or order them online or by mail (see Mail-Order Sources on page 305). A typical rack of bison long ribs contains eight to ten ribs, each 6 to 8 inches long, and weighs 5 to 6 pounds; it will serve two or three people. One bison short rib makes a meaty feast as each weighs about three quarters of a pound.

How to cook bison ribs: I cook bison long ribs just like I cook beef long ribs. Using marinades and basting or mop sauces and/or wrapping the ribs in aluminum foil can all help keep them from drying out. You'll find a recipe for bison long ribs on page 215.

As for bison short ribs, again, I'd use the same methods as for beef short ribs: Tenderize them by smoking, stewing, braising, low and slow indirect grilling, or smoke roasting.

FISH RIBS

Yes, if you look hard enough, you can even find fish ribs (no, this isn't a fish story). The Amazonian fish tambaqui can grow to be up to a yard long and weigh 66 pounds. It has teeth like a horse, which it uses to chew nuts and seeds. And its bones are strong enough that its ribs can be cooked and served just like, well, ribs. Keep that in mind the next time you pull a Harrison Ford on the Amazon.

EIGHT ESSENTIAL TECHNIQUES FOR PREPPING & COOKING RIBS

Ribs are easy to cook, but there's more to the process than simply throwing them on the grill. A proper rack needs to be trimmed and peeled, seasoned or marinated, and mopped and sauced at the right intervals. You also have to know when they're done. Here's an eight-point game plan.

1 TRIM THE RIBS

Chances are, if you buy pork baby backs or beef ribs at the supermarket, they'll come already trimmed. If you see any large lumps of fat, sinews, or loose pieces of bone, cut them off with a paring knife.

Spareribs, on the other hand, often come with the rib tips (cartilaginous ends) and point (a triangle of small bones and sinewy meat at the loin end of the rack) attached. Using a sharp knife and following the line of fat at the base of the ribs, cut off the rib tips. Then cut off the pointed end of the rack of ribs. This will give the rack a neat, rectangular appearance (the point and the rib tips can be cooked separately—see the recipe on page 156 for rib tips). And, if the rack has one, remove the tough flap of meat (the skirt or flap) from the bone side. You can use it to flavor baked beans or for making stock. The more evenly you shape the rectangle of the rack, the more evenly the ribs will cook.

2 REMOVE THE MEMBRANE

Most racks of ribs come with a papery membrane on the bone side. I recommend removing this for a couple of reasons. It impedes the absorption of spice and smoke flavors, and it's tougher than the rest of the rib meat. Two good tools to help you get under the membrane so you can pull it off are a butter knife or the tip of a meat thermometer. You'll find detailed instructions for removing the membrane in each recipe.

3 SEASON THE RIBS WITH A RUB OR MARINADE

You *can* cook ribs seasoned with nothing more than salt and pepper (and on page 174, you'll find a great recipe for salt and pepper beef ribs). Most pit masters opt for the more complex flavors of a full-blown rub or marinade. Rubs are blends of spices, herbs, and often salt. You sprinkle one over the ribs, then rub it onto the meat, which is why it's called a rub. Rubs can be applied right before cooking, in which case, they act like a seasoned salt. Or they can be applied four to six hours—or even a half day—ahead, in which case, the rub cures the meat in addition to seasoning it. Throughout the book, you'll find many recipes for rubs.

A marinade is a wet seasoning, comprised of flavorful liquids, like wine, soy sauce, fruit juice, or olive oil, to name a few, plus spices and aromatic vegetables, like garlic, ginger, or chiles. Marinades are often used to make Asian-style ribs (for example, the Chinatown Ribs on page 77), but they're also frequently used by pit masters in North America. I like disposable heavy aluminum foil drip pans or large resealable plastic bags for marinating.

Always keep meats in the refrigerator as they marinate. Avoid reactive metal containers—unlined aluminum, for example, or cast iron—for marinating, especially with such acidic ingredients as tomatoes, citrus juice, or vinegar. And, *never* reuse a marinade that's been in contact with raw meat as a baste or as a sauce unless you boil it briskly for three minutes to kill any bacteria. Strain the boiled marinade before using.

A wet rub features the best of both; it's a seasoning paste that's thicker than a normal marinade and wetter than a rub. One great example is the wet rub in the Sake-Grilled Short Ribs on page 188.

4 USE A RIB RACK

Only two racks of ribs will fit flat on most kettle grills, but there's an easy way to double the capacity (and the number of people you can feed): Cook the ribs upright in a rib rack. See page 52 for a description.

5 MOP THE RIBS

Direct and indirect grilling and smoking are inherently dry cooking methods. One option for keeping ribs moist is to mop them with a mop sauce. Mop sauces contain little or no sugar, so you can apply them throughout the cooking process without them burning. Use a barbecue mop (see page 50) or basting brush for applying mop sauces. Or, you can pour the mop sauce into a spray bottle and squirt it on the ribs.

6 WRAP THE RIBS, IF NECESSARY

Depending on the size and weight of the ribs, the heat of your grill, and the intensity of the smoke, among other factors, ribs may start to dry out before they've reached the optimal tenderness. Don't worry if this happens—there's an easy solution: Wrap them tightly in aluminum foil and continue grilling. Wrapping seals in moisture because the steam captured will help tenderize the ribs. Be careful when you unwrap the ribs; the escaping steam can burn your fingers.

7 SAUCE THE RIBS—OR NOT

Purists will argue that a great rib doesn't need sauce (see Great Debates in the Realm of Ribs on page 59). Nonetheless, most people prefer their ribs with at least a light basting of barbecue sauce. What I often do is grill the ribs indirectly until they reach the desired tenderness, then lightly baste them with sauce and move them directly over the fire to sizzle the sauce into the meat. The idea is to use the sauce as a sort of light varnish for the ribs, rather than a thick gloppy coating that camouflages the meat.

8 LEARN TO RECOGNIZE WHEN THE RIBS ARE COOKED

The two keys to master grillmanship are learning to control the fire (and consequently the heat) and to tell when the ribs are done. We use a three-part doneness test at Barbecue University. Here's what to look for:

A. An exterior that's darkly browned and crusty.

B. Meat that has shrunk back about ¼ inch from the ends of the bones (or a little more on large beef ribs). I call this a rib's built-in "pop-up thermometer."

C. Meat that's tender enough to tear apart with your fingers. Remember, a rib should have some chew to it.

In addition, if you're smoking ribs, when you cut into one you'll see a layer of reddish pink just beneath the surface. This is called the smoke ring, and it occurs naturally when you expose meat to wood smoke for an extended period of time. I call it the "red badge of honor" of barbecue: If your ribs have one, you've done them right. Display the smoke ring proudly to your guests, taking full advantage of your bragging rights.

■ ■ ■ ■

HOW TO COOK RIBS:
SIX GREAT LIVE-FIRE TECHNIQUES

O K, you've prepped your ribs. The next step is to pick the right method for cooking them perfectly. Fortunately, there are six live-fire methods to choose from. Each one is suited to particular kinds of ribs, and each produces a unique texture and taste.

DIRECT GRILLING

Cooking ribs directly over glowing embers or on a gas-fired grill may not be the first technique that comes to mind for most American pit masters. After all, don't ribs have a lot of fat and connective tissue? If you grill them using the direct method, won't the exterior burn before the meat becomes tender? And won't the dripping fat turn your grill into a blazing inferno? Not according to pit masters in Mexico, Italy, and Japan, where ribs are routinely grilled right over the fire. The lively heat produces a crusty, smokily charred exterior (especially when cooking over wood) and a moist interior with a mercifully firm, meaty consistency.

Of course, you cannot just throw any slab of ribs over a raging fire and expect the best. You must pick a rib properly suited to direct grilling, such as a tender rack like baby back pork ribs or lamb or veal ribs. Next, you need to work over a medium-low to medium fire and have a fire-free safety zone where you can move the ribs should you get flare-ups (see Direct Grilling: Two- and Three-Zone Fires, on page 31). Finally, it's important to take your time—twelve to twenty minutes per side—and not to crowd the grill. Follow these simple steps, and you'll be rewarded with ribs that have as much in common with steak as they do with traditional barbecue.

Instructions for setting up charcoal and gas grills for direct grilling are found on pages 29 and 30.

Ribs well suited for direct grilling include:
Pork—top loin baby backs, "true" baby backs, St. Louis–cut, and country-style ribs; *beef*—Korean-style thinly sliced short ribs (*kalbi kui*) and Argentinean-style crosscut short ribs (*tira de asado*); *veal* ribs; and *lamb* ribs.

MODIFIED DIRECT GRILLING

I'm not sure you'll find the term *modified direct grilling* in barbecue textbooks, but it seems the best way to describe a technique that bridges direct and indirect grilling. It's the method of choice at one of America's landmark barbecue restaurants, the Rendezvous in Memphis, Tennessee. In modified direct grilling, the ribs cook directly over glowing coals but on a grate positioned high above the fire. This unique configuration allows the ribs to grill without burning; the temperature is more akin to that of indirect grilling than direct. And thanks to the distance from the heat source, dripping fat never really develops into threatening flare-ups.

If you own a table grill or have a built-in stone or brick barbecue, you may be able to lift the grate high enough above the fire to adapt it to modified direct grilling (it should be 12 to 24 inches from the fire). Another way to achieve the same effect is to grill the ribs in a kamado cooker (see page 41), which has a fixed grate positioned well above the coals.

Ribs well suited for modified direct grilling include: *Pork*—top loin baby backs, "true" baby backs, St. Louis–cut, and country-style ribs; *beef*—Korean-style thinly sliced short ribs (*kalbi kui*) and Argentinean-style cross-cut short ribs (*tira de asado*); *veal* ribs; and *lamb* ribs.

INDIRECT GRILLING

This (and smoke roasting, see facing page) are probably my personal favorite ways to cook most ribs. Admittedly, the cooking is done at a higher temperature than the pit smoking done by the "low and slow" boys on the barbecue circuit. But if you're cooking a relatively tender, well-marbled rib, like a baby back or beef long rib, you want a higher heat, so you can melt out the fat while you sizzle and crisp the meat fibers. Ribs grilled using the indirect method will have crust, chew, and character; a smoked rib is mere tender perfection (not that there's anything wrong with mere tender perfection).

Instructions for setting up charcoal and gas grills for indirect grilling are found on page 33.

Ribs well suited for indirect grilling include: *Pork*—top loin baby backs, spareribs, St. Louis–cut, and rib tips; *beef*—long ribs and short ribs; *veal* ribs; *bison* ribs; *lamb* ribs.

SMOKE ROASTING

This may be a new term for many of you, and yet it's something you might have done for years. Smoke roasting, simply defined, is indirect grilling with wood smoke. So why bother making the distinction? Well, in many cultures, wood smoke is not part of the barbecue tradition. Turks, Thais, and Taiwanese, to name a few, cook ribs over charcoal but do not use wood for smoke.

Indirect grilling can be done on a gas or charcoal grill; successful smoke roasting can only be done over charcoal or on a wood-burning grill. While I use the indirect method to cook Asian-style (smokeless) ribs, smoke roasting is one of the ways I make true-blue American barbecue. Instructions for setting up a charcoal grill for smoke roasting are found on page 33.

Ribs well suited for smoke roasting include: *Pork*—top loin baby backs, spareribs, and rib tips; *beef*—long ribs and short ribs; *veal* ribs; *bison* ribs; *lamb* ribs.

SMOKING

This is the traditional way to cook ribs in the American South and Midwest. When it comes to softening the tough connective tissue in ribs, melting out the fat, and imbuing the meat with smoke flavor, no other cooking method comes close. True smoking is an indirect method: The ribs cook next to, not directly over, the fire (or if they're over the fire, they're so high above it, they don't face full-on heat). What distinguishes smoking is the low cooking temperature, typically 225° to 250°F, and the long cooking time, four to six hours for pork spareribs or beef long or short ribs. The low, slow smoking produces traditional American barbecue at its best.

Descriptions of a variety of smokers are found beginning on page 43.

Ribs well suited for true smoking include: *Pork*—top loin baby backs, spareribs, St. Louis–cut ribs, rib tips, and riblets; *beef*—long and short ribs; *bison* ribs; *veal* ribs; and *lamb* ribs.

SPIT ROASTING

The rotisserie is ideal for grilling ribs. This method has two advantages: The lateral heat sizzles and crisps the meat fibers while melting out the fat, without burning or overcooking. And, the gentle rotation bastes the ribs in their own juices and that melting fat, keeping them amazingly moist. Not surprisingly, rotisserie ribs turn up often on the world's barbecue trail. I've enjoyed them in countries as diverse as France, Italy, Turkey, Singapore, and Brazil. What's surprising is that you don't find them more in the United States.

If you own a charcoal grill, you can buy a rotisserie attachment for it. In any case, follow the manufacturer's instructions for setting the rotisserie up. For what to look for in a rotisserie, see page 47.

Ribs well suited for spit roasting include: *Pork*—top loin baby backs, "true" baby backs, and St. Louis–cut ribs; *veal* ribs; and *lamb* ribs.

COOKING METHODS YOU'LL FIND IN OTHER BOOKS

Not every cook—or culture—has ready access to grilling outdoors. So, human culinary ingenuity has devised a number of techniques for cooking ribs indoors. Here's a quick overview.

BOILING

Cooking ribs in a pot of boiling water or other liquid—if that's your rib-cooking tradition, OK. But boiling can be the starting point for many misguided barbecuers, who believe that because ribs are tough and fatty, they need to be tenderized and purged of fat by hot water. True, boiling accomplishes these goals, but it also robs the ribs of their flavor, character, and soul. Some pit masters try to recover these qualities by searing boiled ribs on a hot grill with barbecue sauce. The simple truth is, you can achieve perfect tenderness and cook out excess fat by smoking, smoke roasting, indirect grilling, direct grilling, or spit roasting—with infinitely more flavor and style.

BAKING

Unlike boiling, the method of baking ribs in the oven at least features a dry heat. This is more likely to caramelize the meat proteins and brown the meat, generating flavor. Indirect grilling accomplishes everything that baking does, again with a lot more flavor and style.

BRAISING

Braising combines the advantages of boiling and baking: The ribs cook in a covered roasting pan with aromatic root vegetables, herbs, spices, and just a little liquid. The French and Italians are masters of this technique. And, the good news for aspiring pit masters is that you can braise in an aluminum foil pan on the grill—and add wood smoke to boot (for an example, see Beppe's Ribs on page 147).

DEEP-FRYING

The Chinese often finish cooking baked or braised pork ribs by deep-frying them in oil, producing a crackling crisp crust and lacquerlike finish. It's hard to argue with the incredibly tasty results, except to say: It may be delicious—but it's not barbecue.

HOW TO MAKE GRILL-QUALITY RIBS INDOORS

Warning: Do not read this unless you are an apartment dweller with absolutely no access to a grill or a smoker outdoors. No hibachi on the fire escape or grill in your condominium's recreation area. No in-laws in the suburbs or former frat buddy with a grill on his deck. Ribs really do taste better when cooked and served outdoors. Use the following techniques only if outdoor grilling or smoking is not an option.

STOVE-TOP SMOKER METHOD

The stove-top smoker is a device of cunning simplicity; it's a rectangular stainless steel box with a drip pan, a wire rack for holding the food, and a tight-fitting metal lid. One infallible brand is Camerons, available at many cookware shops and via mail order.

To use a stove-top smoker, you place one or two tablespoons of hardwood smoking chips (also available from Camerons) in the bottom of the smoker. Line the drip pan with aluminum foil and place it on top. Insert the food rack and arrange the rubbed, marinated, or otherwise seasoned ribs on top. The smoker will accommodate one large or two small racks of baby backs; you may need to cut a large rack in half to make it fit. Place the smoker over high heat for three minutes, then reduce the heat to medium and smoke the ribs until they're cooked through. They'll be done in less than an hour.

COUNTERTOP ROTISSERIE METHOD

"Set it and forget it." With these words—and with a cleverly designed countertop rotisserie, the prototype of which was an aquarium with a heating element—master pitchman Ron Popeil launched a revolution in spit roasting. His Showtime rotisserie may seem simple, but it does a bang-up job of spit roasting ribs. Spit roasting is a great way to brown and crisp the meat and cook out the excess fat. All you need is one of those Showtime rotisseries with a flat wire rotisserie basket. I'm sure you can pay for it in three easy installments.

To spit roast ribs, season them with your preferred rub and cut them into sections that will fit in the rotisserie basket. Tightly close the basket and attach it to the spit. If your rotisserie has a temperature control, set it to 400°F. Turn on the motor and cook the ribs until they are dark brown and crusty and the meat has shrunk back about a quarter inch from the ends of the bones, forty minutes to an hour. You can also cook pork, beef, and lamb ribs in this fashion. Countertop spit roasting will not give you a smoke flavor; for that, baste the cooked ribs with Steve's Smoky Butter Baste (page 28).

OVEN METHOD

Yes, you can even cook acceptable ribs in the oven. Hundreds of chain restaurants do this. After all, what is an oven, but a gas (or electric) grill marooned indoors and set up for permanent indirect grilling?

To bake ribs, preheat the oven to 350°F. Season the ribs with your favorite rub or seasoning. Place a wire rack in a roasting pan and arrange the ribs, bone side down, in a single layer on top. Bake the ribs until browned and tender and the meat has shrunk back from the ends of the bones about a quarter inch. Pork baby backs will take $1\frac{1}{4}$ to $1\frac{1}{2}$ hours; spareribs will take $1\frac{1}{2}$ to 2 hours. Beef ribs will take $1\frac{1}{2}$ to 2 hours. And, lamb ribs will take forty-five minutes to $1\frac{1}{2}$ hours depending upon their size. During the last half hour, start basting the ribs with Steve's Smoky Butter Baste (page 28), basting them two or three times.

To sizzle the ribs with barbecue sauce, like you can do when grilling outdoors, brush the cooked ribs with the sauce of your choice. Preheat the broiler to high, then broil the ribs until the sauce is sizzling and browned, two to four minutes per side.

Just one thing: Under no circumstances does cooking ribs indoors give you license to boil them first.

STEVE'S SMOKY BUTTER BASTE

Desperate times call for desperate measures. A few years ago, I found myself on the set of a Japanese television show, about to face Iron Chef Rokusaburo Michiba in a "Battle of the Barbecue Gods." I had a rudimentary grill, but no smoker. I also had some butter and a bottle of liquid smoke, which I combined to make this smoky butter baste.

Liquid smoke has a bad rep in barbecue circles, in part because people are tempted to use it as an alternative to achieving a smoke flavor the traditional way, with smoldering hardwood. Liquid smoke is, in fact, a natural product, made by burning logs, condensing the smoke in a still, and mixing it with water. Used judiciously, liquid smoke makes terrific barbecue sauces (for example, see the Lemon Brown Sugar Barbecue Sauce on page 57). If you have to cook your ribs on a gas grill or indoors, the smoky butter baste here will bring you closer to the full glory of ribs slowly smoked in a pit. Just ask the Iron Chef.

4 tablespoons ($^1/_2$ stick) salted butter
2 teaspoons liquid smoke

Melt the butter in a small saucepan over medium heat. Remove the saucepan from the heat and stir in the liquid smoke. Use the baste sparingly. (Remember, as you ascend the ladder of barbecue enlightenment, your ultimate goal is to learn to achieve a profound smoke flavor with actual logs or wood chunks.)

HOW TO SET UP A GRILL

Whether you favor charcoal or gas, you need to know how to set up the grill. You'll find basic instructions here, followed by guidelines on how to use charcoal and gas grills for direct and indirect grilling, smoke roasting, and smoking. For an overview of the merits of a variety of specific types of grills, see What to Cook Your Ribs On: A Quick Guide to Grills and Smokers, on page 39.

CHARCOAL GRILLS

In the old days, or at any rate, when I was growing up, lighting a grill was easy. You dumped the charcoal in the grill, doused it with lighter fluid, and threw on a match. The coals in the center generally lit; the coals on the periphery generally did not. And unless you had the patience to wait until all the coals were glowing red and ashed over, your food may or may not have had a petroleum taste that many people of my generation associated with the taste of barbecue.

Today, we use a device called a chimney starter—an upright metal cylinder or box with a wire or perforated metal partition in it. You put the charcoal in the top, then place a sheet of crumpled newspaper or a paraffin starter (a waxy, white, nonpetroleum fire starter the size and shape of an ice cube) in the bottom and touch a match to it. The coals will become neatly lit in the chimney.

There are three advantages to using a chimney starter: It eliminates the need for petroleum-based lighter fluid. The chimney's upright shape fosters even burning—no more unlit coals on the edges. And, the chimney starter allows you to move the coals easily and dump them where you want.

This is a good place for a word about natural lump charcoal versus charcoal briquettes. Lump charcoal consists of logs or pieces of wood that have been burnt long enough in an oxygen-free kiln to cook out the water and most of the smoke-producing compounds. The result is lightweight and burns clean and hot, although not for quite as long as briquettes.

Briquettes are made by combining ground-up charcoal, coal dust, wood scraps, sawdust, borax, and petroleum binders. Briquettes burn more evenly than lump charcoal and hold a consistently high heat for longer.

I personally prefer lump charcoal, but as long as you completely light briquettes and allow the lighter fluid to burn off, you'll get fine results. Just for the record, a lot of highly decorated pit masters still use the old briquette and lighter fluid method and produce prizewinners.

GAS GRILLS

Gas grills light with little more than the turn of a knob and the push of a button, but there are several points to keep in mind for cooking safely and efficiently with propane.

Have enough propane on hand. There's nothing worse than running out of gas in the middle of cooking ribs for twenty. I recommend keeping an extra full cylinder on hand at all times.

Store all propane cylinders in an upright position, away from heat and certainly away from your grill.

When you hook a propane cylinder up to the grill, make sure there are no leaks. You can do this by smelling for gas or by making a gas detection liquid. This is a mixture of equal parts liquid dish soap and water. You brush it onto the hoses and couplings: If there are any leaks, you'll see bubbles.

Once the cylinder is attached, turn on the valve at the top of the tank. Then turn on the control knob on the grill and push the starter.

Always have the lid open when lighting a gas grill. Failure to do so may result in a gas buildup and explosion. This is not a joking matter. I've seen it happen.

Finally, make sure the grill is really lit. Hold your hand over the lit portion until you can feel heat. If ignition fails the first few times, turn off the grill control knob as well as the valve at the top of the tank. Disconnect and reconnect the tank, then try again.

DIRECT GRILLING: TWO- AND THREE-ZONE FIRES

Many pit masters—especially in Europe and Latin America—grill ribs directly over the fire. The result is ribs with a sizzling crispy crust and firm meaty texture. But, how do you direct grill a tough, fatty cut of meat like ribs without burning them or causing flare-ups? The secret is to build a multizone fire. You control how quickly the ribs cook by moving them from a hot zone to a cooler zone. If the ribs start to burn or cause flare-ups, you can transfer them to the safety zone. A multizone fire can have either two or three zones.

FOR A TWO-ZONE FIRE

You'll want to use a two-zone fire when grilling "true" baby back and St. Louis–cut pork ribs, veal ribs, and lamb ribs.

THE THREE RULES OF DIRECT GRILLING

When it comes to direct grilling, I have a little mantra for success: Keep it hot. Keep it clean. Keep it lubricated.
  Which is to say, start with a hot grill grate. Brush it clean with a stiff wire brush. Then, oil it well with a tightly folded paper towel you've dipped in a small bowl of vegetable oil. Hold the paper towel with tongs and draw it across the bars of the grill grate.
  I call this practicing good grill hygiene. It makes your life easier in three ways:
  A hot grate is easier to clean than a cool grate.
  Food sears better on a hot grate than on a cool grate.
  Food is less likely to stick to a hot grate than a cool grate.

To build a two-zone fire in a **charcoal grill,** light charcoal in a chimney starter (see page 29). Dump out the coals on one side of the grill and rake them into a single layer covering half the firebox (the bottom of the grill). Use a grill hoe (see page 50) or garden hoe to rake out the coals. Leave the other side of the grill bare. You'll need more coals for a medium fire (325° to 350°F), fewer for a low fire (225° to 250°F). As a general rule, a double-thick layer of coals will produce a hot fire; a single layer of coals will produce a medium fire; and a single layer of coals spread out more sparsely will produce a low fire. Use the Mississippi test to check the heat (see page 35).

To build a two-zone fire on a **gas grill,** if your grill has two burners, set one burner to the temperature you need and leave the other burner turned off. On a front-to-back three-burner gas grill, turn on the rear two burners and leave the front burner off. With four- or six-burner gas grills, set half of the burners to the desired temperature.

FOR A THREE-ZONE FIRE

Use a three-zone fire for grilling country-style pork ribs, thinly sliced beef short ribs, and cross-cut beef short ribs.

To build a three-zone fire in a **charcoal grill,** light charcoal in a chimney starter (see page 29). Dump out the coals on one side of the grill and rake roughly two thirds of them into a double-thick layer over one third of the firebox. Rake the remaining third into a single layer in the center of the firebox. Leave one third of the firebox bare. The double-thick layer of coals is a hot zone for searing. The single layer is a medium zone for cooking. The coal-free part is the safety zone. Use the Mississippi test to check the heat (see page 35).

To build a three-zone fire on a **gas grill,** if your grill has two burners, set one burner on high and the other one on medium. Use the warming rack as the safety zone. On a front-to-back three-burner gas grill, set the rear burner on high, the middle burner on medium, and leave the front burner turned off. With a four- or six-burner gas grill, set two burners on high, one or two on medium, and leave the others turned off as a safety zone.

INDIRECT GRILLING

The foolproof method for cooking ribs, indirect grilling is easy to do, utterly reliable, and practiced by millions of American grill masters. You can grill using the indirect method on a gas or a charcoal grill, and if you add wood chips or chunks to the fire, the process becomes smoke roasting (see below).

To set up a **charcoal grill** for indirect grilling, light charcoal in a chimney starter (see page 29). Dump or rake the lit coals into two mounds on opposite sides of the grill. Place an aluminum foil drip pan in the center under the grate. You'll grill the ribs on the grate that's over the drip pan, away from the heat, making sure to cover the grill. Any time you grill for longer than one hour, you'll need to replenish the coals. You can do this by lighting fresh charcoal in a chimney starter.

To set up a **gas grill** for indirect grilling, if your grill has two burners, set one burner to the temperature you want. Place the ribs over the other, unlit burner and cover the grill. You'll need to rotate the ribs several times, so they cook evenly. On a three-burner gas grill, set the outside or front and rear burners to the desired temperature. Cook the ribs over the center, unlit burner, with the grill covered. To use the indirect grill method on a four- or six-burner gas grill, set the outside burners on the temperature you need. Cook the ribs over the center, unlit burners, covering the grill.

SMOKE ROASTING WITHOUT A SMOKER

Smoke roasting is a fancy way of saying smoking at a moderate temperature on a charcoal (or, if you must, a gas) grill. So what's the big deal? Smoke roasting differs from smoking in that it's done at a higher temperature—325° to 350°F as opposed to 225° to 250°F. A higher temperature produces a crisper crust and moister, chewier meat (chewy in a satisfying way). It takes a heck of a lot less cooking time. Smoking "low and slow" is something you need to plan for and start a half day before serving. Smoke roasting is actually something you can do when you get home from work. Both methods give you the wonderful smoke flavor of traditional barbecue.

Previously, I've provided instructions for smoking ribs and other meats on a gas grill, but my philosophy has changed. If you want ribs with an authentic smoke flavor, you really must cook them with wood chips or chunks on a charcoal grill. In what follows you'll find instructions for approximating a smoke flavor with a gas grill. But no matter how much you love grilling with gas, I strongly recommend investing in an inexpensive charcoal grill, like a 22½-inch kettle grill, for smoking (for more about kettle grills, see page 40).

Of course, for smoke you need wood. You can use either hardwood chips or chunks. When smoke roasting most ribs, you'll need about a cup and a half for two racks. Soak the wood in water to cover for an hour, then drain it a few minutes before you put it on the coals. Soaked wood chips smolder rather than catching fire; this gives you more smoke.

To use a **charcoal grill** for smoke roasting, set it up as you would for indirect grilling. You produce smoke by tossing the drained wood chips or chunks on the mounds of coals and cooking with the grill covered, but the top and bottom vents open. If you are cooking for more than an hour, you'll need to replenish the coals.

You can get some of the smoke flavor cooking on a **gas grill** by using a smoker box or smoker pouch. If the grill has a smoker box (a shallow metal drawer for holding wood chips or chunks), fill it with the drained wood. Set the smoker box burner on high and turn on the grill

HOW HOT IS IT?
THE MISSISSIPPI TEST

The recipes throughout this book specify a level of heat for grilling—low, medium-low, medium, and so on. The chart here gives the specific temperature or temperature range in degrees for each of these levels of heat.

If your grill has a built-in thermometer, of course you can use this to determine the temperature. However the readings of these thermometers can be somewhat approximate. A reliable way of gauging the heat—one you can use even if your grill doesn't have a thermometer—is the Mississippi test. Hold your hand three to four inches above the hot grill grate and start counting: "One Mississippi, two Mississippi . . ." When the fire is burning on high, you will be able to count to only two or three Mississippis before the intense heat forces you to snatch you hand away. When the fire is low, you'll be able to count to as many as twelve Mississippis. Here's a breakdown of the Mississippi count for the various heat levels.

HEAT	TEMPERATURE	MISSISSIPPI COUNT
High	450° to 650°F	2 to 3 Mississippis
Medium-high	400°F	4 Mississippis
Medium	325° to 350°F	5 to 6 Mississippis
Medium-low	300°F	7 to 8 Mississippis
Low	225° to 250°F	9 to 12 Mississippis

burners as you would for indirect grilling. When you see smoke, put on the ribs and cover the grill.

If your gas grill does not have a smoker box, you can make a smoker pouch by wrapping one and a half to two cups of drained wood chips or chunks in heavy-duty aluminum foil, making a pillow-shaped pouch. Poke holes in the top of the pouch with the point of a meat thermometer so the smoke can escape. Place this smoker pouch under the grate over one of the burners (generally, the hottest part of the grill is in one of the back corners). Preheat the grill to high and run it on high until you see smoke. Then, reduce the heat to the desired temperature, setting the burners as you would for indirect grilling. Put on the ribs and cover the grill.

HOW TO SMOKE ON A GAS GRILL—SOME EXTREME METHODS

Gas grills have many advantages—the convenience of push-button ignition, for example, or turn-of-the-knob heat control. There's the ability to maintain a consistent temperature and the general "neatness" of propane. Gas grills are great for both direct and indirect grilling and for spit roasting. But, the one area in which just about every gas grill falls short is smoking.

This is true of even the most sophisticated stainless steel gas super grills, the ones with built-in smoker boxes that have dedicated burners. True, these may generate a lot of smoke, but that rarely translates into ribs (or anything else) that taste smoky. The problem has to do with the way a gas grill is vented. It needs lots of air, and this necessitates wide vents in the back. No matter how much smoke the smoker box produces, most of it ends up pouring out of those vents.

If you're really serious about smoking on your gas grill, there are three possible solutions. The first is to buy an accessory called Sam's Smoker Pro. The device looks like a large, heavy, flat metal candy box, and it fits under the grate directly over the burners. Following the manufacturer's instructions, you fill the box with wood chips that have been soaked in water and drained, then you place the box in a preheated grill. The rising smoke subtly flavors the ribs. Because this device has a wide surface area, it's more efficient for smoking than the average smoker box.

The second possibility for smoking with gas is to put a cast-iron skillet or metal pie pan filled with eight to ten lit charcoals on the grate next to the ribs. Place a hardwood log, three or four wood chunks, or a cup and a half of soaked and drained wood chips on top of the hot coals. This will pump out lots of smoke. After turning off the grill's burners, you can plug up the vents in the back of the grill with crumpled aluminum foil to keep some of the smoke in, letting the ambient heat do the cooking. You may need to remove the foil from the vents and fire up the grill again to finish cooking (don't forget to open the grill when you light it).

The third option for smoking on a gas grill has been suggested by no less a grill master than radio host Howard Stern: Fill the grill's smoker box with soaked wood chips and run the smoker burner on high to produce lots of wood smoke, then turn off all the gas burners and plug the vents in the back of the grill with crumpled aluminum foil. Let the ribs smoke for fifteen or twenty minutes, then open the grill lid, remove the aluminum foil from the vents, light the burners again, and finish cooking the ribs. You may want to repeat the smoking process. But remember, *never* run a propane grill with the vents plugged up.

TRUE SMOKING— LOW AND SLOW

True smoking is traditionally done low and slow—at a low temperature and for a long time, frequently in a water smoker or horizontal barrel smoker. What you may not realize is that you can smoke low and slow in a kettle or front-loading **charcoal grill**. To do this, set up the grill the way you would for smoke roasting, but use only half as much charcoal as you would normally, so you can keep the temperature low. The Bad to the Bone Ribs (page 128), Princess Ribs (page 133), Porkosaurus Ribs (page 138), Dinosaur Ribs (page 183), and Rabbi's Ribs (page 204) recipes all give specific instructions for using a charcoal grill as a smoker.

Using a **gas grill** as a smoker is almost impossible, but you'll find some extreme methods in the box on page 36.

If you are interested in finding out more about actual smokers, see pages 43 through 47.

WHAT TO COOK YOUR RIBS ON: A QUICK GUIDE TO GRILLS AND SMOKERS

First, the good news—you can cook ribs on any sort of grill: On gas. On charcoal. In a front loader, water smoker, or kettle grill. In a kamado cooker or in a trailer-size smoker. Even on a Lilliputian hibachi.

Now, the not so good news. If you want to be a true rib master, you need to own a charcoal grill. The reason is simple: Most ribs taste best when assertively scented with wood smoke. It's easy to smoke on a charcoal grill or in a smoker and virtually impossible to do so effectively on a gas grill. That's not to say that there aren't gas grills with elaborate smoke systems, smoker drawers or boxes with dedicated burners. The problem is, no matter how big these grills are and how much they cost, most of the smoke spills out the vent slots and holes in the back.

There's a simple answer. If you own a gas grill (and for about 70 percent of American families, that's the grill of choice), use it for direct and indirect grilling and for spit roasting. But invest in an inexpensive charcoal grill (you can buy a 22½-inch Weber kettle grill for less than $100) and use it exclusively for smoke-roasting and smoking.

Gas and charcoal grills are just a start, because ribs have been cooked on just about everything that relies on live fire. Here's a scorecard to help you keep the players straight and let you know how to get the best out of each. For the lowdown on getting the grill started, see How to Set Up a Grill on page 29. For full descriptions of the various cooking methods, see How to Cook Ribs: Six Great Live-Fire Techniques on page 21.

CHARCOAL GRILLS

I'm going to assume you already own a charcoal grill. Or will shortly. If you're looking to buy one, charcoal grills come in many different shapes and sizes. Here are the most common.

KETTLE GRILL

The kettle grill, pioneered by Weber, is one of the most perfect live-fire cooking devices ever invented. You can use it for virtually every rib cooking technique: direct grilling, indirect grilling, smoke-roasting, smoking, even spit roasting. (OK, spit roasting does require the purchase of a rotisserie ring and motor.) A 22$\frac{1}{2}$-inch kettle grill (don't buy anything smaller) will hold two racks of baby backs, but by using a rib rack (see page 52), you can increase the grill capacity to four racks. One of the biggest kettle-style grills is the Weber Ranch, which measures three feet across and can accommodate at least twelve racks of ribs.

A kettle grill consists of a bowl-shaped firebox on legs, with a rounded lid and vent holes in the top and bottom to control the heat (for a hotter fire, you open the vent holes; for a cooler fire, you partially close them). Kettle grills are good for ribs cooked using the direct and indirect method and for ribs that are smoke roasted, smoked, and spit roasted.

What to look for when buying a kettle grill:

- A grill that measures at least 22$\frac{1}{2}$ inches across (anything smaller won't be tall enough to hold a rib rack)

- Side baskets to hold the mounds of coals for indirect grilling

- A grill grate with hinges at opposite sides that lift so you can add fresh coals and/or wood chips

- An ash catcher under the firebox

- A built-in thermometer

- Side tables for work space

FRONT LOADER

A front loader looks like a rectangular metal box on legs or built into a cart. A door in the front panel of the grill lets you add fresh coals, wood chips or chunks, or even logs, without having to lift off the grill grate. Thus, they're well suited to wood grilling and smoking, as well as direct and indirect grilling and smoke roasting.

Another advantage: Front loaders tend to have more surface area on the grate than kettle grills, desirable for people who like to cook for a crowd. Two good front loaders are the Bar-B-Chef by Barbeques Galore and the CB940 by Char-Broil.

What to look for when buying a front loader:

• A heavy cast-iron grate

• A mechanism for raising and lowering the coal pan— for example, a screw and crank

• A built-in temperature gauge

• Side tables for work space

KAMADO COOKER

The kamado, or ceramic cooker, looks like a giant egg with a sturdy hinge about two thirds of the way up the side so you can open it. Its thick ceramic walls (typically $3/4$ to 1 inch thick) make it highly thermodynamically efficient. A large vent at the bottom and a top vent with multiple settings allow you to cook on a very low heat (225°F); a very high heat (700°F, not that you'd ever grill ribs at a heat that hot); and every temperature in between.

The advantages of kamado-style cookers are their even heat and ability to hold in moisture. And, they don't need much fuel; one batch of charcoal will burn for several hours. There are also several disadvantages: You have to remove the grill grate to add fresh charcoal or wood chips; the grate is relatively small; and some models tend to leave traces of ash on the food. Nonetheless, their partisans (and there are many) swear by these big, heavy cookers. Kamado grills are good for ribs cooked using the direct and indirect methods and for ribs that are smoke-roasted or smoked. The best-known brand is the Big Green Egg; Viking contributed to the market with its stylish, stainless steel C4.

What to look for when buying a kamado cooker:

• Thick ceramic walls

• A strong hinge with a locking mechanism to hold up the heavy lid

• Side tables or other auxiliary work space

TABLE GRILL

Table grills are large, open, shallow metal boxes on legs. Most are filled with charcoal to grill, although some models use gas-fired lava stones. You tend to see table grills at street fairs and block parties. Most people rent them from party supply houses, rather than buy them outright (there are no major brand-name home-use table grills). The main virtue of table grills is their size; they're designed for serving a crowd. The disadvantage—from a rib master's point of view at least—is that they are open. You can grill ribs on a table grill using the direct method and you can spit roast if it comes with a rotisserie, but there's no lid and no way to cover them for indirect grilling or smoking.

What to look for when selecting a table grill:

• Sturdy construction

• An adjustable grate with one setting fairly high above the coals so you can grill with minimal flare-ups

• A rotisserie fitting

HIBACHI

Yes, you can even grill ribs on a tiny hibachi (that's what they do in Japan). However, the ribs must be cut into one- or two-bone sections and can only be grilled using the direct method. One good hibachi brand made here in the United States is Lodge.

What to look for when buying a hibachi:

• Heavy cast-iron construction

• A heavy grate with legs or a way of adjusting the grate's height from the coals

• A trapdoor in the front for adding fresh coals

GAS GRILLS

The most popular grills in America are gas; they're available in almost any size or price range. You'll want a gas grill with at least two burners and preferably three, four, or six (a single-burner gas grill is OK for direct grilling, but you need to be able to shut one burner off before you can grill using the indirect method). Well-known brands for gas grills include Weber, Barbeques Galore, Fiesta, Char-Broil, Vermont Castings, KitchenAid, and Viking.

Gas grills are useful for ribs cooked using the direct and indirect methods and for spit-roasted ribs. While it's nice to have one with a dedicated smoker box, you'll never get the optimum smoke flavor from it (for more about smoking in a gas grill, see page 36).

What to look for when buying a gas grill:

• At least two burners, and preferably three or four

• A heavy cast-iron or stainless steel grate

• A built-in thermometer

• A built-in gas gauge

• A rotisserie

• Side tables for work space

SMOKERS

Smokers run at a lower temperature than either charcoal or gas grills, typically 225° to 275°F. This enables you to prepare a true barbecued rib—cooked low and slow.

UPRIGHT BARREL SMOKER

Also known as a water smoker, the upright barrel smoker looks a bit like the *Star Wars* character R2-D2. It's a vertical metal cylinder with a rounded base and lid and a metal door in the front. Most models have a metal bowl that fits in the center below the food being smoked. You fill this with water (or another liquid, like cider or wine), which helps keep ribs moist as they smoke. (It also creates a barrier between the fire and the meat.) Traditional models burn charcoal, but you can also buy gas-fired and electric barrel smokers (see below). The charcoal models are beloved by purists, but they do require hourly tending. Weber's Smokey Mountain Cooker (affectionately nicknamed "The Bullet") is a good example of a charcoal-burning water smoker.

To use a charcoal-fueled upright barrel smoker, you light charcoal in a chimney starter. When the coals are hot, you dump them in the firebox (the bottom section of the smoker; the Weber comes with a perforated metal ring for holding the coals). The smoke chamber, a large metal cylinder, goes on top of the base of the smoker. Then you insert the water bowl; you can fill it with liquid if you like (I like to dry-smoke ribs, so I don't usually add water). The cooking grate gets placed over the water bowl, and the ribs are arranged on top. Once the smoker is covered with its lid, you adjust the top and bottom vent holes to obtain the desired temperature. You can add soaked wood chips or chunks to the fire through the metal door in the smoke chamber (use long-handled tongs). And, you'll need to add fresh coals and wood every hour.

What to look for when buying an upright barrel smoker:

• A door in the front of the smoke chamber

• Multiple racks, so you can smoke ribs and other foods on several levels

HORIZONTAL BARREL OR BOX SMOKER

Home versions of the big rigs used by competition and professional pit masters, these smokers have two parts: a horizontal barrel that serves as the smoke chamber and a smaller firebox set at a lower level and welded to one side of the smoke chamber. This design keeps the heat away from the meat, so ribs cook low and slow, bathed in clouds of wood smoke. Good brands include the Classic made by Horizon Smokers and Barbeques Galore's Bar-B-Chef offset smoker. Some manufacturers, like Brinkmann, make a horizontal smoker with a smoke chamber and firebox that are box shaped.

When using a horizontal barrel or box smoker, you light charcoal in a chimney starter, then dump the coals into the firebox. You place the ribs in the smoke chamber and toss drained, soaked wood chips or chunks on the coals in the firebox. The heat is controlled by opening or closing the vents on the firebox door and chimney. Some models have a metal baffle in the bottom of the smoke chamber to spread the heat more evenly.

What to look for when buying a horizontal barrel or box smoker:

• Heavy, thick-walled construction (ideally $\frac{1}{4}$ inch)

• A built-in thermometer

• A drip spout and bucket to collect the dripping fat

DRUM SMOKER

Picture a 55-gallon metal barrel set on its side, with a door cut in the front or top and a chimney welded to one end—that's a drum smoker. Some enterprising people make their own. Drum smokers are not only good for smoking ribs, you can also use them for direct and indirect grilling. Drum smokers are most often sold at grill shops and hardware stores.

You use a drum smoker by dumping hot coals at one or both ends of the drum and tossing drained, soaked wood chips on them. The ribs cook at the coal-free end or between the mounds of coals (the process is very similar to indirect grilling).

One interesting variation on the drum smoker is the BDS (Big Drum Smoker), an upright version made by

Rocky Richmond. The coals and wood go in the bottom, making it function in a way similar to the upright water smoker.

What to look for when buying a drum smoker:

• Sturdy construction with stable legs

• Adjustable vents on the bottom, side, and chimney

• A heavy-duty cast-iron or stainless steel grate

PELLET SMOKER

Popular in the South and Midwest, pellet smokers look like horizontal barrel smokers or front- or top-loading charcoal grills. What sets them apart is the use of hardwood pellets as both the source of smoke *and* the fuel. A worm gear inside feeds wood pellets into the fire chamber. (John Willingham, a winner of multiple Memphis in May grand championships, uses a pellet smoker.) One respected commercial brand is Traeger.

THE BIG RIG

The sort of smoker towed behind a 4x4 to barbecue competitions, a big rig is used to serve ribs or briskets to a couple hundred of your best friends. If you own one, you likely know how to use it. If you're in the market for one, the National Barbecue News (www.nationalbarbecuenews.com) is a good source of information about them, including where to purchase a used one.

ELECTRIC AND GAS SMOKERS

Some of these look like the traditional upright water smoker kind; others resemble metal boxes or miniature refrigerators. In any case, the heat is generated by an electric or gas heating element. The smoke comes from wood chips, chunks, or pellets, which you place on the heating element. Gas and electric smokers offer plug-in or turn-of-the-knob convenience, a near-constant temperature, and virtually effort-free smoking. Then again, you don't get to play with fire with these models, and that's a serious shortcoming for many pit masters. Two good manufacturers of electric smokers are Meco and Cookshack.

What to look for when buying an electric or gas smoker:

• Sturdy construction, with a tightly fitting door

• Racks and a drip pan that can be easily removed for cleaning

• A warranty on moving and/or electrical parts

ROTISSERIES

The oblique heat of spit roasting is ideal for melting out fat, while the slow gentle turning bastes ribs in their own juices. Most gas grills come with rotisseries; the more elaborate ones have special dedicated infrared burners. If you own a charcoal grill, you can buy a rotisserie attachment, a metal collar that fits over the kettle section and has holes for a motor-driven spit. The recipes for spit-roasted ribs on pages 116, 119, 208, and 235 include instructions for threading ribs onto a rotisserie spit.

What to look for when buying a rotisserie attachment:

• A stainless steel spit with heavy prongs

• A heavy-duty motor

WOOD-BURNING GRILLS

Wood imparts a unique flavor to ribs, and that doesn't just have to come from smoke. There are grills that are specifically designed for grilling over burning hardwood chunks or logs. These grills have a shallow firebox, usually with an open front through which you can add more wood. Above the firebox is a heavy grate that can be raised or lowered by means of a screw mechanism or can be positioned in a slotted frame. As with table grills, you can grill ribs directly over the wood fire but there's generally no lid and no way to cover the grill for indirect grilling or smoking. Two good wood-burning grill manufacturers are The Grillery and Kalamazoo.

TOOLS AND ACCESSORIES
FOR COOKING RIBS

Some tools are indispensable and some accessories just look cool, but all can help you do a better job when grilling ribs. Here's the lowdown.

TOOLS FOR PREPARING RIBS

BAKING SHEETS WITH RAISED SIDES: Great for holding ribs while you peel off the membrane and season them, the raised sides of the baking sheet will keep spices from going all over the place.

LARGE HEAVY-DUTY RESEALABLE PLASTIC BAGS: Heavy-duty zip-top plastic bags are useful for holding ribs as they marinate in wet rubs and liquid marinades.

MARINADE TURBOCHARGER: A spring-loaded device with one or more rows of razor-sharp needles, marinade turbochargers make small holes in the meat, aiding in the absorption of the marinade.

MORTAR AND PESTLE: Used by pit masters from Mexico City to Manila, the mortar and pestle is the premier device for pounding garlic, chiles, herbs, and other flavorings into aromatic seasoning pastes or wet rubs. This gives you a very different—and much richer—flavor than pureeing the same ingredients in a food processor, although a food processor is adequate if you're pressed for time.

SPICE MILL: Resembling a propeller-style coffee grinder, a spice mill is indispensable for grinding whole spices. Freshly ground spices have a much more robust flavor than store-bought ground ones.

TOOLS FOR SETTING UP THE GRILL

ALUMINUM FOIL DRIP PANS: Disposable aluminum foil drip pans are indispensable for rib masters. Not only do they catch dripping fat, but when placed between the mounds of coals, they also help define the zone for indirect grilling. Be sure to place a drip pan under the turning ribs when you're spit roasting. Foil drip pans are handy for holding ribs as you season and/or marinate them, too. I buy them by the case; you can never have enough

CHIMNEY STARTER: The preferred way to ignite charcoal, a chimney starter is an upright metal cylinder or box that has a wire mesh or perforated metal partition inside. The charcoal goes in the top part. Light a crumpled newspaper or a paraffin starter in the bottom, and the coals will be evenly lit in fifteen to twenty minutes.

CHIP SOAKER: A set of wire baskets or perforated metal trays that fit into a watertight plastic or metal soaker box and hold wood chips or chunks as they soak before being used for smoking. The purpose of this arcane device is to facilitate draining the wood; when you're ready to grill, you lift up the wire baskets or metal trays and let the water run off. With some models, you can place the basket or tray full of chips right on the mounds of coals.

DO-IT-YOURSELF CHIP SOAKERS

To make your own chip soaker, use a sharp object, like the point of a meat thermometer, to poke a dozen or so holes in a small aluminum foil drip pan. Fill the pan with wood chips, then place it in another drip pan and fill it with water. When the chips are finished soaking, simply lift the top pan out of the bottom and let the water drain out.

GRILL BRUSH: A good grill brush is essential for the second of the Three Rules of Direct Grilling (see page 31): Keep it clean. Whenever you put ribs—or any other food—on the grill, brush the grate first with a long-handled, stiff-wire grill brush. The long handle keeps you away from the fire; the stiff wire of the brush effectively removes any burnt-on debris. Cleaning the bars of the grate helps prevent food from sticking and produces first-rate grill marks.

GRILL HOE: A grill-size version of a garden hoe, grill hoes are used for raking burning embers into two- or three-zone fires. They're available at barbecue shops— or you can use a regular metal garden hoe.

TOOLS FOR COOKING RIBS

BARBECUE MOP AND MOP BUCKET: The perfect tool for applying mop sauces (thin, flavorful liquids that are swabbed on ribs as they cook to keep them moist and add flavor), barbecue mops look like miniature cotton floor mops. Some models come with miniature plastic-lined buckets for holding the mop sauce.

TONGS: Tongs are indispensable for handling ribs on the grill without piercing the meat and letting the juices run out. Buy the longest pair you can find, and look for ones with rolled-steel arms and a spring-loaded hinge.

GRILL LIGHT OR FLASHLIGHT: The best pit master is a well-informed pit master, one who can actually see what's going on inside the grill or smoker. A lot of barbecue is cooked and served at night. A grill light clips onto the grill or smoker, enabling you to see when the ribs are ready to serve. A flashlight is useful for peering in as food smokes. You can even buy tongs with built-in lights.

INSTANT-READ MEAT THERMOMETER: Most pit masters determine the doneness of ribs by how they look, what they feel like, and how much the meat has shrunk, not by internal temperature. However, you *can* use an instant-read meat thermometer, and it never hurts to double check. To do this, starting at the bone end of the meat, insert the slender metal probe of the thermometer into the meat parallel to the ribs, taking care not to let it touch the bones (the bones conduct heat and will give you a false reading). You'll be able to read the exact internal temperature.

MISTER OR SPRAY BOTTLE: Another way to keep ribs moist and add more flavor is to spray them with wine, beer, apple cider, cola, or another flavorful but thin liquid. A clean spray bottle or plant mister works great for this. Don't try to use a spray bottle when grilling with thick or oil-based basting mixtures or ones that contain large bits of spices; any of these can clog the spray mechanism.

HEAVY-DUTY LEATHER OR SUEDE GRILL GLOVES: Leave the cloth oven mitts to the indoor cooks. Leather or suede gloves are perfect for keeping your hands cool while lifting lit chimney starters, hot grill grates, rib racks, etc. Note: Be sure to buy a model that comes high up your arms. They may cost a bit more, but your forearms will be happy you paid the extra amount.

RIB RACK: A metal or wire device with vertical slots designed to hold racks of ribs upright, a rib rack enables you to fit four full-size racks of ribs in the space that would be filled by only two racks of ribs lying flat. When buying a rib rack, look for sturdy construction, rustproof metal, and a rack that's long enough to accommodate eleven-bone racks of baby backs, along with compartments wide enough to hold the thickest pork spareribs or beef long ribs. Of course, I'm partial to the Best of Barbecue rib rack (visit www.bestofbarbecue.com).

■ ■ ■ ■ ■

PORK BABY BACKS

The baby back is America's most popular rib—and a remarkable meat department success story. When I was a kid, butchers could hardly give these ribs away. Today, they command prime shelf space and top dollar. The reasons for this development are simple: Baby backs are flavorful, tender, well-marbled, and quick and easy to cook. You can use virtually any live fire method to grill them. The first recipe here is designed for neophytes—foolproof First-Timer's Ribs. From there you graduate to Thailand's sweet chile baby back ribs, coffee-crusted redeye ribs, and even mint julep ribs with a bourbon and mint barbecue sauce. In the process you'll learn how to indirect grill, direct grill, fast smoke, slow smoke, and spit roast this extraordinarily succulent rack. In no time you'll be eating high off the hog.

FIRST-TIMER'S RIBS

METHOD: Indirect grilling, followed by direct grilling
ADVANCE PREP: None
SERVES: 4

There are certain dishes every grill master should know how to cook without thinking—a perfect steak, a beer-can chicken, a fish dish you can actually lift off the grill grate in one piece. But the most essential thing of all is knowing how to cook ribs. Ribs are the ur-barbecue—iconic and elemental—and if there's only one dish you master, it should be ribs.

So what makes a perfect rib? It should be handsome and dark, like polished mahogany, with a rough surface, like centennial tree bark. The ribs themselves should be tender enough to pull apart with your fingers, but not so soft the meat falls off the bone. (It should have some chew to it—that's why you have teeth.) The meat should be fragrant with spice and smoke but not overpowered by either. Yes, you want to feel the heat of pepper and mustard and enjoy the soothing sweetness of brown sugar and molasses, but at the end of the day, the rib should taste like pork.

TIPS: *This recipe calls for indirect grilling with wood smoke rather than using a smoker. The reason is twofold. First of all, a lot more people have grills than smokers. Second, when cooking baby back ribs, I prefer the higher heat of indirect grilling (350°F) over smoking's lower temperature (250°F); the more intense heat melts out the fat, crisping the meat and giving the ribs a more interesting texture. Of course, there are legions of old-school pit masters who will disagree with me (their mantra is "low and slow"). If you happen to be one of them, these ribs can be cooked in a smoker following the instructions on page 57.*

Well, if this is your idea of the perfect rib (and it should be), here's your master recipe. It will teach you the principles of first-class ribsmanship—skinning the ribs, rubbing the meat, using a mop sauce, glazing with a barbecue sauce, and harnessing the mouth-watering powers of wood smoke. But ultimately, it's so simple you can prepare it from start to finish in about an hour and a half, only ten minutes of which is actual work.

For the mop sauce:

3 tablespoons unsalted butter

1 cup apple cider

3 tablespoons bourbon, or 3 more tablespoons apple cider

3 tablespoons soy sauce

For the rub and ribs:

2 tablespoons coarse salt (kosher or sea)

2 tablespoons brown sugar

2 tablespoons sweet paprika

1 tablespoon freshly ground black pepper

2 teaspoons dry mustard (preferably Colman's)

2 teaspoons garlic powder

$^1/_2$ teaspoon celery seed

2 racks baby back pork ribs (4 to 5 pounds total)

Lemon Brown Sugar Barbecue Sauce (recipe follows) or
    another favorite barbecue sauce

You'll also need:

$1^1/_2$ cups wood chips or chunks (preferably hickory or
    apple), soaked for 1 hour in water to cover, then drained;
    barbecue mop

1. Make the mop sauce: Melt the butter in a nonreactive saucepan over medium heat. Stir in the cider, bourbon, and soy sauce. Keep warm until ready to use.

2. Make the rub: Place the salt, brown sugar, paprika, pepper, mustard, garlic powder, and celery seed in a small bowl and mix with your fingers, breaking up any lumps in the brown sugar or garlic powder.

3. Prepare the ribs: Place a rack of ribs meat side down on a baking sheet. Remove the thin, papery membrane from the back of the rack by inserting a slender implement, such as a butter knife or the tip of a meat thermometer, under it. The best place to start is on one of the middle bones. Using a dishcloth, paper towel, or pliers to gain a secure grip, peel off the membrane. Repeat with the remaining rack.

4. Set aside 1 tablespoon of rub for serving. Sprinkle the remaining rub over both sides of the ribs, rubbing it onto the meat. Cover the ribs with plastic wrap and refrigerate them while you set up the grill.

5. Set up the grill for indirect grilling (see page 33) and preheat to medium (325° to 350°F). Place a large drip pan in the center of the grill under the grate. (For instructions on smoking on a gas grill see page 36.)

6. When ready to cook, brush and oil the grill grate. Place the ribs bone side down in the center of the grate over the drip pan and away from the heat. (If your grill has limited space, stand the racks of ribs upright in a rib rack; see page 52.) If cooking on a charcoal grill, toss half of the wood chips on each mound of coals. Cover the grill and cook the ribs for 45 minutes.

7. Mop the ribs on both sides with the mop sauce. Re-cover the grill and continue cooking the ribs until well browned, cooked through, and tender enough to pull apart with your fingers, 45 minutes to 1 hour longer, $1\frac{1}{4}$ to $1\frac{1}{2}$ hours in all. When the ribs are cooked, the meat will have shrunk back from the ends of the bones by about $\frac{1}{4}$ inch. Mop the ribs again every 15 minutes and, if using a charcoal grill, replenish the coals as needed.

8. Just before serving, brush the ribs on both sides with some of the Lemon Brown Sugar Barbecue Sauce and move them directly over the fire. Grill the ribs until the barbecue sauce is browned and bubbling, 1 to 3 minutes per side.

9. Transfer the ribs to a large platter or cutting board. Let the ribs rest for a few minutes, then cut the racks in half or into individual ribs. Sprinkle a little of the reserved rub over the ribs and serve at once with the remaining barbecue sauce on the side.

Variation

How to cook First-Timer's Ribs in a smoker: Set up and light the smoker according to the manufacturer's instructions (for more on smokers, see page 43) and preheat it to low (225° to 250°F). Place the ribs in the smoker bone side down and smoke until cooked through, 4 to 5 hours. Start mopping the ribs with the mop sauce after 1 hour, then mop the ribs again once every hour. Brush the ribs with the Lemon Brown Sugar Barbecue Sauce a half hour before they are done smoking. You'll need to replenish the wood chips or chunks after the first and second hour of smoking and to replenish the coals every hour.

LEMON BROWN SUGAR BARBECUE SAUCE

If you like your barbecue sauce sweet and smoky like they do in Kansas City, this condiment is for you. The lemon zest and juice add brassy notes of tartness, balancing the sweetness of the molasses and brown sugar. Were it not for the other delicious sauces in this book, I'd say that this suave, sweet, lemony slather is the only barbecue sauce you'd ever need.

MAKES ABOUT 3 CUPS

2 cups ketchup

$^1/_2$ cup brown sugar

1 teaspoon grated lemon zest

6 tablespoons fresh lemon
   juice, or more to taste

2 tablespoons molasses

1 tablespoon Worcestershire
   sauce

$1^1/_2$ teaspoons liquid smoke

2 teaspoons dry mustard
   (preferably Colman's)

1 teaspoon onion powder

$^1/_2$ teaspoon freshly ground
   black pepper

1. Combine the ketchup, brown sugar, lemon zest and juice,

molasses, Worcestershire sauce, liquid smoke, mustard, onion powder, and pepper in a nonreactive saucepan and whisk to mix.

2. Gradually bring the sauce to a simmer over medium heat and let simmer until thick and flavorful, 8 to 10 minutes. Taste for seasoning, adding more lemon juice if necessary. Transfer the sauce to a bowl or clean jars and let cool to room temperature. Refrigerate the sauce, covered, until serving time; let it return to room temperature before using. The sauce can be refrigerated for several weeks.

TIP: *The zest is the oil-rich outer rind of a citrus fruit. The easiest way to grate it is with a Microplane or the fine side of a box grater. Take care not to also remove the bitter white pith.*

THE GREAT DEBATES IN THE REALM OF RIBS

For many of us, barbecue is a true religion—especially when it comes to ribs. And, like all religions, it has its theological debates. Much the way theologians of old would argue over the number of angels that could dance on the head of a pin, fervent pit masters debate which are higher and holier: baby backs versus spareribs, "dry" rubs versus "wet," smoking versus grilling, and so on. To this add such age-old questions as whether to boil or not to boil ribs and whether to cook them over charcoal or gas, and you've got enough theological tinder to fire a Sunday sermon. My job here is to lay out the arguments. You'll have plenty of time to debate the fine points while waiting for the ribs to cook.

SMOKED OR GRILLED?

Ask a barbecue team at the Memphis in May or Kansas City American Royal festivals this question, and you'll almost certainly be told smoked—low and slow, in the presence of fragrant clouds of wood smoke. How low? 225° to 275°F, with most pros aiming for 250°F. How slow? Typical cooking time at this temperature is five to six hours for spareribs. The low and slow method produces ribs of supreme tenderness—not quite fall-off-the-bone, but almost—with a dense, moist, rich, compressed texture. In short, textbook ribs.

But while you're at Memphis in May, be sure to visit the city's most famous rib joint, the Rendezvous. There, in the heart of the South, you'll find a rib of a very different character:

bones that have been grilled directly over charcoal as quickly as possible—twenty to thirty minutes per side. Grilled ribs are seared and crusty, but not particularly smoky, possessing a forthright pork flavor and chewy, meaty texture that make them a pleasure to sink your teeth into. Not better or worse, just different.

If you really want to watch sparks fly, expand this debate to include the merits of smoke roasting, spit roasting, and grill-top braising.

CHARCOAL VERSUS GAS

This is more a question of how you approach live fire cooking at home. Charcoal has the obvious advantage of allowing you to play with fire, and it's also much easier to smoke on a charcoal grill. Gas grills offer the convenience of push-button ignition and turn-of-a-knob heat control and do a fine job with smokeless methods, such as direct grilling and spit roasting. Actually, traditionalists believe the best fuel for cooking ribs is neither charcoal nor gas, but wood.

BABY BACKS OR SPARERIBS?

The polls are in and baby back ribs (also known as top loin ribs) are the public's first choice, prized for their tenderness, generous marbling, and even their rectilinear shape. That means they come in slabs that are more or less the same width at the top and bottom. And that means they cook evenly. No matter which end of the rack you're served, you'll get a rib that's tender and meaty. Spareribs are bigger, fatter, and tougher than baby backs, but they also have a richer "porkier" flavor. Bottom line? Both are terrific. (For a full description of pork ribs, see page 7.)

"WET" VERSUS "DRY"

Most ribs are seasoned with a rub—or at least salt and pepper—before cooking. The debate here centers on whether the slabs are then slathered with barbecue sauce as they cook and just before they're served or are cooked and served "dry," with sauce, if any, on the side. Often, this dry style calls for an extra sprinkling of rub or spice mix on the cooked ribs in lieu of sauce. The dry rib was pioneered at the Rendezvous in Memphis. It's also popular in Texas and among pit masters who want their ribs to be about smoke and fire, not sauce. Wet ribs are associated with the Deep South and Kansas City. In my temple, there's room at the altar for both.

TO BOIL OR NOT TO BOIL?

OK, it's hard for me to maintain theological impartiality on this one, as I believe a rib's tenderness should come from long, slow grilling or smoking. But lots of rib enthusiasts—both professional and home grillers—boil their bones before grilling or smoking on the theory that boiling melts out the fat and tenderizes the meat. I never like to argue with success, and if you've got a rib recipe people love that involves boiling, go for it.

SHOULD A RIB REALLY BE FALL-OFF-THE-BONE TENDER?

Again, it's hard for me to be impartial here, because I believe a rib should have some chew to it. But some pit masters have built multimillion-dollar empires on ribs that are meltingly tender. The recipes in this book all produce ribs that are a little chewy. My only request, if you adhere to the fall-off-the-bone tender school, is that you give ribs with a little more chew a chance.

THE ORIGINAL MEMPHIS DRY RUB RIBS

RENDEZVOUS RIBS

METHOD: Indirect grilling, followed by direct grilling
ADVANCE PREP: None
SERVES: 4

L et's get the record straight. Charlie Vergos did not set out to invent the dry rub rib. For that matter, the founder of the legendary Rendezvous in Memphis didn't even plan to serve ribs, period. And he certainly never called the stuff barbecue. These are just three of the paradoxes surrounding the most famous "barbecue" joint in Memphis and the birth of one of America's most distinctive rib dishes: dry rub baby backs. Charlie was in the sandwich business, and he'd never even cooked a rib until a meat salesman gave him a free case of baby backs. This was back in the 1950s, when ribs sold for not much more per pound than the box in which they were packed. Good Greek American that he was, Vergos seasoned the ribs with salt, pepper, oregano, and garlic and grilled them over charcoal. "Tastes great, but looks awful," opined the salesman, informing Vergos that proper barbecue was supposed to be red. So Charlie reddened the seasoning mixture with chili powder and paprika and the rest, as they say, is history.

TIP: *The Vergos family is very specific as to the fuel (Royal Oak lump charcoal), the grilling method (direct), the temperature of the fire (325° to 350°F), and even the distance between the ribs and the coals (18 inches). Which amounts to a method I call modified direct grilling (for a full definition see page 22). The ribs are cooked over the embers, as in classic direct grilling, but are high enough above the fire to avoid burning and flare-ups, just as in indirect grilling. You can use this method if you have a grill with a grate that can be positioned high above the fire, like a Big Green Egg or other kamado cooker or some front-loading or wood-burning grills (see the variation on page 65 for cooking instructions).*

The Rendezvous ribs defy the traditional notion of American barbecue on several counts: They're grilled, not smoked; cooked over charcoal, not wood; and the seasonings (which the owners take pains to call just that, not a rub) are applied only after the ribs are completely cooked. To this day, the Vergos family takes care not to label the result barbecue. As the restaurant's marquee and menu clearly state, the Rendezvous house specialty is charcoal-grilled ribs. Such distinctions don't seem to trouble the 3,500 or so customers who jam the basement dining rooms on a typical weeknight.

Here's my re-creation of the Rendezvous "rub" and ribs. You'll have more seasoning mixture than you need for two racks of ribs, but it keeps well in a sealed jar away from heat and light, and it's nice to have around for everything from chicken to lamb to steak.

$1/3$ **cup sweet paprika**

2 tablespoons chile powder

1 tablespoon garlic powder

1 tablespoon dried oregano (preferably Greek)

1 tablespoon coarse salt (kosher or sea)

2 teaspoons coarsely ground black pepper

2 teaspoons mustard seeds

1 teaspoon celery seed

1 cup distilled white vinegar

2 racks baby back pork ribs (4 to 5 pounds total)

Memphis Mustard Slaw (recipe follows),
   for serving

1. Place the paprika, chile powder, garlic powder, oregano, salt, pepper, mustard seeds, and celery seed in a small bowl and mix with your fingers, breaking up any lumps in the paprika and garlic powder. Set the seasoning mixture aside.

2. Place the vinegar in a nonreactive bowl, add 2 tablespoons of the seasoning mixture and 1 cup of water, and whisk until the salt dissolves. Set the mop sauce aside.

3. Prepare the ribs: Place a rack of ribs meat side down on a work surface. Remove the thin, papery membrane from the back of the rack by inserting a slender implement, such as a butter knife or the tip of a meat thermometer, under it. The best place to start is on one of the middle bones. Using a dishcloth, paper towel, or pliers to gain a secure grip, peel off the membrane. Repeat with the remaining rack.

> **TIP:** *Grilling a fatty cut of meat like ribs directly over the heat is trickier on a conventional charcoal grill, so I recommend starting by cooking the ribs using the indirect method, then moving the ribs over the fire for the last few minutes to brown them. This is the method you'll find here. Finally, because there's no wood smoke involved, these ribs are well suited to cooking on a gas grill.*

4. Set up the grill for indirect grilling (see page 33) and preheat to medium (325° to 350°F). Place a large drip pan in the center of the grill under the grate.

5. When ready to cook, brush and oil the grill grate. Place the ribs bone side down in the center of the grate over the drip pan and away from the heat. (If your grill has limited space, stand the racks of ribs upright in a rib rack; see page 52.) Cover the grill and cook the ribs for 30 minutes.

6. Mop the ribs with some of the mop sauce. Re-cover the grill and continue cooking the ribs until well browned, cooked through, and tender enough to pull apart with your fingers, 45 minutes to 1 hour longer, $1\frac{1}{4}$ to $1\frac{1}{2}$ hours in all. When the ribs are done, the meat will have shrunk back from the ends of the bones by about $\frac{1}{4}$ inch. After the ribs have cooked for an hour, mop them once more and, if using a charcoal grill, replenish the coals as needed.

7. Just before serving, move the ribs directly over the heat and grill them until brown and sizzling, 1 to 3 minutes per side.

8. Transfer the ribs to a large platter or cutting board. Let the ribs rest for a few minutes, then generously mop each rack of ribs with the remaining mop sauce. Cut the racks in half or into individual ribs. Thickly sprinkle some of the remaining seasoning mixture on top. Serve at once with the mustard slaw.

Variation

How to grill the ribs on a kamado cooker: If you have a kamado cooker, like a Big Green Egg, build a charcoal fire in the bottom and let it burn down to glowing embers. Arrange the ribs bone side down on the grate. Cover the cooker and adjust the vents to maintain a medium-low temperature (about 300°F). Grill the ribs until well browned and tender, 15 to 20 minutes per side. Monitor the cooking to make sure the ribs don't burn, closing the vents to lower the heat as needed. Mop the ribs each time you turn them, plus one final time just before serving.

MEMPHIS MUSTARD SLAW

Part of what makes Memphis barbecue Memphis barbecue is the slaw—it's not a mayonnaise-based slaw in the style of the Northeast, nor a vinegar-based slaw in the style of North Carolina. No, Memphis slaw is mustard based and the spice and vinegar are just what you need to counterpoint the richness of the pork.

MAKES ABOUT 4 CUPS

TIP: This is a chopped, not shredded, slaw. Use a food processor fitted with a metal chopping blade to chop the cabbage.

3 tablespoons Dijon mustard

3 tablespoons sugar

3 tablespoons distilled white vinegar, or more to taste

3 tablespoons vegetable oil

1 tablespoon hot sauce, such as Texas Pete

Coarse salt (kosher or sea) and freshly ground black pepper

1 small or $^{1}/_{2}$ large green cabbage, cored and cut into 1-inch pieces (for about 4 cups finely chopped)

1 medium-size carrot, peeled

TIP: *While tradition calls for using an inexpensive ballpark-style mustard, I like the salty sharpness of Dijon mustard instead.*

1. Place the mustard and sugar in a nonreactive mixing bowl and whisk to mix. Gradually whisk in the vinegar, oil, and hot sauce. Season with salt and pepper to taste; the dressing should be highly seasoned. Set the dressing aside.

2. Finely chop the cabbage in a food processor fitted with a metal chopping blade, running the machine in short bursts; this is a chopped, not a shredded, slaw. Work in several batches so as not to overcrowd the processor bowl (overprocessing will reduce the cabbage to mush). Finely grate the carrot by hand or using the shredding disk of the food processor.

3. Add the cabbage and carrot to the dressing and toss to mix. Taste for seasoning, adding more salt and/or vinegar as necessary. The slaw tastes best served within a few hours of being made but can be refrigerated, covered, for a day or two. Taste for seasoning before serving, adding more salt and/or vinegar as necessary, and toss to remix.

BUFFALO RIBS

METHOD: Indirect grilling
ADVANCE PREP: None
MAKES: about 20 ribs; serves 4 to 6 as an appetizer

The barbecue bus pulled into Buffalo, New York, recently, and I can tell you this: The locals really are still obsessed with wings. From the Anchor Bar on Main Street (where the buffalo wing was invented on October 30, 1964) to Ralph Wilson Stadium tailgate parties, Buffalonians grill everything from shrimp to scallops the way they prepare Buffalo wings. Many of you are familiar with the "Buffa-que" wings in my book *BBQ USA,* which are smoked on the grill instead of deep-fried. After all, what makes a wing "Buffalo" is the generous slathering of hot sauce and butter, not to mention the accompanying celery stalks and blue cheese dip. I'm not sure anyone has ever made a Buffalo rib before, but I think you'll find that pork, smoke, and fire make a hellish twist on the Buffalo classic.

For the rub and ribs:

2 teaspoons coarse salt (kosher or sea)

2 teaspoons lemon pepper

2 teaspoons garlic powder

2 teaspoons dry mustard

$1/2$ teaspoon cayenne pepper, or more to taste

2 racks baby back pork ribs (4 to 5 pounds total)

1 to 2 lemons, cut in half and seeded

Louisiana-style hot sauce, to taste

For the butter sauce:

8 tablespoons (1 stick) salted butter

$1/2$ cup Louisiana-style hot sauce

> **TIP:** There are many options for hot sauce, such as Tabasco (the classic), Crystal, and Frank's RedHot.

For serving:

Gorgonzola Cheese Dip (recipe follows)

4 ribs celery, rinsed

You'll also need:

$1^1/2$ cups wood chips or chunks (optional; preferably hickory), soaked for 1 hour in water to cover, then drained

1. Make the rub: Place the salt, lemon pepper, garlic powder, mustard, and cayenne in a small bowl and mix with your fingers, breaking up any lumps in the garlic powder or dry mustard.

2. Prepare the ribs: Place a rack of ribs meat side down on a baking sheet. Remove the thin, papery membrane from the back of the rack by inserting a slender implement, such as a butter knife or the tip

of a meat thermometer, under it. The best place to
start is on one of the middle bones. Using a dishcloth,
paper towel, or pliers to gain a secure grip, peel off
the membrane. Repeat with the remaining rack.

3. Sprinkle the rub over both sides of the ribs,
rubbing it onto the meat. Squeeze the lemon juice over
the ribs on both sides, patting it onto the meat with a
fork. Drizzle a tablespoon or two of hot sauce over the
ribs, patting it onto the meat with a fork. Cover the ribs
with plastic wrap and refrigerate them while you make
the sauces and set up the grill.

4. Make the butter sauce: Melt the butter in a small
saucepan over medium-high heat. Stir in the $1/2$ cup of
hot sauce and bring to a boil. Remove from the heat and
set the butter sauce aside.

5. Make the Gorgonzola Cheese Dip, then prepare
the celery. Cut the ribs in half lengthwise, then cut each
half crosswise into roughly 3-inch sticks. Stand the celery
sticks upright in a small bowl or ramekin. Refrigerate the
dip and celery until ready to serve.

6. Set up the grill for indirect grilling (see page 33)
and preheat to medium (325° to 350°F). Place a large
drip pan in the center of the grill under the grate.
(For instructions on smoking on a gas grill, see page 36.)

7. When ready to cook, brush and oil the grill grate.
Place the ribs bone side down in the center of the grate
over the drip pan and away from
the heat. (If your grill has limited
space, stand the racks of ribs
upright in a rib rack; see page 52.)
If cooking on a charcoal grill and
using wood chips, toss half of
them on each mound of coals.
Cover the grill and cook the ribs
until well browned, cooked

TIP: *To experience the
ribs at their best, smoke-
roast them on a charcoal
grill. You can also use gas
(see How to Smoke on a
Gas Grill on page 36), but
the smoke flavor will be
less pronounced.*

inspired by Quebec TV cooking show host Ricardo Larrivée, and they owe their inviting sweetness to a flame-charred glaze made with Quebec's superb maple sugar and syrup.

TIP: *The ribs acquire their candylike crust from caramelized maple sugar. This distinctive sweetener is available at natural foods markets and specialty food stores; or see the Mail-Order Sources (page 305). A turbinado sugar, such as Sugar In The Raw, will work in a pinch.*

For the rub and ribs:

2 tablespoons maple sugar,
    turbinado sugar,
    or light brown sugar

1 tablespoon dry mustard

2 teaspoons coarse salt (kosher or sea)

1 teaspoon freshly ground black pepper

1 teaspoon crumbled or powdered dried sage

2 racks baby back pork ribs (4 to 5 pounds total)

For the maple glaze:

1 cup real maple syrup

3 tablespoons ketchup

2 tablespoons Worcestershire sauce

1 tablespoon Dijon mustard

1 tablespoon cider vinegar

1 tablespoon prepared horseradish

$^1/_2$ cup maple sugar or turbinado sugar

You'll also need:

$1^1/_2$ cups wood chips or chunks (optional; preferably maple),
    soaked for 1 hour in water to cover, then drained

1. Make the rub: Place the maple sugar, dry mustard, salt, pepper, and sage in a small bowl and mix with your fingers, breaking up any lumps in the maple sugar or dry mustard.

2. Prepare the ribs: Place a rack of ribs meat side down on a baking sheet. Remove the thin, papery membrane from the back of the rack by inserting a slender implement, such as a butter knife or the tip of a meat thermometer, under it. The best place to start is on one of the middle bones. Using a dishcloth, paper towel, or pliers to gain a secure grip, peel off the membrane. Repeat with the remaining rack.

3. Sprinkle the rub over both sides of the ribs, rubbing it onto the meat. Cover the ribs with plastic wrap and refrigerate them while you make the glaze and set up the grill.

4. Make the glaze: Place the maple syrup, ketchup, Worcestershire sauce, Dijon mustard, vinegar, and horseradish in a heavy nonreactive saucepan. Bring to a boil over high heat, whisking to mix. Reduce the heat to medium and let the glaze simmer gently until thick and syrupy, 3 to 5 minutes, whisking as needed. Set the glaze aside.

5. Set up the grill for indirect grilling (see page 33) and preheat to medium (325° to 350°F). Place a large drip pan in the center of the grill under the grate. (For instructions on smoking on a gas grill, see page 36.)

6. When ready to cook, brush and oil the grill grate. Place the ribs bone side down in the center of the grate over the drip pan and away from the heat. (If your grill has limited space, stand the racks of ribs upright in a rib rack; see page 52.) If cooking on a charcoal grill and using wood chips, toss half of them on each mound of coals. Cover the grill and cook the ribs for 45 minutes.

7. Brush the ribs on both sides with some of the maple glaze. Re-cover the grill and continue cooking the ribs until well browned, cooked through, and tender enough to pull apart with your fingers, 30 to 45 minutes longer, $1\frac{1}{4}$ to $1\frac{1}{2}$ hours in all. When the ribs are done, the meat will have shrunk back from the ends of the bones by about $\frac{1}{4}$ inch. Brush the ribs once or twice more with glaze and, if using a charcoal grill, replenish the coals as needed.

8. Just before serving, brush the ribs once more on both sides with maple glaze and sprinkle both sides with the maple sugar. Move the ribs directly over the fire and grill until the glaze is browned and caramelized, 1 to 3 minutes per side.

9. Transfer the ribs to a large platter or cutting board. Let the ribs rest for a few minutes, then cut the racks in half or into individual ribs. Serve at once with any remaining maple glaze on the side.

Variation

How to cook Maple-Glazed Ribs in a smoker: Set up and light the smoker according to the manufacturer's instructions (for more on smokers, see page 43) and preheat it to low (225° to 250°F). Place the ribs in the smoker bone side down and smoke until cooked through, 4 to 5 hours. Start brushing the ribs with glaze after 2 hours and repeat every 30 minutes. Sprinkle the maple sugar over the ribs 30 minutes before you plan on serving them. You'll need to replenish the wood chips or chunks after the first and second hour of smoking and to replenish the coals every hour.

MINT JULEP RIBS
WITH BOURBON MINT BARBECUE SAUCE

METHOD: Indirect grilling
ADVANCE PREP: None
SERVES: 4

I've created these ribs to pay homage to two classic Southern beverages—the mint julep and "sweet tea," the region's preternaturally sweet iced tea. In the contemporary spirit of deconstruction/reconstruction, the rub is based on mint, sugar, and iced tea mix.

(Rest assured: It tastes much better than it sounds.) The mint jelly glaze and bourbon and mint barbecue sauce reinforce the mint flavor. Serve the ribs at a Derby party and wash them down with the Mint Juleps on page 266.

For the mint glaze:

3 tablespoons mint jelly

3 tablespoons fresh lemon juice

3 tablespoons salted butter

3 tablespoons bourbon

2 tablespoons sugar

1 teaspoon liquid smoke (optional; use only if cooking the ribs on a gas grill)

For the rub and ribs:

2 teaspoons iced tea mix
   (made with sugar, not an artificial sweetener)

2 teaspoons sugar

2 teaspoons dried mint
   (peppermint or spearmint)

2 teaspoons sweet paprika

2 teaspoons coarse salt (kosher or sea)

1 teaspoon freshly ground black pepper

2 racks baby back pork ribs
   (4 to 5 pounds total)

Bourbon Mint Barbecue Sauce
   (recipe follows)

TIP: *If dried mint's not in your supermarket spice rack, there's a readily available source: a couple of spearmint or peppermint tea bags. Use pure mint tea, not mint-flavored tea.*

You'll also need:

$1^1/2$ cups wood chips or chunks (optional; preferably hickory), soaked for 1 hour in water to cover, then drained

1. Make the glaze: Place the mint jelly, lemon juice, butter, bourbon, 2 tablespoons of sugar, and the liquid smoke, if using, in a small nonreactive saucepan and stir to mix. Bring to a boil over medium heat, whisking often, and cook until the mint jelly dissolves and the glaze is syrupy, about 5 minutes. Set the mint glaze aside.

2. Make the rub: Place the iced tea mix, 2 teaspoons

of sugar, dried mint, paprika, salt, and pepper in a small bowl and mix with your fingers, breaking up any lumps in the paprika.

3. Prepare the ribs: Place a rack of ribs meat side down on a baking sheet. Remove the thin, papery membrane from the back of the rack by inserting a slender implement, such as a butter knife or the tip of a meat thermometer, under it. The best place to start is on one of the middle bones. Using a dishcloth, paper towel, or pliers to gain a secure grip, peel off the membrane. Repeat with the remaining rack.

4. Sprinkle the rub over both sides of the ribs, rubbing it onto the meat. Cover the ribs with plastic wrap and refrigerate them while you set up the grill.

5. Set up the grill for indirect grilling (see page 33) and preheat to medium (325° to 350°F). Place a large drip pan in the center of the grill under the grate. (For instructions on smoking on a gas grill, see page 36.)

TIP: As always, it's easier to smoke ribs on a charcoal grill than a gas one.

6. When ready to cook, brush and oil the grill grate. Place the ribs bone side down in the center of the grate over the drip pan and away from the heat. (If your grill has limited space, stand the racks of ribs upright in a rib rack; see page 52.) If cooking on a charcoal grill and using wood chips, toss half of them on each mound of coals. Cover the grill and cook the ribs for 1 hour.

7. Brush the ribs on both sides with some of the mint glaze. Re-cover the grill and continue cooking the ribs until well browned, cooked through, and tender enough to pull apart with your fingers, 15 to 30 minutes longer, $1\frac{1}{4}$ to $1\frac{1}{2}$ hours in all. When the ribs are done, the meat will have shrunk back from the ends of the bones by about ¼ inch. Brush the ribs once or twice more with the glaze and, if using a charcoal grill, replenish the coals as needed.

8. Transfer the ribs to a large platter or cutting board. Let the ribs rest for a few minutes, then cut the racks in half or into individual ribs. Serve at once with the Bourbon Mint Barbecue Sauce on the side.

Variation

How to cook Mint Julep Ribs in a smoker: Set up and light the smoker according to the manufacturer's instructions (for more on smokers, see page 43) and preheat to low (225° to 250°F). Place the ribs in the smoker bone side down and smoke until cooked through, 4 to 5 hours, lightly basting the ribs with the Bourbon Mint Barbecue Sauce during the last 30 minutes of cooking. You'll need to replenish the wood chips or chunks after the first and second hour of smoking and to replenish the coals every hour.

BOURBON MINT BARBECUE SAUCE

If a mint julep were a barbecue sauce, this is what it would taste like. Sweet, mint-scented, and boozy, it's as unexpected as it is delectable. You don't need a ten-year-old barrel-aged sipping whiskey for the barbecue sauce, but you should use a bourbon you wouldn't mind drinking straight. **MAKES ABOUT 1½ CUPS**

¹/₂ cup ketchup

¹/₂ cup chili sauce (see Note)

¹/₃ cup mint jelly

¹/₄ cup bourbon

2 tablespoons cider vinegar, or more to taste

2 tablespoons brown sugar, or more to taste

1 tablespoon Worcestershire sauce

1 teaspoon liquid smoke

Coarse salt (kosher or sea) and freshly ground black pepper

Place the ketchup, chili sauce, mint jelly, bourbon, vinegar, brown sugar, Worcestershire sauce, and liquid smoke in a heavy nonreactive saucepan and stir to mix. Bring to a boil over medium heat, whisking often. Reduce the heat to medium-low and let the sauce simmer gently until thick and richly flavored, 8 to 10 minutes, whisking from time to time. Taste for seasoning, adding a little more vinegar for tartness and/or brown sugar for sweetness as necessary and salt and pepper to taste. The sauce can be refrigerated, covered, for several weeks. Let it return to room temperature before using.

Note: The chili sauce called for here is the ketchuplike condiment, not a tongue burner from Texas or Thailand. One good brand is Heinz.

CHINATOWN RIBS

METHOD: Indirect grilling
ADVANCE PREP: At least 4 hours for marinating the ribs
SERVES: 4

These ribs were inspired by a popular appetizer common in Chinese restaurants. You know what I'm talking about—spareribs that are dark, shiny, and supernaturally crimson, with a candy-sweet crust and a meaty but tender inside. The ribs play the anisey sweetness of five-spice powder and hoisin sauce against the earthy taste of roast pork. Both are classic Chinese seasonings. Five-spice powder is a blend of star anise, fennel seeds, cinnamon, cloves, and pepper (and sometimes other spices); hoisin sauce is a thick purplish brown condiment (there's something plummy about its sweet flavor). Put them together and you get some of the tastiest ribs on the planet, all the more remarkable because they're roasted in an oven and/or deep-fried—with nary a whiff of wood smoke.

Another version of this recipe appeared in my book *Indoor! Grilling;* the ribs were spit roasted to give them the air-dried crust of the Chinese original. Then someone at Barbecue University had the brilliant idea to smoke the ribs. Remember when *The Wizard of Oz* goes from black and white to color? That's the same thing that happens when you smoke a Chinese rib.

TIP: *Five-spice powder and hoisin sauce are available in the ethnic foods section of most supermarkets; good brands of hoisin sauce include Koon Chun and Lee Kum Kee. Chinese rice wine may require a trip to an Asian market, but you can also use Japanese sake, dry sherry, or even dry white wine. The recipe calls for more marinade than you actually need: The excess makes a nice dipping sauce.*

Which goes to prove my old adage: If something tastes good baked, fried, or sautéed, it probably tastes even better hot off the grill.

1 cup hoisin sauce

$1/2$ cup sugar

$1/2$ teaspoon Chinese five-spice powder

$1/2$ cup soy sauce

$1/3$ cup Chinese rice wine or dry sherry

3 tablespoons Asian (dark) sesame oil

5 cloves garlic, peeled and gently crushed with
   the side of a cleaver

5 slices fresh ginger (each $1/4$ inch thick),
   peeled and gently crushed with the side
   of a cleaver

3 scallions, trimmed, white parts gently crushed
   with the side of a cleaver, green parts minced

2 racks baby back pork ribs (4 to 5 pounds total)

You'll also need:

$1^1/2$ cups wood chips or chunks (preferably cherry),
   soaked for 1 hour in water to cover, then drained

1. Place the hoisin sauce, sugar, and five-spice powder in a nonreactive mixing bowl and whisk to mix. Add the soy sauce, rice wine, and sesame oil and whisk until the sugar dissolves. Stir in the garlic, ginger, and scallion whites. Set one third of the marinade aside to make a sauce.

TIP: When I demonstrate this recipe at the Barbecue University, I smoke the ribs on a kettle grill (I find the higher heat of indirect grilling tends to crisp the meat fibers). When our resident pit master prepares the ribs, he cooks them low and slow in a smoker. Both are fantastic. You'll find instructions for smoking the ribs in the variation on page 80. You can also use a gas grill, but you won't get as much smoke flavor.

2. Prepare the ribs: Place a rack of ribs meat side down on a work surface. Remove the thin, papery membrane from the back of the rack by inserting a slender implement, such as a butter knife or the tip of a meat thermometer, under it. The best place to start is on one of the middle bones. Using a dishcloth, paper towel, or pliers to gain a secure grip, peel off the membrane. Repeat with the remaining rack.

3. Place the ribs in a nonreactive roasting pan or baking dish just large enough to hold them. Pour the remaining marinade over the ribs and spread it all over the racks with a rubber spatula, turning to coat both sides. Let the ribs marinate, covered, in the refrigerator for at least 4 hours or as long as overnight, turning them 3 or 4 times. The longer the ribs marinate, the richer the flavor will be. (The ribs can also be marinated in large heavy resealable plastic bags.)

4. Set up the grill for indirect grilling (see page 33) and preheat to medium (325° to 350°F). Place a large drip pan in the center of the grill under the grate. (For instructions on smoking on a gas grill see page 36.)

5. When ready to cook, brush and oil the grill grate. Drain the ribs well and place them in the center of the grate bone side down over the drip pan and away from the heat. (If your grill has limited space, stand the racks of ribs upright in a rib rack; see page 52.) If cooking on a charcoal grill, toss half of the wood chips on each mound of coals. Cover the grill and cook the ribs until dark brown and very crisp on the outside and tender enough to pull apart with your fingers, 1¼ to 1½ hours. When the ribs are done, the meat will have shrunk back from the ends of the bones by about ¼ inch. If using a charcoal grill, replenish the coals as needed.

6. Meanwhile, transfer the reserved marinade to a nonreactive saucepan, let come to a gentle simmer over medium heat, and cook until thick and flavorful, about 3 minutes. Let the resulting sauce cool to room temperature, then strain it into an attractive serving bowl.

7. Transfer the ribs to a large platter or cutting board. Let the ribs rest for a few minutes, then cut the racks in half or into individual ribs. Brush or drizzle the ribs with some of the sauce and sprinkle the scallion greens on top. Serve at once with the remaining sauce on the side.

Variation

How to cook Chinatown Ribs in a smoker: Set up and light the smoker following the manufacturer's instructions (for more on smokers, see page 43) and preheat to low (225° to 250°F). Place the ribs in the smoker bone side down and smoke until cooked through, 4 to 5 hours. You'll need to replenish the wood chips or chunks after the first and second hour of smoking and to replenish the coals every hour.

BUCCANEER BABY BACKS

METHOD: Indirect grilling, followed by direct grilling
ADVANCE PREP: At least 6 hours for marinating the ribs
SERVES: 4

In the sixteenth and seventeenth centuries, an unruly band of pirates, petty criminals, deserters, and runaway slaves took refuge on the uninhabited coasts of Haiti and the Dominican Republic. From the Indians they learned a technique called *boucan*—seasoning and preserving meats with fiery chiles and spices and smoke roasting them over smoldering fruitwoods. They were the first European pit masters in the New World, and in time they came to be called buccaneers. Their memory lives on at a popular watering hole and restaurant in St. Barts called La Route des Boucaniers. Founded by one of the foremost experts on French West Indian cooking, Francis Delage, La Route des Boucaniers borders Gustavia harbor, and if the tables were any closer to the water, you'd have to dine in your swimsuit. Delage uses a three-step process to create his buccaneer baby back ribs: First he marinates them for twenty-four hours in an aromatic mixture of Caribbean spices and soy sauce. Then he grills them over allspice wood, using the indirect method. And finally, he quickly sizzles them with a rum-laced barbecue sauce directly over the fire.

TIPS: *The Scotch bonnet is one of the world's hottest chiles, of course, and French West Indian chefs have developed an ingenious technique for holding the chiles without burning their fingertips: They carve, seed, and mince them at the end of a fork.*

For smoky bones, cook the ribs in a charcoal grill or smoker. But there's so much flavor in the marinade and sauce, your ribs will have plenty of taste cooked on a gas grill, too.

1 large orange

1 small onion, coarsely chopped

2 cloves garlic, coarsely chopped

$^1/_2$ bunch chives, or 2 scallions, both white and green parts,
    trimmed and coarsely chopped (3 to 4 tablespoons)

$^1/_2$ to 1 Scotch bonnet chile, seeded and minced

2 tablespoons coarsely chopped fresh flat-leaf parsley

3 tablespoons red wine vinegar

3 tablespoons soy sauce

3 tablespoons vegetable oil

$^1/_2$ teaspoon freshly ground black pepper

4 allspice berries, or $^1/_4$ teaspoon ground allspice

$^1/_4$ teaspoon whole cloves or ground cloves

2 racks baby back pork ribs (4 to 5 pounds total)

Rumbullion Barbecue Sauce (recipe follows)

You'll also need:

$1^1/_2$ cups wood chips or chunks (preferably apple or cherry),
    soaked for 1 hour in water to cover, then drained

1. Using a vegetable peeler, remove 2 strips of orange zest (the oil-rich outer rind). Place them in the bowl of a food processor or blender. Cut the orange in half and squeeze out the juice, discarding any seeds. Set 2 tablespoons of orange juice aside for the Rumbullion Barbecue Sauce and add the remaining orange juice to the food processor for the marinade.

2. Add the onion, garlic, chives, Scotch bonnet, parsley, vinegar, soy sauce, oil, pepper, allspice, and cloves to the food processor and puree until smooth.

3. Prepare the ribs: Place a rack of ribs meat side down on a work surface. Remove the thin, papery membrane from the back of the rack by inserting a slender implement, such as a butter knife or the tip of a meat thermometer, under it. The best place to start is on one of the middle bones. Using a dishcloth, paper towel, or pliers to gain a secure grip, peel off the membrane. Repeat with the remaining rack.

4. Place the ribs in a large nonreactive roasting pan or baking dish and pour the marinade over them, turning the racks to coat both sides. Let the ribs marinate, covered, in the refrigerator for at least 6 hours or as long as 24, turning them 3 or 4 times. The longer the ribs marinate, the richer the flavor will be. (The ribs can also be marinated in large heavy resealable plastic bags.)

5. Set up the grill for indirect grilling (see page 33) and preheat to medium (325° to 350°F). Place a large drip pan in the center of the grill under the grate. (For instructions on smoking on a gas grill, see page 36.)

6. When ready to cook, brush and oil the grill grate. Place the ribs bone side down in the center of the grate, over the drip pan and away from the heat. (If your grill has limited space, stand the racks of ribs upright in a rib rack; see page 52.) If cooking on a charcoal grill, toss half of the wood chips on each mound of coals. Cover the grill and cook the ribs until tender, 1¼ to 1½ hours. When the ribs are done, they'll be handsomely browned and the meat will have shrunk back from the ends of the bones by about ¼ inch. If using a charcoal grill, replenish the coals as needed.

7. Just before serving, lightly brush the ribs on both sides with a little of the Rumbullion Barbecue Sauce. Move the ribs directly over the fire and grill until the sauce is sizzling and browned, 1 to 3 minutes per side.

8. Transfer the ribs to a large platter or cutting board. Let the ribs rest for a few minutes, then cut the racks in half or into individual ribs. Serve the remaining barbecue sauce on the side.

Variation

How to cook Buccaneer Baby Backs in a smoker: Set up and light the smoker according to the manufacturer's instructions (for more on smokers, see page 43) and preheat it to low (225° to 250°F). Place the ribs in the smoker bone side down and smoke until cooked through, 4 to 5 hours, lightly basting the ribs with the Rumbullion Barbecue Sauce during the last 30 minutes of cooking. You'll need to replenish the wood chips or chunks after the first and second hour of smoking and to replenish the coals every hour.

RUMBULLION BARBECUE SAUCE

Rum is the spirit of the Caribbean both literally and figuratively, distilled from sugar or molasses, which in turn derive from a plant Columbus took to the West Indies on his second voyage: sugar cane. The first rums were harsh stuff, at least to judge from their nicknames: kill devil, skull-rattle, rumbullion. This barbecue sauce owes its musky sweetness to dark Guadaloupean rum, but any dark rum will do. You'll have more sauce than you need for the Buccaneer Baby Backs, but it keeps well. It's great slathered on chicken and grilled pork.

MAKES ABOUT 2 CUPS

$^1/_4$ *cup dark rum, or more to*
    taste
$^1/_4$ *cup honey*
$^1/_4$ *cup firmly packed dark*
    brown sugar, or more
    to taste
$^1/_4$ *cup fresh lime juice,*
    or more to taste
3 tablespoons soy sauce,
    or more to taste
2 tablespoons fresh orange
    juice (reserved from
    Buccaneer Baby Backs)
$^1/_2$ *teaspoon ground cinnamon*
$^1/_2$ *teaspoon ground nutmeg*
1 cup ketchup

1. Place the rum, honey, brown sugar, lime juice, soy sauce, orange juice, cinnamon, and nutmeg in a heavy nonreactive saucepan and bring to a boil over high heat. Reduce the heat to medium and let the mixture simmer until syrupy, 3 to 5 minutes.

2. Stir in the ketchup and 2 to 3 tablespoons of water and let the sauce simmer gently until thick and flavorful, 6 to 10 minutes. Taste for seasoning, adding more soy sauce if a saltier flavor is desired, more brown sugar if sweetness is desired, more lime juice if tartness is desired, and more rum if you agree with Mark Twain's claim that "too much" liquor is "barely enough."

3. Let the sauce cool to room temperature before serving. It can be refrigerated, covered, for several weeks. Let it come to room temperature before serving.

THAI SWEET CHILE RIBS

METHOD: Indirect grilling, followed by direct grilling
ADVANCE PREP: At least 2 hours for marinating the ribs
SERVES: 4

Ribs aren't really part of the traditional Thai grill repertory, but that hasn't prevented numerous Thai restaurants in the United States from adding them to the menu. The ribs usually get a double dose of flavor—first from a spice paste or marinade, then from a generous slathering of Thai chile sauce. That sauce is about the tastiest stuff to come along since Kansas City–style

TIPS: *These Thai ribs are seasoned with a wet rub—a sort of spice paste that's wetter than a conventional rub but not as soupy as a marinade. To be strictly authentic, you'd make it using the roots of the coriander (cilantro) plant; these have an earthy flavor that lies somewhere between that of cilantro leaves and celery root. You can find coriander plants with the roots attached at Asian and Indian markets and some farmers' markets. Rinse and dry them before mincing. If they're unavailable, it's OK to substitute chopped fresh cilantro leaves.*

This is another good recipe to cook on a gas grill, as smoke is not part of the Thai barbecue palate.

barbecue sauce (of which, it's the Asian counterpart). It's sweet, piquant, garlicky, and spicy, but not particularly fiery. It's hard to imagine a food that doesn't taste better with a shot of this thick red condiment poured on top. Thai sweet chile sauce (not to be confused with Sriracha, a sort of spicy but not sweet Thai ketchup) is available at specialty food stores and most natural foods stores and supermarkets. Good brands include Mae Ploy and Mae Pranom. Another good commonly available brand is Taste of Asia.

> 6 cloves garlic, coarsely chopped
> $1/4$ cup minced cilantro roots, or $1/4$ cup fresh
>   cilantro leaves
> 1 tablespoon coarse salt (kosher or sea)
> 2 teaspoons freshly ground black or white pepper
> 2 teaspoons ground coriander
> 2 tablespoons fresh lime juice
> 3 to 4 tablespoons vegetable oil
> 2 racks baby back pork ribs (4 to 5 pounds total)
> 1 cup Thai sweet chile sauce, for basting and serving
> $1/4$ cup finely chopped or coarsely ground dry roasted
>   peanuts

1. Place the garlic, cilantro, salt, pepper, and coriander in a food processor and finely chop them. Add the lime juice and enough oil to obtain a thick paste. Alternatively, you can pound the garlic and cilantro with the salt and pepper in a mortar, using a pestle, then work the lime juice and oil into the wet rub.

2. Prepare the ribs: Place a rack of ribs meat side down on a baking sheet. Remove the thin, papery membrane from the back of the rack by inserting a slender implement, such as a butter knife or the tip of a meat thermometer, under it. The best place to start is on one of the middle bones. Using a dishcloth, paper towel, or pliers to gain a secure grip, peel off the membrane. Repeat with the remaining rack.

3. Using a rubber spatula, spread the wet rub on both sides of the racks. Cover the ribs with plastic wrap and let marinate in the refrigerator for at least 2 hours or as long as overnight, turning them 3 or 4 times. The longer the ribs marinate, the richer the flavor will be.

4. Set up the grill for indirect grilling (see page 33) and preheat to medium (325° to 350°). Place a large drip pan in the center of the grill under the grate.

5. When ready to cook, brush and oil the grill grate. Place the ribs bone side down in the center of the grate over the drip pan and away from the heat. (If your grill has limited space, stand the racks of ribs upright in a rib rack; see page 52.) Cover the grill and cook the ribs until well browned, cooked through, and tender enough to pull apart with your fingers, 1¼ to 1½ hours. When the ribs are done, the meat will have shrunk back from the ends of the bones by about ¼ inch. If using a charcoal grill, replenish the coals as needed.

6. Just before serving, brush the ribs on both sides with some of the chile sauce and move them directly over the fire. Grill the ribs until the sauce is sizzling and browned, 1 to 3 minutes per side.

7. Transfer the ribs to a large platter or cutting board. Let the ribs rest for a few minutes, then cut the racks in half or into individual ribs. Brush the ribs with more chile sauce and sprinkle the peanuts on top. Serve any remaining chile sauce on the side.

WILL THE REAL BABY BACK RIB STAND UP?

Baby backs are America's favorite rib—with good reason: They're meaty, but well marbled. They're tender, but extremely flavorful. And the rectangular shape of the rack ensures even cooking and egalitarian serving (in other words, no matter which end of the rack you're served, you'll have plenty of meat).

You might be surprised to learn that in butchers' and meat cutters' parlance, the rack most of us call baby back is actually known as a top loin rib. *Top* refers to its position on the hog, at the highest part of the back. *Loin* refers to the lean, tender cylinder of muscle located just on top of the ribs. Traditionally, the loin was the most prized part of the pig, hence the phrase "eating high off the hog." A typical rack of American baby back, or top loin, ribs weighs about 2 to $2\frac{1}{2}$ pounds (some weigh even more) and comfortably feeds two. They're tender enough to be cooked by the direct grilling method (grilled over a medium fire, they're done after fifteen to twenty minutes per side) but sturdy enough to hold up to four to five hours of smoking.

To complicate matters, there's another use of the term *baby back*—to describe a very small rack of top loin ribs cut from a young pig. These baby backs really are baby, weighing $3\!/\!4$ to $1\frac{1}{4}$ pounds and serving one person per rack. Most of them come from Denmark, and they're so tender, direct grilling or spit roasting are the preferred grilling methods.

Most of the "baby backs" you see at the supermarket are the larger top loin ribs. Almost always they'll be labeled *baby backs,* which is what I call them in this book. Don't worry, it's a lot less confusing than it sounds. One glance at the size and weight of the ribs will tell you whether you're dealing with supersized American baby backs or small European baby backs.

In deference to the Danes and to encourage you to try a rib you may not be familiar with, on page 113 I have included a recipe that calls for the smaller baby backs, which I refer to as "true" baby back ribs. If you like the results and want to experiment with other ways of cooking "true" baby backs, you can substitute four of the smaller racks for two racks of full-size top loin ribs in any of the recipes in this chapter. Indirect grilling time for "true" baby back ribs will be forty minutes to one hour at 325° to 350°F; direct grilling time will be twelve to twenty minutes per side over a medium-low fire. Smoking time "low and slow" will be two to three hours.

So, where do you buy "true" baby backs? Start with a specialty food shop or a butcher. Or check out the Mail-Order Sources on page 305. And, of course, if you ever get to Scandinavia, be sure to try them there.

CHINO-LATINO BARBECUED RIBS
WITH GUAVA BARBECUE SAUCE

METHOD: Indirect grilling, followed by direct grilling
ADVANCE PREP: None
SERVES: 4

C hino-Latino refers to the fusion of Asian and Hispanic flavors popularized by trendy restaurants like New York's Sushi Samba and Asia de Cuba in Los Angeles. You may be surprised to learn that the concept originated with the rough-and-tumble eateries opened by Chinese railroad workers and their descendants in nineteenth-century Cuba. The Asian influence in these ribs comes through in the rub— fragrant with licoricy five-spice powder and fiery with Chinese mustard—not to mention the rice wine sprayed on the ribs to keep them moist. So where's the Latino? The sauce is based on guava, a tropical fruit with a perfumed musky flavor that's beloved not just in Cuba but throughout the Caribbean and in Miami. Put them together and you get the sticky sweet ribs that define the genre for many Americans, but that dance to a Latin rhythm.

TIPS: *Chinese mustard is sold dried at Asian markets and many supermarkets. If you can't find it, a dry mustard, like Colman's, works fine.*

You have several grill choices for this recipe. Spanish Caribbean pit masters don't go in for the heavy smoke flavor favored by their Jamaican and North American neighbors. But smoke harmonizes well with the richness of pork and the sweetness of guava. A gas grill will keep the focus on the sweetness of the guava sauce, while a charcoal grill and wood chips will bring the ribs into the camp of Kansas City.

2 tablespoons sugar

1 tablespoon coarse salt (kosher or sea)

1 tablespoon Chinese dry mustard

1 teaspoon Chinese five-spice powder

$1/2$ teaspoon freshly ground black pepper

$1/2$ teaspoon ground cinnamon

$1/4$ teaspoon ground cloves

1 cup Chinese rice wine, sake, or cream sherry

2 racks baby back pork ribs (4 to 5 pounds total)

Guava Barbecue Sauce (recipe follows)

You'll also need:

$1^1/2$ cups wood chips or chunks
(optional; preferably hickory), soaked
for 1 hour in water to cover, then
drained; mister or spray bottle

1. Place the sugar, salt, mustard, five-spice powder, pepper, cinnamon, and cloves in a small bowl and mix with your fingers, breaking up any lumps in the sugar or mustard powder. Set the rub aside.

2. Place the rice wine in a mister or spray bottle and set aside.

3. Prepare the ribs: Place a rack of ribs meat side down on a baking sheet. Remove the thin, papery membrane from the back of the rack by inserting a slender implement, such as a butter knife or the tip of a meat thermometer, under it. The best place to start is on one of the middle bones. Using a dishcloth, paper towel, or pliers to gain a secure grip, peel off the membrane. Repeat with the remaining rack.

4. Sprinkle the rub over both sides of the ribs, rubbing it onto the meat. Cover the ribs with plastic wrap and refrigerate them while you set up the grill.

5. Set up the grill for indirect grilling (see page 33) and preheat to medium (325° to 350°F). Place a large drip pan in the center of the grill under the grate. (For instructions on smoking on a gas grill see page 36.)

6. When ready to cook, brush and oil the grill grate. Place the ribs bone side down in the center of the grate over the drip pan and away from the heat. (If your grill has limited space, stand the racks of ribs upright in a rib rack; see page 52.) If cooking on a charcoal grill and using wood chips, toss half of them on each mound of coals. Cover the grill and cook the ribs for 30 minutes.

7. Spray the ribs with rice wine. Re-cover the grill and continue cooking the ribs until well browned, cooked through, and tender enough to pull apart with your fingers, 45 minutes to 1 hour longer, $1\frac{1}{4}$ to $1\frac{1}{2}$ hours in all. When the ribs are cooked, the meat will have shrunk back from the ends of the bones by about $\frac{1}{4}$ inch. Spray the ribs once or twice more with rice wine and, if using a charcoal grill, replenish the coals as needed.

8. Just before serving, brush the ribs on both sides with a little of the Guava Barbecue Sauce and move them directly over the fire. Grill the ribs until the sauce is browned and bubbling, 1 to 3 minutes per side.

9. Transfer the ribs to a large platter or cutting board. Let the ribs rest for a few minutes, then cut the racks in half or into individual ribs. Serve at once with the remaining Guava Barbecue Sauce on the side.

GUAVA BARBECUE SAUCE

Guava is one of the most distinctive fruits of the tropics—almost impossible to eat fresh (it's riddled with a multitude of rock-hard tiny seeds) but irresistible when boiled down with sugar to make a thick crimson jelly called guava paste. It's so musky and perfumed, you can smell it clear across a room. Guava paste comes in flat metal cans and long slender cardboard boxes. The canned guava is the one you want. This makes much more sauce than you need for the Chino-Latino ribs on page 90, but you'll be glad you have the leftover sauce in your refrigerator. It's also delicious with grilled or smoked poultry, pork, or ham. **MAKES ABOUT 2 CUPS**

8 ounces guava paste (about 1 cup; see Note), cut into ¹/₂-inch pieces

¹/₃ cup rice vinegar or cider vinegar

¹/₄ cup dark rum

3 tablespoons tomato paste

3 tablespoons fresh lime juice

1 tablespoon soy sauce

1 tablespoon Worcestershire sauce

2 teaspoons minced peeled fresh ginger

2 teaspoons minced scallion white

1 clove garlic, minced

Coarse salt (kosher or sea) and freshly ground black pepper

Place the guava paste, vinegar, rum, tomato paste, lime juice, soy sauce, Worcestershire sauce, ginger, scallion, and garlic in a heavy nonreactive saucepan. Add ¹/₄ cup of water. Gently bring the sauce to a simmer over medium heat and cook until thick and richly flavored, about 10 minutes, whisking to break up the pieces of guava paste. The sauce should be thick but pourable; add more water if necessary. Season the sauce with salt and pepper to taste. The barbecue sauce can be refrigerated, covered, for at least a week. Let it return to room temperature before using.

Note: Guava paste can be found in Latino markets and in the ethnic food section of most supermarkets. Goya is a good brand.

BABY BACK RIBS
WITH CHERRY BEER BARBECUE SAUCE

METHOD: Indirect grilling, followed by direct grilling
ADVANCE PREP: At least 4 hours for marinating the ribs
SERVES: 4

The sweet, rich meat of pork has a natural affinity for fruit—a combination appreciated by anyone who has basted ribs with cider, slathered them with peach jam (page 207), or simply stuck an apple between the jaws of a whole hog. This brings us to these cherry barbecued ribs, served at a beer seminar at COPIA (the American Center for Wine, Food & the Arts in Napa, California). The fruit is present not only in the cherry preserves in the sauce but also in a marinade of kriek lambic, an amazing cherry-flavored beer from Belgium. Kriek lambic is one of the world's few beers that can require a corkscrew to open (some bottles come stoppered with corks), and its fruity acidity and complex layering of flavors have as much in common with wine as with beer. Ribs and beer are common enough companions in barbecue, but I wager this is the first time you've ever had bones and cherry beer.

TIPS: *The main challenge in preparing this recipe will be finding kriek lambic. It's available in some upscale liquor stores, wine shops, and natural foods markets. You can buy an imported brew, such as Lindemans from Belgium, or use a domestic cherry beer, like the Ommegang brewery's Three Philosophers, made in upstate New York. Alternatively, you can make a pretty fair approximation by mixing two parts regular beer or ale with one part cherry juice or cherry cider.*

For the best results, cook these ribs on a charcoal grill with wood chips or chunks.

2 racks baby back pork ribs (4 to 5 pounds total)

Coarse salt (kosher or sea) and freshly ground black pepper

2 cups kriek lambic or other cherry-flavored beer

1 onion, thinly sliced

5 cloves garlic, peeled and gently crushed with the side
    of a cleaver

2 bay leaves

4 allspice berries

10 black peppercorns

$1/2$ cup cherry juice or cherry cider (optional),
    in a spray bottle

Cherry Lambic Barbecue Sauce (recipe follows)

You'll also need:

$1^1/2$ cups wood chips or chunks (optional; preferably cherry),
    soaked for 1 hour in water to cover, then drained

1. Prepare the ribs: Place a rack of ribs meat side
down on a work surface. Remove the thin, papery
membrane from the back of the rack of ribs by inserting
a slender implement, such as a butter knife or the tip
of a meat thermometer, under it. The best place to
start is on one of the middle bones. Using a dishcloth,
paper towel, or pliers to gain a secure grip, peel off
the membrane. Repeat with the remaining rack.

2. Generously season the ribs on both sides with salt
and pepper and arrange them, bone side down, in a
roasting pan or baking dish. Pour the beer over the ribs.
Add the onion, garlic, bay leaves, allspice berries, and
peppercorns. Let the ribs marinate, covered, in the
refrigerator for 4 to 6 hours, turning them 2 or 3 times.
The longer the ribs marinate, the richer the flavor will be.
(The ribs can also be marinated in large heavy resealable
plastic bags.)

3. Set up the grill for indirect grilling (see page 33) and
preheat to medium (325° to 350°F). Place a large drip pan
in the center of the grill under the grate. (For instructions
on smoking on a gas grill, see page 36.)

4. When ready to cook, brush and oil the grill grate. Place the ribs bone side down in the center of the grate over the drip pan and away from the heat. (If your grill has limited space, stand the racks of ribs upright in a rib rack; see page 52.) If cooking on a charcoal grill and using wood chips, toss half of them on each mound of coals. Cover the grill and cook the ribs for 45 minutes.

5. If using cherry cider, spray the ribs on both sides. Re-cover the grill and continue cooking the ribs until well browned, cooked through, and tender enough to pull apart with your fingers, 30 to 45 minutes longer, $1\frac{1}{4}$ to $1\frac{1}{2}$ hours in all. When the ribs are done, the meat will have shrunk back from the ends of the bones by about $\frac{1}{4}$ inch. Spray the ribs once or twice more with cherry cider, if using, and if working on a charcoal grill, replenish the coals as needed.

6. Just before serving, generously brush the ribs on both sides with Cherry Lambic Barbecue Sauce and move them directly over the fire. Grill the ribs until the sauce is sizzling, 1 to 3 minutes per side.

7. Transfer the ribs to a large platter or cutting board. Let the ribs rest for a few minutes, then cut the racks in half or into individual ribs. Serve at once with the remaining Cherry Lambic Barbecue Sauce on the side or drizzled over the ribs.

Variation

How to cook Baby Back Ribs with Cherry Lambic Barbecue Sauce in a smoker: Set up and light the smoker according to the manufacturer's instructions (for more on smokers, see page 43) and preheat to low (225° to 250°F). Place the ribs in the smoker bone side down and smoke until cooked through, 4 to 5 hours, lightly basting the ribs with sauce during the last 30 minutes of cooking. You'll need to replenish the wood chips or chunks after the first and second hour of smoking and to replenish the coals every hour.

CHERRY LAMBIC BARBECUE SAUCE

This sauce offers a triple whammy of lush fruit flavor—from whole cherries, cherry preserves, and cherry beer. In the best of all worlds, you'd use fresh cherries, pitted with a cherry pitter (they're available at cookware stores). You can also make a highly tasty sauce with frozen cherries or even drained canned cherries. If you'd prefer the sauce to be chunky, don't run it through the blender. In the unlikely event you have sauce left over, it goes well on grilled or smoked chicken, duck, ham, or pork. **MAKES ABOUT 3 CUPS**

2 tablespoons unsalted butter

3 shallots, or 1 medium-size onion, finely chopped (about 1 cup)

2 cups pitted black or sour cherries, drained if canned, thawed if frozen, or $^3/_4$ cup dried cherries (see Note)

$1^1/_2$ cups (12 ounces) kriek lambic or other cherry beer

$^1/_2$ cup ketchup

$^1/_2$ cup cider vinegar

6 tablespoons brown sugar, or more to taste

2 tablespoons honey

$^1/_4$ cup cherry preserves

$1^1/_2$ tablespoons Worcestershire sauce

Coarse salt (kosher or sea) and freshly ground black pepper

1. Melt the butter in a heavy nonreactive saucepan over medium heat. Add the shallots and cook until translucent but not brown, 3 to 4 minutes. Add the cherries and cook until soft, about 2 minutes. (If using dried cherries, add 2 to 3 tablespoons of water.)

2. Add the beer and increase the heat to high. Let the beer simmer briskly until the liquid is reduced by about half, 4 to 6 minutes. Reduce the heat to medium and add the ketchup, vinegar, brown sugar, honey, cherry preserves, Worcestershire sauce, and a little salt and pepper. Let the sauce simmer gently until richly flavored and slightly thickened, 4 to 6 minutes.

3. Remove the pan from the heat and let the

sauce cool slightly, then puree it in a blender. Taste for seasoning, adding more brown sugar, salt, and/or pepper (or any other ingredient) as necessary; the sauce should be highly seasoned. Let the sauce cool to room temperature before serving. The sauce can be refrigerated, covered, for at least a week. Let it return to room temperature before using.

Note: You can you use sweet black bing cherries or sour Montmorency or yellow cherries—all will be great in the sauce. A drained 1½ pound jar of cherries will give you 2 cups. If you use canned cherries, save a little of the juice for thinning the sauce in Step 3, if necessary.

REDEYE RIBS
WITH CAFE AU LAIT BARBECUE SAUCE

METHOD: Indirect grilling, followed by direct grilling
ADVANCE PREP: At least 1 hour for curing the ribs
SERVES: 4

C all it the Starbucks syndrome—it's hard to pick up a food magazine these days without reading about some trendy coffee-based sauce or spice mix. Actually, the practice of combining coffee and meat (especially pork) belongs to a centuries-old tradition in the Deep South, where cooks routinely add coffee to the frying pan in which ham steaks or pork chops have been cooked

TIPS: Any coffee will do for the rub and mop sauce (provided it's not instant); for a really interesting flavor, use a coffee with chicory from Louisiana.

Like all good Southern barbecue, these ribs show best under a fragrant veil of hickory smoke. For the optimum results, cook them on a charcoal grill or in a smoker.

to make a robust, beloved sauce known as redeye gravy. That's the inspiration for these ribs, and if you've never combined java with baby backs, well, wake up and smell the coffee.

For the rub and ribs:

2 tablespoons ground dark roast coffee

2 teaspoons coarse salt (kosher or sea)

1 teaspoon pure chile powder

1 teaspoon onion powder

1 teaspoon garlic powder

1 teaspoon ground coriander

$1/2$ teaspoon freshly ground black pepper

$1/4$ teaspoon ground cinnamon

2 racks baby back pork ribs (4 to 5 pounds total)

For the mop sauce:

2 tablespoons butter

$1/4$ cup brewed coffee, cooled to room temperature

2 tablespoons cider vinegar

2 tablespoons bourbon

Coarse salt (kosher or sea) and freshly ground black pepper

Café au Lait Barbecue Sauce (recipe follows)

You'll also need:

$1^1/2$ cups wood chips or chunks (preferably hickory), soaked for 1 hour in water to cover, then drained

1. Make the rub: Place the ground coffee, salt, chile powder, onion powder, garlic powder, coriander, pepper, and cinnamon in a small bowl and mix with your fingers, breaking up any lumps.

2. Prepare the ribs: Place a rack of ribs meat side down on a baking sheet. Remove the thin, papery membrane from the back of the rack by inserting a slender implement, such as a butter knife or the tip of a meat thermometer, under it. The best place to start is on one of the middle bones. Using a dishcloth, paper towel, or pliers to gain a secure grip, peel off the membrane. Repeat with the remaining rack.

3. Sprinkle the rub over both sides of the ribs, rubbing it onto the meat. Cover the ribs with plastic wrap and let cure in the refrigerator at least 1 hour or as long as 4. The longer the ribs cure, the richer the flavor will be.

4. Meanwhile, make the mop sauce: Melt the butter in a nonreactive saucepan over medium heat. Add the brewed coffee, vinegar, and bourbon and let simmer gently until blended, about 1 minute. Whisk in salt and pepper to taste. Let the mop sauce cool to room temperature.

5. Set up the grill for indirect grilling (see page 33) and preheat to medium (325° to 350°F). Place a large drip pan in the center of the grill. (For instructions on smoking on a gas grill, see page 36.)

6. When ready to cook, brush and oil the grill grate. Place the ribs bone side down in the center of the grate over the drip pan and away from the heat. (If your grill has limited space, stand the racks of ribs upright in a rib rack; see page 52.) If cooking on a charcoal grill and using wood chips, toss half of them on each mound of coals. Cover the grill and cook the ribs for 45 minutes.

7. Mop or brush the ribs on both sides with some of the mop sauce. Re-cover the grill and continue cooking the ribs until well browned, cooked through, and tender enough to pull apart with your fingers, 30 to 45 minutes longer, $1\frac{1}{4}$ to $1\frac{1}{2}$ hours in all. When the ribs are done, the meat will have shrunk back from the ends of the bones by about $\frac{1}{4}$ inch. Mop the ribs once or twice more with the sauce and, if using a charcoal grill, replenish the coals as needed.

8. Just before serving, brush both sides of the ribs with some of the Café au Lait Barbecue Sauce. Move the ribs directly over the fire and grill until the sauce is sizzling, 1 to 3 minutes per side.

9. Transfer the ribs to a large platter or cutting board. Let the ribs rest for a few minutes, then cut the racks in half or into individual ribs. Serve at once with the remaining Café au Lait Barbecue Sauce on the side or, if desired, drizzled over the ribs.

CAFE AU LAIT BARBECUE SAUCE

Like thousands of other visitors to New Orleans (and the locals themselves), I start each day I'm there with a beignet and café au lait at the Café du Monde. A beignet is a crisp pillow of fried dough dusted with confectioners' sugar, which you dip into the coffee—a steaming cup of dark, strong, chicory-flavored brew laced with hot milk. Chicory is a root with a sweet-bitter flavor used as a coffee additive or substitute. (New Orleanians likely acquired a taste for it during the Civil War, when blockading Yankee ships interrupted the coffee supply.) That earthy, bitter, sweet flavor makes it a perfect base for a barbecue sauce. **MAKES ABOUT 1 $1/_2$ CUPS**

1 tablespoon butter

1 large shallot, finely chopped (about 3 tablespoons)

1 clove garlic, minced

1 tablespoon minced celery

$1/_2$ cup brewed coffee with chicory (see Note)

$1/_2$ cup ketchup

2 tablespoons heavy (whipping) cream

2 tablespoons soy sauce

2 tablespoons bourbon

1 tablespoon Worcestershire sauce

1 tablespoon cider vinegar

1 tablespoon Dijon mustard

1 teaspoon liquid smoke

2 tablespoons dark brown sugar, or more to taste

Coarse salt (kosher or sea) and freshly ground black pepper to taste

1. Melt the butter

in a heavy nonreactive saucepan. Add the shallot, garlic, and celery and cook over medium heat until lightly browned, 3 to 4 minutes. Stir in the coffee, ketchup, cream, soy sauce, bourbon, Worcestershire sauce, vinegar, mustard, liquid smoke, and brown sugar and bring to a boil.

2. Reduce the heat

slightly and let the sauce simmer until thick and richly flavored, 8 to 10 minutes, whisking from time to time. Taste for seasoning, adding salt and pepper to taste and more brown sugar (or any other ingredient) as necessary. The sauce can be refrigerated, covered, for several weeks. Let it return to room temperature before using.

Note: Two good brands of coffee with chicory are Luzianne and Café du Monde, both available in most supermarkets.

DINOSAUR BABY BACKS
(MOJO MARINATED RIBS WITH PINEAPPLE BARBECUE SAUCE)

METHOD: Indirect grilling, followed by direct grilling
ADVANCE PREP: At least 4 hours for marinating the ribs
SERVES: 4

It was a hard day on the barbecue trail. Relief came as we pulled up to a rambling brick building with hundreds of Harley-Davidson motorcycles lined up out front. Welcome to Dinosaur Bar-B-Que in Syracuse, New York, and don't let the tattooed bikers spook you. This is a food-focused and, dare I say, family-friendly restaurant run by a pit master who got his start grilling on a 55-gallon barrel drum at biker meets. Today, John Stage blasts his Harley between restaurants in Syracuse, Rochester, and most recently Harlem, adding just the right number of hickory logs to his all-wood burning pits and transforming slabs of ribs and pork shoulders into smoky hunks of carnivorous bliss. John spent a lot of time in Miami (Cuban girlfriend—it's a long story). One happy outcome was these baby

TIP: *John's original recipe called for baking the ribs in the oven. You know how I feel about that, so here you'll find them grilled using the indirect method and wood smoke.*

back ribs marinated with a garlic, orange, and lime marinade (modeled on Cuban adobo) and served with a *muy* tropical pineapple and guava barbecue sauce. This recipe has been adapted from John's book, *Dinosaur Bar-B-Que: An American Roadhouse.*

$1/3$ cup extra-virgin olive oil

6 cloves garlic, minced

$1/2$ medium-size onion, finely chopped

$1^1/2$ cups fresh orange juice

$1/2$ cup fresh lime juice

1 teaspoon coarse salt (kosher or sea)

1 teaspoon freshly ground black pepper

1 teaspoon ground cumin

1 teaspoon dried oregano

3 tablespoons finely chopped fresh cilantro

2 racks baby back pork ribs (4 to 5 pounds total)

Pineapple Barbecue Sauce (recipe follows)

You'll also need:

$1^1/2$ cups wood chips or chunks (optional; preferably hickory), soaked for 1 hour in water to cover, then drained

1. Heat the olive oil in a deep, heavy saucepan over medium heat. When the oil is hot but not smoking, add the garlic and onion and cook until lightly browned, 3 to 4 minutes. Add the orange and lime juice. Increase the heat to high and let boil for 30 seconds. Add the salt, pepper, cumin, oregano, and cilantro and boil for 30 seconds. Let the marinade cool to room temperature, then puree it in a food processor or blender. Or don't—you'll still get plenty of flavor.

2. Prepare the ribs: Place a rack of ribs meat side down on a work surface. Remove the thin, papery membrane from the back of the rack by inserting a slender implement, such as a butter knife or the tip of a meat thermometer, under it. The best place to start is on one of the middle bones. Using a dishcloth, paper towel, or pliers to gain a secure grip, peel off the membrane. Repeat with the remaining rack.

3. Place the ribs in a large nonreactive roasting pan or baking dish and pour three quarters of the marinade over them, turning the ribs to coat both sides. Set the remaining marinade aside for basting or mopping. Let the ribs marinate in the refrigerator, covered, for at least 4 hours or as long as 24, turning 3 or 4 times. The longer the ribs marinate, the richer the flavor will be. (The ribs can also be marinated in large resealable plastic bags.)

4. Meanwhile, make the Pineapple Barbecue Sauce.

5. Set up the grill for indirect grilling (see page 33) and preheat to medium (325° to 350°F). Place a large drip pan in the center of the grill under the grate. (For instructions on smoking on a gas grill, see page 36.)

6. When ready to cook, brush and oil the grill grate. Place the ribs bone side down in the center of the grate over the drip pan and away from the heat. (If your grill has limited space, stand the racks of ribs upright in a rib rack; see page 52.) If cooking on a charcoal grill and using wood chips, toss half of them on each mound of coals. Cover the grill and cook the ribs until well browned, cooked through, and tender enough to pull apart with your fingers, $1\frac{1}{4}$ to $1\frac{1}{2}$ hours in all. When the ribs are done, the meat will have shrunk back from the ends of the bones by about $\frac{1}{4}$ inch. Start basting or mopping the ribs with the reserved marinade after they have cooked for 45 minutes and mop them again every 15 minutes.

7. Just before serving, brush the ribs on both sides with a little of the Pineapple Barbecue Sauce and move them directly over the fire. Grill the ribs until the sauce is sizzling and browned, 1 to 3 minutes per side.

8. Transfer the ribs to a large platter or cutting board. Let the ribs rest for a few minutes, then cut the racks in half or into individual ribs. Serve the ribs at once with the remaining Pineapple Barbecue Sauce on the side.

Variation

How to cook Dinosaur Baby Backs in a smoker: Set up and light the smoker according to the manufacturer's instructions (for more on smokers, see page 43) and preheat to low (225° to 250°F). Place the ribs in the smoker bone side down and smoke until cooked through, 4 to 5 hours, lightly basting them with Pineapple Barbecue Sauce during the last 30 minutes.

PINEAPPLE BARBECUE SAUCE

This barbecue sauce owes its sweet, hot, musky flavor to four tropical ingredients: fresh pineapple, ginger, Scotch bonnet chile, and guava paste. Guava paste is a sort of ruby-colored preserve made from fruit grown in Florida. The best grade is sold in flat, round cans and found in the ethnic foods sections of most supermarkets.

Don't be put off by the large number of ingredients in the sauce. Remember, barbecue sauces are *supposed* to be complicated. The recipe most likely makes more sauce than you need for one batch of Dinosaur Baby Backs. It keeps well and would also be great with grilled (or smoked) beef, pork, poultry, or seafood—it's pretty versatile. **MAKES ABOUT 3 CUPS**

1 tablespoon vegetable oil

$1/4$ medium-size onion,
coarsely chopped
(about $1/4$ cup)

$1/4$ green bell pepper,
coarsely chopped
(about 3 tablespoons)

2 cloves garlic, coarsely
chopped

1 tablespoon coarsely
chopped peeled fresh
ginger

$1/4$ to 1 Scotch bonnet chile,
seeded and coarsely
chopped (see Note)

$3/4$ cup diced fresh pineapple
with its juice

$1/4$ cup canned pineapple
juice or water

2 tablespoons guava paste or
apricot preserves

$3/4$ cup canned tomato sauce

$1/2$ cup ketchup

$1/3$ cup fresh lime juice

3 tablespoons Worcestershire
sauce

1 tablespoon molasses

1 tablespoon spicy mustard

3 tablespoons dark brown
sugar, or more to taste

1 teaspoon chile powder

$1/4$ teaspoon ground allspice

3 tablespoons finely chopped
fresh cilantro

1 teaspoon liquid smoke

1. Heat the oil in a heavy nonreactive saucepan over medium heat. Add the onion, bell pepper, garlic, ginger, and Scotch bonnet and cook until the mixture is golden brown, 3 to 4 minutes, stirring with a wooden spoon. Stir in the diced pineapple, pineapple juice, and guava paste and cook until the pineapple juice boils, about 1 minute.

2. Add the tomato sauce, ketchup, lime juice, Worcestershire sauce, molasses, mustard, brown sugar, chile powder, and allspice and gradually bring to a boil, whisking to mix. Reduce the heat slightly and let the sauce simmer gently until thick and richly flavored, 5 to 8 minutes. Remove the pan from the heat and let the sauce cool to room temperature. Stir in the cilantro and liquid smoke, then puree the sauce in a blender or food processor. Any leftover sauce can be transferred to clean jars and refrigerated; it will keep for several weeks. Let the sauce return to room temperature before using.

Note: Scotch bonnets are among the world's hottest

chiles, so wear rubber gloves when handling them. A quarter of a Scotch bonnet will give you a sauce with some warmth; a whole chile makes a sauce with serious heat.

PEANUT BUTTER RIBS

METHOD: Indirect grilling
ADVANCE PREP: At least 4 hours for marinating the ribs
SERVES: 4

A while ago, we ran a Lip-Smackin' Rib Recipe Contest on www.barbecuebible.com. Call it the Elvis factor: A surprisingly large number of people submitted rib recipes that called for peanut butter. The notion is not as strange (or off-putting) as it might initially seem; pork is often paired with peanut sauce in Southeast Asia. This recipe emphasizes the savory, not sweet, qualities of peanut butter, thanks to the addition of garlic, ginger, and soy sauce for a sauce that doubles as a marinade. It was inspired by a recipe from one of our contest runners-up, Renata Stanko. I've tinkered with the recipe a little (I always tinker with recipes a little), but I think you'll find it spot-on.

TIPS: *In keeping with the Asian inspiration of this recipe, the ribs are not smoked. This is a good time to fire up your gas grill.*

By coconut milk, I mean the unsweetened kind, sold canned in the ethnic foods section of the supermarket. Two good brands include Chaokoh and Taste of Thai.

Sriracha is a garlic chile sauce used in Thailand the way we use ketchup in the States. It's available at supermarkets and specialty food stores.

1 cup creamy peanut butter

1 cup chicken stock (preferably homemade)

$^1/_2$ cup unsweetened coconut milk

2 tablespoons soy sauce, or more to taste

2 tablespoons fresh lime juice, or more to taste

1 tablespoon Thai chile garlic sauce, such as Sriracha,
    or 1 tablespoon of your favorite hot sauce

1 tablespoon minced peeled fresh ginger

3 cloves garlic, minced

1 scallion, both white and green parts, trimmed
    and minced

1 tablespoon brown sugar

Freshly ground black pepper

2 racks baby back pork ribs (4 to 5 pounds total)

Garlic powder

$^1/_4$ cup finely chopped fresh cilantro, for serving

1. Place the peanut butter, chicken stock, coconut milk, soy sauce, lime juice, chile garlic sauce, ginger, garlic, scallion, brown sugar, and $1/4$ teaspoon pepper in a large heavy nonreactive saucepan. Gradually bring the sauce to a boil over medium heat, whisking to mix. Reduce the heat slightly and let the sauce simmer gently until thick and richly flavored, 10 to 15 minutes, whisking to mix. Remove the pan from the heat and taste for seasoning, adding more soy sauce, lime juice, and/or pepper as necessary. Let the sauce cool completely.

2. Prepare the ribs: Place a rack of ribs meat side down on a work surface. Remove the thin, papery membrane from the back of the rack by inserting a slender implement, such as a butter knife or the tip of a meat thermometer, under it. The best place to start is on one of the middle bones. Using a dishcloth, paper towel, or pliers to gain a secure grip, peel off the membrane. Repeat with the remaining rack.

3. Place the ribs in a nonreactive roasting pan or baking dish just large enough to hold them and season them on both sides with garlic powder and pepper. Pour half of the peanut butter sauce over the ribs, turning to coat both sides and spreading the marinade all over the ribs with a rubber spatula. Cover and refrigerate the remaining peanut butter sauce; you'll use it for basting and serving.

4. Let the ribs marinate in the refrigerator, covered, for at least 4 hours or as long as overnight, turning them 3 or 4 times. The longer the ribs marinate, the richer the flavor will be. (The ribs can also be marinated in large heavy resealable plastic bags.)

5. Set up the grill for indirect grilling (see page 33) and preheat to medium (325° to 350°F). Place a large drip pan in the center of the grill under the grate.

6. When ready to cook, brush and oil the grill grate. Place the ribs bone side down in the center of the grate over the drip pan and away from the heat. (If your grill has limited space, stand the racks of ribs upright in a rib rack; see page 52.) Cover the grill and cook the ribs for 45 minutes.

7. Brush the ribs on both sides with a little peanut butter sauce. Re-cover the grill and continue cooking the ribs until well browned, cooked through, and tender enough to pull apart with your fingers, 30 to 45 minutes longer, $1\frac{1}{4}$ to $1\frac{1}{2}$ hours in all, basting the ribs with peanut butter sauce 2 or 3 times. When the ribs are done, the meat will have shrunk back from the ends of the bones by about $\frac{1}{4}$ inch. If using a charcoal grill, replenish the coals as needed.

8. Transfer the ribs to a large platter or cutting board. Let the ribs rest for a few minutes, then cut the racks in half or into individual ribs. Pour the remaining peanut butter sauce over the ribs and sprinkle the cilantro on top. Serve at once.

COUSIN DAVE'S CHOCOLATE CHIPOTLE RIBS

METHOD: Indirect grilling
ADVANCE PREP: At least 4 hours for marinating the ribs
SERVES: 4

My cousin Dave is the other professional griller in the family—with a PhD, he's a university anthropologist by day and a barbecue fanatic at night and on the weekends. (He helped finance his graduate school studies in Austin, Texas, by smoking whole hogs for weddings and cookouts.) Dave contributed the *muy fabuloso* Grill-Top Shrimp "Boil" recipe in *BBQ USA,* and it was only natural that I touch base with him for ribs. He and his barbecue buddy Russ Glass responded with these chipotle and chocolate flavored bones, which certainly sound bizarre—until you pause to consider that chiles and chocolate are the backbone of the classic Mexican sauce *mole poblano.*

TIPS: Chipotle peppers (smoked jalapeños) come canned and dried, and this is one instance where I actually recommend the canned product. The reason is simple: Canned chipotles come in a spicy vinegar sauce called adobo, and they have a lot more flavor than the dried.

Like all good Tex-Mex barbecue, these ribs turn out best when cloaked in fragrant wood smoke. For the optimal results, cook them on a charcoal grill or in a smoker (you'll find instructions on page 112 for preparing these ribs in a smoker).

3 to 6 canned chipotle peppers, with
   1 tablespoon of their juice
$^1/_2$ medium-size onion, coarsely chopped
   ($^1/_2$ cup)
2 cloves garlic, coarsely chopped
$^1/_4$ cup chopped fresh cilantro, plus $^1/_4$ cup
   chopped cilantro for garnish
$^1/_2$ ounce semisweet chocolate, coarsely grated
   or cut into pieces
2 strips (each $^1/_2$ by $1^1/_2$ inches) fresh lemon zest,
   coarsely chopped
2 tablespoons brown sugar
1 tablespoon pure chile powder, such as
   ancho chile powder
2 teaspoons coarse salt (kosher or sea)
1 teaspoon lemon pepper
2 to 3 tablespoons vegetable oil
2 racks baby back pork ribs (4 to 5 pounds total)
Lime wedges, for serving

You'll also need:

$1^1/_2$ cups wood chips or chunks
   (preferably oak), soaked for 1 hour in water to cover,
   then drained

1. Place the chipotles and their juice, onion, garlic, $^1/_4$ cup of cilantro, chocolate, lemon zest, brown sugar, chile powder, salt, and lemon pepper in a food processor and puree, adding enough oil to obtain a thick paste.

2. Prepare the ribs: Place a rack of ribs meat side down on a baking sheet. Remove the thin, papery membrane from the back of the rack by inserting a slender implement, such as a butter knife or the tip of a meat thermometer, under it. The best place to start is on one of the middle bones. Using a dishcloth, paper towel, or pliers to gain a secure grip, peel off the membrane. Repeat with the remaining rack.

3. Using a rubber spatula, spread the chipotle paste on both sides of the racks. Cover the ribs with plastic wrap and let marinate in the refrigerator for at least 4 hours or as long as overnight. The longer the ribs marinate, the richer the flavor will be.

4. Set up the grill for indirect grilling (see page 33) and preheat to medium (325° to 350°F). Place a large drip pan in the center of the grill under the grate. (For instructions on smoking on a gas grill see page 36.)

5. When ready to cook, brush and oil the grill grate. Place the ribs bone side down in the center of the grate over the drip pan and away from the heat. (If your grill has limited space, stand the racks of ribs upright in a rib rack; see page 52.) If cooking on a charcoal grill and using wood chips, toss half of them on each mound of coals. Cover the grill and cook the ribs until well browned, cooked through, and tender enough to pull apart with your fingers, 1$\frac{1}{4}$ to 1$\frac{1}{2}$ hours. When the ribs are done, the meat will have shrunk back from the ends of the bones by about $\frac{1}{4}$ inch. If using a charcoal grill, replenish the coals as needed.

6. Transfer the ribs to a large platter or cutting board. Let the ribs rest for a few minutes, then cut the racks in half or into individual ribs. Sprinkle the ribs with the remaining cilantro. Serve at once with lime wedges.

Variation
How to cook Chipotle Chocolate Ribs in a smoker:
Set up and light the smoker according to the manufacturer's instructions (for more on smokers, see page 43) and preheat to low (225° to 250°F). Place the ribs in the smoker bone side down and smoke until cooked through, 4 to 5 hours. You'll need to replenish the wood chips or chunks after the first and second hour of smoking and to replenish the coals every hour.

GRILLED "TRUE" BABY BACK RIBS
WITH ST. BARTS SEASONINGS

METHOD: Direct grilling
ADVANCE PREP: At least 3 hours for marinating the ribs
SERVES: 4

It never fails to amaze me how a single cut of meat, seasoned in a similar way and cooked on the same grill (either charcoal or gas), can taste so utterly different depending on whether it's grilled using the direct or indirect method. Case in point: baby back ribs flavored with French West Indian seasonings. The ribs here, from the Pipiri Palace restaurant on St. Barthélemy, are grilled directly over the fire. Try comparing them with the smoky indirectly grilled—and equally delicious— Buccaneer Baby Backs on page 81.

And, if you're wondering why the tiny island of St. Barts in the French West Indies appears often in my books, the reason is simple—my wife and I ran a cooking school called Cooking in Paradise there in the 1980s. As for Pipiri Palace, it's a mercifully unpretentious eatery where you dine under palm trees and the stars. It's also a wonderful relief from the stratospherically priced St. Barts restaurants. Owner-chef Pierre Montalti keeps the seasonings and sauce simple, putting the focus on the taste of the pork. Here's my version of his ribs.

TIPS: *"True" baby backs are small racks of ribs from young hogs. Each rack weighs $3/4$ to $1^1/4$ pounds. They cook quickly, and you want to serve a whole rack per person. Most "true" baby backs are imported from Denmark. For more information, see page 88.*

Whenever you grill a fatty cut of meat, like ribs, directly over the heat, you want to build a two-zone fire. Half of the grill should be preheated to medium and the other half—the safety zone—should be left bare or unlit. If the dripping fat starts to cause flare-ups, simply move the ribs from the hot zone to the safety zone.

For the marinade:

1 piece (2 inches) fresh ginger, peeled and coarsely chopped

2 cloves garlic, peeled and coarsely chopped

2 scallions, both white and green parts,
   trimmed and coarsely chopped

1 cup chopped canned tomatoes

$^1/_2$ cup cider vinegar

3 tablespoons honey

3 tablespoons extra-virgin olive oil

For the ribs:

4 racks "true" baby back pork ribs ($^3/_4$ to 1$^1/_4$ pounds each,
   3 to 5 pounds total), or 2 large racks baby back pork ribs
   (4 to 5 pounds total)

Coarse salt (kosher or sea) and freshly ground black pepper

Creole Sauce (recipe follows)

1. Make the marinade: Place the ginger, garlic, scallions, and tomatoes in a food processor and puree until smooth. With the motor running add the vinegar, honey, and olive oil and process until a coarse puree forms.

2. Prepare the ribs: Place a rack of ribs meat side down on a work surface. Remove the thin, papery membrane from the back of the rack if necessary (some "true" baby backs come already peeled). Insert a slender implement, such as a butter knife or the tip of a meat thermometer, under it. The best place to start is on one of the middle bones. Using a dishcloth, paper towel, or pliers to gain a secure grip, peel off the membrane. Repeat with the remaining rack(s).

3. Generously season the ribs on both sides with salt and pepper. Place the ribs in a nonreactive roasting pan or baking dish and pour the marinade over them, turning to coat both sides. Let the ribs marinate, covered, in the refrigerator for 3 to 4 hours, turning them once or twice. (The ribs can also be marinated in large heavy resealable plastic bags.)

4. Set up the grill for direct grilling, building a two-zone fire (see page 31), and preheat the lit zone to medium (325° to 350°F). Use the Mississippi test to check the heat (see page 35). If a flare-up occurs, you can move the ribs to the unlit part of the grill.

5. When ready to cook, brush and oil the grill grate. Place the ribs over the hot zone bone side down and cook until that side is sizzling and golden brown, 12 to 20 minutes. Turn the ribs and cook them meat side down until the second side is sizzling and golden brown, 12 to 20 minutes longer, 24 to 40 minutes in all. When fully cooked, the ribs will be nicely browned and tender enough to pull apart with your fingers; the meat will have shrunk back from the ends of the bones by about ¼ inch. If flare-ups occur or the ribs start to brown too quickly, move them to the unlit portion of the grill for a few minutes.

6. Transfer the grilled ribs to a platter or plates and let rest for a few minutes. If you're using true baby backs, serve the racks whole. If you've cooked larger racks, cut them in half. Serve the Creole Sauce spooned over the ribs or on the side.

CREOLE SAUCE

Creole sauces are served throughout the French Caribbean, and every cook has his or her own version. It can be as simple as a sort of vinaigrette, pepped up with lime juice and Scotch bonnet chiles, or as complex as a long-simmered tomato sauce perfumed with fresh thyme and whole allspice. Pipiri Palace's Creole Sauce takes the simple approach, to emphasize the fresh flavor of grilled pork, without a lot of spices or sweeteners. **MAKES ABOUT 1 CUP**

1 clove garlic, minced

1 scallion, white part only, finely chopped

Coarse salt (kosher or sea)

2 tablespoons chopped fresh chives or scallion greens

1 ripe tomato, seeded and finely diced

1 piece ($^1/_2$ inch) Scotch bonnet chile, seeded and minced

3 tablespoons fresh lime juice, or more to taste

$^1/_3$ cup vegetable oil

Freshly ground black pepper

Place the garlic, scallion, and $^1/_2$ teaspoon of salt in a nonreactive mixing bowl and mash well with the back of a wooden spoon. Add the chives, tomato, Scotch bonnet, and lime juice and whisk to mix. Whisk in the oil in a thin stream; the sauce should thicken slightly. Taste for seasoning, adding pepper and additional salt and/or lime juice as necessary.

HULI HULI RIBS

METHOD: Spit roasting
ADVANCE PREP: None
SERVES: 4

The rotisserie is ideally suited to cooking tough, fatty cuts of meats, like ribs. The indirect heat melts out the fat and softens tough connective tissue, while the gentle, slow rotation bastes the ribs, keeping them moist as they sizzle. Many European grill cultures from Italian to French to Greek back me on this. America's most singular homegrown spit-roasted dish is *huli huli* chicken from Hawaii (*huli* means "to turn" in the Hawaiian language). That's the inspiration for this recipe and its Polynesian roots are obvious in the glazing sauce, a sweet, salty, fruity mixture of soy sauce, honey, and pineapple juice that cooks to a lacquerlike glaze on the pork.

For the rub and ribs:

1 tablespoon coarse salt (kosher or sea)

1 tablespoon sugar

1 teaspoon freshly ground black pepper

1 teaspoon ground ginger

1 teaspoon garlic powder

1 teaspoon fresh or freeze-dried chives

2 racks baby back pork ribs (4 to 5 pounds total)

2 tablespoons Asian (dark) sesame oil

For the glaze:

2 cups canned pineapple juice

1 cup dark or regular soy sauce

$1/2$ cup honey

$1/2$ cup firmly packed brown sugar

$1/4$ cup fresh lime juice

2 tablespoons Thai chile sauce

2 cloves garlic, lightly crushed with the side of a cleaver

2 slices peeled fresh ginger (each $1/4$ inch thick), crushed with the side of a cleaver

2 scallions, trimmed, white parts crushed with the side of a cleaver, green parts finely chopped

1. Make the rub: Place the salt, sugar, pepper, ground ginger, garlic powder, and chives in a small bowl and mix with your fingers, breaking up any lumps in the garlic powder.

2. Prepare the ribs: Place a rack of ribs meat side down on a baking sheet. Remove the thin, papery membrane from the back of the rack by inserting a slender implement, such as a butter knife or the tip of a meat thermometer, under it. The best place to start is on one of the middle

TIPS: *The trick to this recipe is weaving the ribs on the spit; you'll find instructions in Step 5. Some grill rotisseries have a flat basket attachment, in which case you can cut the rib racks in half and cook them in it.*

You can make this recipe on either a gas or charcoal grill fitted with a rotisserie. If you don't have a rotisserie, you'll find instructions for grilling the ribs using the indirect method in the variation on page 119.

bones. Using a dishcloth, paper towel, or pliers to gain a secure grip, peel off the membrane. Repeat with the remaining rack of ribs.

3. Brush the ribs on both sides with the sesame oil and sprinkle both sides with the rub. Cover the ribs with plastic wrap and refrigerate them while you make the glaze and set up the grill.

4. Make the glaze: Place the pineapple juice in a heavy nonreactive saucepan over high heat and boil until reduced by half. Lower the heat to medium and add the soy sauce, honey, brown sugar, lime juice, chile sauce, garlic cloves, fresh ginger, and scallion whites. Let the mixture simmer over medium-high heat until thick and syrupy, about 5 minutes.

5. Thread the ribs onto the rotisserie spit: Place a rack of ribs bone side up on a work surface. Using a sharp, slender knife, make starter holes in the center of the meat between every two ribs. Twist the knife blade to widen the holes; this will make it easier to insert the spit. Repeat with the remaining rack of ribs. Use an over and under weaving motion to thread the spit through the holes in the racks of ribs.

6. Set up the grill for spit roasting following the manufacturer's instructions and preheat to high. If you are cooking on a charcoal grill, use the Mississippi test to check the heat (see page 35). Place a large drip pan in the center of the grill directly under the spit.

7. When ready to cook, attach the spit to the rotisserie mechanism, turn on the motor, and cover the grill. Cook the ribs until they are golden brown, tender, and cooked through, 40 minutes to 1 hour, depending on their size. When the ribs are done the meat will have shrunk back from the ends of the bones by about $1/4$ inch. During the last 15 minutes of cooking, start basting the ribs with some of the glaze and baste several times.

8. Transfer the spit with the ribs to a cutting board. Carefully remove the spit, then let the ribs rest for a few minutes. Cut each rack of ribs in half or into individual ribs and serve at once, with the remaining glaze drizzled over them (remove the garlic, ginger, and scallion whites from the glaze with a fork and discard them). Sprinkle the scallion greens on top of the ribs and serve at once.

Variation

How to cook Huli Huli Ribs using the indirect method: Set up the grill for indirect grilling (see page 33) and preheat it to medium (325° to 350°F). Place the ribs bone side down in the center of the grill. The ribs will be cooked through and tender after $1\frac{1}{4}$ to $1\frac{1}{2}$ hours. Wood chips are optional—use them if smoky ribs are desired.

BRAZILIAN COCONUT ROTISSERIE RIBS
WITH PIRI-PIRI RELISH

METHOD: Spit roasting
ADVANCE PREP: At least 4 hours for marinating the ribs
SERVES: 4

When I began writing about barbecue, *churrasco,* Brazil's superb grilled meats, could only be found in Brazil. Today *churrascarias* (Brazilian steak houses) are springing up like the proverbial mushrooms after a rainstorm, epitomized by such lively restaurant chains as Fogo de Chão. At the heart of the experience is the *rodizio,* an ingenious wall-mounted rotisserie, with multiple spits extending perpendicularly from a metal wall over a trough of burning charcoal. In a stroke of theatrical genius, the spits of grilled meat are carried like raised swords through the dining room to be carved directly onto patrons' plates.

It would cost tens of thousands of dollars to reproduce a Brazilian rotisserie at home (not that that will stop a few die-hard pit masters from trying), but you can achieve a similar effect, at least as far as ribs are concerned, by spit roasting them on your grill's rotisserie. Although it's not widely practiced in this country, spit roasting is a great way to cook ribs: The lateral heat melts out the fat without flare-ups, while the gentle rotation bastes the meat with its natural fats and juices. A coconut and lime marinade adds an electrifying flavor without overpowering the taste of the pork. (If you don't have a rotisserie, you'll find instructions for grilling the ribs using the indirect method in the variation on page 122.)

$^1/_2$ *green bell pepper, cored, seeded, and cut into*
    1-inch pieces (save the other half for the Piri-Piri Relish)
$^1/_2$ *medium-size onion, peeled and cut into 1-inch pieces*
    (save the other half for the Piri-Piri Relish)
3 cloves garlic, peeled and cut in half
1 piece (1 inch) fresh ginger, peeled and
    cut into $^1/_4$-inch slices
2 teaspoons coarse salt (kosher or sea)
1 teaspoon freshly ground black pepper
3 tablespoons fresh lime juice
$^1/_2$ *cup unsweetened coconut milk, or $^1/_4$ cup extra-virgin*
    olive oil
1 bunch fresh cilantro or flat-leaf parsley, rinsed,
    shaken dry, stemmed, and finely chopped ($^1/_2$ to $^3/_4$ cup)
2 racks baby back pork ribs (4 to 5 pounds total)
Piri-Piri Relish (recipe follows)

1. Place the bell pepper, onion, garlic, ginger, salt, and black pepper in a food processor fitted with a metal chopping blade. Puree to a coarse paste, running the machine in short bursts. With the motor running, add the lime juice and coconut milk. Add half of the cilantro to the marinade and pulse the machine just to mix. Set the remaining cilantro aside for serving.

2. Prepare the ribs: Place a rack of ribs meat side down on a work surface. Remove the thin, papery membrane from the back of the rack by inserting a slender implement, such as a butter knife or the tip of a meat thermometer, under it. The best place to start is on one of the middle bones. Using a dishcloth, paper towel, or pliers to gain a secure grip, peel off the membrane. Repeat with the remaining rack.

3. Place the ribs in a nonreactive roasting pan or baking dish. Pour the marinade over them, turning several times to coat both sides. Let the ribs marinate in the refrigerator, covered, for at least 4 hours or as long as overnight, turning them 3 or 4 times. The longer the ribs marinate, the richer the flavor will be. (The ribs can also be marinated in large heavy resealable plastic bags.)

TIP: *Coconut milk is the heavy cream of the tropics, and it lends these ribs a suave texture and subtle flavor that gently hints at coconut. Coconut milk is easy to use and readily available canned in the ethnic foods section of most supermarkets. It comes from Brazil, Puerto Rico, and Thailand (Thai is the most common where I shop; two good brands are Chaokoh and Taste of Thai). Be sure you get unsweetened coconut milk, not a sweet coconut cream, like Coco López. In the unlikely event you can't find coconut milk, I suggest you substitute olive oil—it has a similar mouthfeel, and the other ingredients in the marinade will give you plenty of flavor.*

4. Drain the ribs well, then thread them onto the rotisserie spit. Place a rack of ribs bone side up on a work surface. Using a sharp, slender knife, make starter holes in the center of the meat between every two ribs. Twist the knife blade to widen the holes; this will make it easier to insert the spit. Repeat with the remaining rack of ribs. Use an over and under weaving motion to thread the spit through the starter holes in the racks of ribs.

5. Set up the grill for spit roasting following the manufacturer's instructions and preheat to high. If you are cooking on a charcoal grill, use the Mississippi test to check the heat (see page 35). Place a large drip pan in the center of the grill directly under the spit.

6. When ready to cook, attach the spit to the rotisserie mechanism, turn on the motor, and cover the grill. Cook the ribs until they are golden brown, tender, and cooked through, 40 minutes to 1 hour, depending on their size. When the ribs are done, the meat will have shrunk back from the ends of the bones by about $\frac{1}{4}$ inch.

7. Transfer the spit with the ribs to a cutting board. Carefully remove the spit, then let the ribs rest for a few minutes. Cut each rack in half or into individual ribs. Spoon a little Piri-Piri Relish over the ribs, serving the rest on the side. Sprinkle the ribs with the reserved cilantro and serve at once.

Variation

How to cook Brazilian ribs using the indirect method:
Set up the grill for indirect grilling (see page 33) and preheat it to medium (325° to 350°F). Place the ribs bone side down in the center of the grill. The ribs will be tender after $1\frac{1}{4}$ to $1\frac{1}{2}$ hours. There's no need to use wood chips; wood smoke is not part of the Brazilian tradition.

PIRI-PIRI RELISH

iri-piri refers to a tiny, fiery chile popular throughout Brazil and Portugal's other former colonies. You'll find it pickled in jars in Brazilian and Latino markets and in specialty food stores (or use one of the Mail-Order Sources on page 305). For a substitute, you might try the pickled cayenne peppers found at lunch counters and barbecue joints in the Deep South, or even fresh jalapeño or serrano peppers. **MAKES ABOUT 1 CUP**

1 large or 2 medium-size ripe
tomatoes, seeded and
finely chopped

$^1/_2$ green bell pepper,
finely chopped

$^1/_2$ medium-size onion (see
Note), finely chopped

2 to 4 piri-piri peppers or
other fresh or pickled hot
peppers, minced

3 tablespoons finely chopped
fresh cilantro or flat-leaf
parsley

3 tablespoons fresh lime
juice, or more to taste

3 tablespoons extra-virgin
olive oil

Coarse salt (kosher or sea)
or freshly ground black
pepper

Place the tomato, bell pepper, onion, piri-piri peppers, cilantro, lime juice, and olive oil in a nonreactive bowl and stir to mix. Taste for seasoning, adding salt and black pepper to taste and more lime juice, if necessary.

Note: For the best results, use a sweet onion, like a Vidalia, Walla Walla, or Maui.

TIP: The relish can be made up to 6 hours ahead and refrigerated, covered. If you make it more than 1 hour in advance, be sure to taste for seasoning, adding more salt and/or lime juice as necessary.

SAUERKRAUT-BRAISED RIBS
WITH SMOKED BEER BARBECUE SAUCE

METHOD: Braising in foil, followed by direct grilling
ADVANCE PREP: None
SERVES: 4

OK, I admit I was dubious when I first heard about this oddball method for cooking ribs. I mean, aluminum foil has a place in keeping ribs warm once they're cooked (or keeping them from burning if they've browned too quickly). But to braise ribs in foil on the grill, then sizzle and brown them on the grate once they're tender—well, that almost seems like cheating. Still, there's room for some unconventional cooking techniques. Besides, I can't think of a better way to bring out the gutsy Alsatian/Germanic flavor of sauerkraut than with pork ribs cooked on the grill.

> **2 racks baby back pork ribs (4 to 5 pounds total)**
>
> **Coarse salt (kosher or sea) and freshly ground**
>> **black pepper**
>
> **$^1/_3$ cup Dijon mustard**
>
> **4 cups drained sauerkraut**
>
> **6 juniper berries lightly crushed with the side of**
>> **a cleaver, or $^1/_4$ cup gin**
>
> **1 cup smoked beer, ale, or pilsner (see Note)**
>
> **Smoked Beer Barbecue Sauce (recipe follows)**

You'll also need:
Heavy-duty aluminum foil

1. Prepare the ribs: Place a rack of ribs meat side down on a baking sheet. Remove the thin, papery membrane from the back of the rack by inserting a slender implement, such as a butter knife or the tip of a meat thermometer, under it. The best place to start is on one of the middle bones. Using a dishcloth, paper towel, or pliers to gain a secure grip, peel off the membrane. Repeat with the remaining rack.

2. Generously season the ribs on both sides with salt and pepper. Using a rubber spatula, spread the mustard on both sides of the ribs.

3. Place 2 large pieces of heavy-duty aluminum foil, one on top of the other, on a work surface, shiny side down. Spoon 1 cup of sauerkraut down the center of the foil in a rectangular mound roughly the size and shape of a rack of ribs. Place a mustard-covered rack of ribs, bone side down, on top of the sauerkraut.

Spread 1 cup of sauerkraut on top of the ribs and dot it with 3 juniper berries or sprinkle it with 2 tablespoons of gin. Fold up the edges of the foil high enough that liquid will not run out. Pour $1/2$ cup of beer over the ribs. Fold the edges of the foil over the ribs and pleat them together to tightly seal in the ribs and sauerkraut. Repeat with the remaining rack of ribs, sauerkraut, juniper berries, and beer.

4. Set up the grill for indirect grilling (see page 33) and preheat to medium (325° to 350°F).

5. Place the packets of ribs on the grill in the center of the grate away from the heat. Cover the grill and cook the ribs until cooked through and tender, $2^1/2$ to 3 hours; replenish the coals as needed.

6. Let the ribs cool for a few minutes, then carefully unwrap them, taking care not to scald yourself with the steam. Drain the sauerkraut in a colander and set it aside, reserving 1 cup of the juices. Place the ribs in a roasting pan. The ribs and sauerkraut can be prepared to this stage up to 2 days ahead. Let them cool to room temperature, then refrigerate them, covered separately, until you are ready to finish grilling.

7. Set up the grill for direct grilling (see page 31) and preheat to high; use the Mississippi test to check the heat (see page 35).

TIPS: *This is a good recipe to make on a gas grill. After all, the ribs are cooked wrapped in aluminum foil, so they wouldn't absorb any smoke flavor anyway.*

Juniper berries are purplish dried berries with a fresh piney flavor that counterbalances the fatiness of pork. Europeans often combine them with sauerkraut. Juniper is one of the primary flavorings in gin (to which it gave its name), so if you can't find juniper berries (which you probably can in a good supermarket spice rack), you can use a couple tablespoons of gin instead.

As for the sauerkraut, try to find the sort sold in bulk at delicatessens. Barring that, bottled sauerkraut is usually better than canned.

8. When ready to cook, brush and oil the grill grate. Brush the ribs on both sides with some of the Smoked Beer Barbecue Sauce, then place them meat side down directly over the fire (if you are using a gas grill, you can turn on all the burners and set them on high). Grill the ribs until nicely browned and heated through, 1 to 3 minutes per side (3 to 5 minutes per side if the ribs are not hot off the grill), basting them with the sauce.

9. Transfer the ribs to a large platter or cutting board and cut the racks in half or into individual ribs. Transfer the ribs to a platter or plates and cover them with aluminum foil to keep warm. Reheat the sauerkraut at the side of the grill in an aluminum foil drip pan or in a saucepan on the stove. Serve the ribs topped with the remaining Smoked Beer Barbecue Sauce and the sauerkraut with its reserved juices spooned alongside.

Note: If you are using an unsmoked ale or pilsner, add $1/2$ to 1 teaspoon of liquid smoke—suit your taste. For more about smoked beer, see below.

SMOKED BEER BARBECUE SAUCE

Beer and sauerkraut—it's one of the classic Central European flavor combinations. The ultimate (or at least ultimately appropriate) beer for barbecue may well be *Rauchbier* from Germany, a powerful dark beer made from wood-smoked barley, so it actually tastes smoked. Look for *Rauchbier* at a liquor store or wine shop that specializes in imported beers or use one of the many smoked beers made by American microbreweries. In a pinch, you could use a good dark beer or ale, plus a little liquid smoke. Don't use a strongly bitter beer, like stout.
MAKES ABOUT 1$1/2$ CUPS

3 tablespoons butter

1 medium-size onion,
    finely chopped

1 clove garlic, minced

1 cup smoked beer

$1/4$ cup ketchup

$1/4$ cup molasses

$1/4$ cup Worcestershire sauce

3 tablespoons Dijon mustard

2 tablespoons brown sugar,
    or more to taste

1 teaspoon red wine vinegar
    or distilled white vinegar

$1/2$ to 1 teaspoon liquid
    smoke (optional; use only
    if using unsmoked beer)

Coarse salt (kosher or sea)
    and freshly ground black
    pepper

1. Melt the butter in a saucepan over medium heat. Add the onion and cook until deep golden brown, 4 to 6 minutes. Add the garlic to the onion after 2 minutes; reduce the heat if it starts to burn.

2. Add the beer and let boil until reduced to about $1/2$ cup. Add the ketchup, molasses, Worcestershire sauce, mustard, brown sugar, vinegar, and $1/2$ teaspoon of liquid smoke, if using. Let the sauce simmer over medium heat until thick and richly flavored, 6 to 10 minutes, stirring often with a wooden spoon. Taste for seasoning, adding salt and pepper to taste, more brown sugar for sweetness and/or more liquid smoke, if necessary; the sauce should be highly seasoned. Let the sauce cool to room temperature before serving. It can be refrigerated, covered, for at least a week. Let return to room temperature before using.

BAD TO THE BONE RIBS
WITH RAZOR BONE SAUCE

METHOD: Smoking in a charcoal grill, followed
by direct grilling
ADVANCE PREP: At least 1 hour for marinating
the ribs
SERVES: 4

I n their many years of competition, the Arkansas-
based Bad to the Bone barbecue team has won
numerous regional grand championships. Each
year, team founders Robert and Pam Satterfield inch
closer to the coveted first place at the American Royal
in Kansas City. One taste of their ribs tells you why.
The Satterfields use a three-step cooking process: First
the ribs are cooked low and slow in a pit to give them
plenty of smoke flavor. Then, they're basted with cider,
brown sugar, and home-harvested honey and grilled
wrapped in aluminum foil to break down the meat
fibers. And finally, they're sizzled directly over the fire
to produce a crisp, caramelized crust. The result is
a sweet, sticky, intensely smoky rib in the finest
Arkansas tradition.

So, is that all there is to it? Not likely, as no self-
respecting barbecue team would show all its cards. But

SMOKING LOW AND SLOW
ON A CHARCOAL GRILL

A ssuming you're like most Americans, you're more likely to have a
charcoal grill than a smoker. So with the recipes for Bad to the
Bone Ribs (page 128), Princess Ribs (page 133), and Porkosaurus Ribs
(page 138), I've given instructions for smoking on a charcoal grill—
that's low, slow smoking as opposed to the indirect grilling with wood
chips you'll see elsewhere in this chapter. The secret to maintaining the
consistent low temperature needed for smoking on a charcoal grill is to
use half as many coals as you normally would. (And if you're one of the
lucky ones with a smoker, you'll find instructions for cooking these ribs
in the variation that follows each recipe.)

here's a home version that will certainly win you kudos at your next grill session.

For the rub and ribs:

2 tablespoons dark brown sugar

1 tablespoon sweet paprika

1^1/$_2$ teaspoons garlic salt

1^1/$_2$ teaspoons onion powder

1 teaspoon lemon pepper

^{1}/$_2$ teaspoon freshly and coarsely ground black pepper

1^1/$_2$ teaspoons ground white pepper

1 teaspoon dry mustard, such as Colman's

^{1}/$_4$ teaspoon celery seed

2 racks baby back pork ribs (4 to 5 pounds total)
   or St. Louis–cut spareribs (see page 9)

^{1}/$_2$ cup fresh lemon juice (from 3 lemons)

For the baste:

^{1}/$_3$ cup unsalted butter, at room temperature

^{1}/$_3$ cup firmly packed dark brown sugar

^{1}/$_3$ cup honey

^{1}/$_3$ cup apple juice

Razor Bone Sauce (recipe follows)

You'll also need:

Clean spray bottle (optional); 3 to 4 cups wood chips
   or chunks (preferably hickory), soaked for 1 hour
   in water to cover, then drained; heavy-duty
   aluminum foil

1. Make the rub: Place the 2 tablespoons of brown sugar and the paprika, garlic salt, onion powder, lemon pepper, black and white peppers, mustard, and celery seed in a small bowl and mix with your fingers, breaking up any lumps in the brown sugar or garlic powder. Set aside 1 tablespoon of the rub for the Razor Bone Sauce.

2. Prepare the ribs: Place a rack of ribs meat side down on a rimmed baking sheet. Remove the thin, papery membrane from the back of the rack by inserting a slender implement, such as a butter knife or the tip of a meat thermometer, under it. The best place to start is on one of the middle bones. Using a dishcloth, paper towel, or pliers to gain a secure grip, peel off the membrane. Repeat with the remaining rack. Pierce the meat along the length of each bone with the tines of a dinner fork to allow the rub to penetrate more deeply (you can also use a Marinade Turbocharger; see page 48).

3. Arrange the ribs in a single layer on the baking sheet. Place the lemon juice in the spray bottle, if using, and thoroughly spray the ribs on both sides with lemon juice. Or, you can brush the ribs on both sides with the lemon juice, using a pastry brush, or pour the juice over the ribs, making sure to cover them all over. Drain and discard any excess lemon juice from the baking sheet.

4. Sprinkle the rub over both sides of the ribs, rubbing it onto the meat. Tightly wrap the ribs in plastic wrap and let marinate in the refrigerator for at least 1 hour or as long as 4 hours. The longer the ribs marinate, the richer the flavor will be.

5. Set up a charcoal grill for smoking (see page 33) and preheat to low (225° to 250°F), using half the number of coals you would normally grill with. Place a large drip pan in the center of the grill under the grate.

6. When ready to cook, brush and oil the grill grate. Pour water to a depth of about 1 inch into the drip pan (you will need to replenish the water each time it has evaporated to a depth of about $1/2$ inch). Place the ribs bone side down in the center of the grate over the drip pan and away from the heat. (If your grill has limited space, stand the racks of ribs upright in a rib rack; see page 52.) Toss $1/2$ cup of

"RIB TIP"

Cook the ribs the way you like to eat them, because you're going to eat a lot of them.

—ROBERT AND PAM SATTERFIELD, BAD TO THE BONE barbecue team

wood chips on each mound of coals, then cover the grill. Smoke the ribs until browned and partially cooked, about 3 hours, adding 1 cup of wood chips and replenishing the coals every hour.

TIPS: *The Satterfields have some interesting theories about wood smoke, using a 3-to-1 blend of cured or dry hickory and green hickory. According to Robert, the green hickory gives the ribs flavor and the cured hickory adds a dark, smoky hue—but neither should dominate. If you cut your own wood, you may be able to find green hickory. If not, I've had success using regular dried hickory chunks or chips.*

If you've got a smoker, this is a great time to use it. Bad to the Bone uses a JR water smoker. Other good options include a Weber Smokey Mountain Cooker.

7. Remove the ribs from the grill, leaving the fire burning. Place 2 large pieces of heavy-duty aluminum foil, one on top of the other, on a work surface, shiny side down. Place a rack of ribs on top, bone side down. Fold up the edges of the foil high enough that liquid will not run out. Repeat with more aluminum foil and the remaining rack of ribs. Spread the top of each rack with half of the butter and sprinkle half of the $\frac{1}{3}$ cup of brown sugar over each. Drizzle half of the honey over each rack and pour half of the apple juice on top. Fold the edges of the foil over the ribs and pleat them together to make a tight seal.

8. Place the wrapped ribs in the center of the grate, re-cover the grill, and continue cooking the ribs until cooked through and tender, 1 to 2 hours longer, 4 to 5 hours in all. When the ribs are done, you will be able to pull them apart with your fingers and the meat will have shrunk back from the ends of the bones by about $\frac{1}{4}$ inch (take care to avoid the scalding steam when you open the foil to check the ribs). Replenish the coals as needed.

9. Unwrap the ribs. Make sure the mounds of coals are hot, then place the ribs directly over the fire and brush them with a little of the Razor Bone Sauce. Grill the ribs until the outside is sizzling and browned, 1 to 3 minutes per side.

10. Transfer the ribs to a large platter or cutting board. Let the ribs rest for a few minutes, then cut the racks in half or into individual ribs. Serve at once with the remaining Razor Bone Sauce on the side.

Variation

How to cook Bad to the Bone Ribs in a smoker: Set up and light the smoker according to the manufacturer's instructions (for more on smokers, see page 43) and preheat to low (225° to 250°F). Place the ribs in the smoker bone side down and smoke for 3 to 4 hours, adding 1 cup of wood chips and replenishing the coals every hour.

Remove the ribs from the smoker and follow the instructions in Step 7 for wrapping them. Place the wrapped ribs back in the smoker and continue cooking until done, 1 to 2 hours longer. Replenish the coals if needed.

Then, if your smoker has a grill over the firebox, preheat it to high. Unwrap the ribs and place them directly over the fire. Brush the ribs with a little of the Razor Bone Sauce and grill them until the outside is sizzling and browned, 1 to 3 minutes per side. If you don't have the option to grill directly over the fire in your smoker, unwrap the ribs after they have cooked 1 hour, brush them with sauce, and cook them unwrapped until done, 30 to 60 minutes longer.

RAZOR BONE SAUCE

This sweet, sticky sauce is what I call a "doctor" sauce, made by doctoring two commercial barbecue sauces with apple juice, honey, and spice rub. For a smokier version, use all KC Masterpiece. In the unlikely event you have any left over, it would be delicious on grilled or smoked chicken or pork tenderloin. **MAKES ABOUT 1$^1/_2$ CUPS**

1 cup commercial tomato-
   based barbecue sauce,
   such as Head Country or
   Open Pit
1/2 cup commercial smoky
   tomato-based barbecue
   sauce, such as
   KC Masterpiece
1/4 cup apple juice or
   apple cider
2 tablespoons honey
2 tablespoons dark brown
   sugar
2 tablespoons cider vinegar
About 2 teaspoons barbecue
   rub, reserved from Bad to
   the Bone Ribs (page 128)

Place the barbecue sauces, apple cider, honey, brown sugar, cider vinegar, and 2 teaspoons of rub in a nonreactive saucepan and whisk to mix. Place over low heat and bring to a gentle simmer (do not let the sauce boil). Cook the sauce until thick and richly flavored, about 10 minutes, whisking it often. Taste for seasoning, adding more rub if necessary. Let the sauce cool to room temperature before serving. It can be stored in a clean glass jar in the refrigerator for several weeks. Let it return to room temperature before using.

PRINCESS RIBS
(SPICE RUBBED AND SMOKED OVER CHERRY WOOD)

METHOD: Smoking in a charcoal grill
ADVANCE PREP: None
SERVES: 8

If you've been to the Kansas City Royal or some of the other barbecue competitions around the Midwest, you've probably seen Dianna Fick. She's the one wearing a sparkling tiara on her head and a red sash emblazoned with the words "It's not easy being a princess." In 2004, Dianna and her barbecue team won first place in the rib division at the Kansas City Royal.

As just about everyone in Kansas City knows, her confident skills in the kitchen and at the pit have garnered dozens of gold medals and trophies for the teams she's worked with. Dianna's the sort of person who gladly helps neophytes. It's also no surprise some of the most macho pit masters in the business have sought her advice. She's someone who wants to make sure her fellow team members get due credit, so here's thanks to Sandy and Danny Crabtree, too. Dianna's ribs get a one-two punch, first from a cumin- and cinnamon-scented rub, then from the kind of thick, sweet sauce for which Kansas City is famous. Tender tongues take note: This princess has a pretty generous hand with cayenne pepper.

$1/2$ cup granulated sugar

$1/3$ cup firmly packed brown sugar

$1/3$ cup coarse salt (kosher or sea)

$1^1/2$ tablespoons chile powder

1 tablespoon ground cumin

1 teaspoon onion powder

1 teaspoon garlic powder

1 teaspoon cayenne pepper

1 teaspoon ground cinnamon

$1/2$ teaspoon ground allspice

4 racks baby back ribs (8 to 10 pounds total)

Sweet and Seriously Hot Barbecue Sauce
    (recipe follows)

You'll also need:

A jar with a shaker lid; 3 to 4 cups wood chips or chunks
    (preferably cherry; if you can get wild cherry,
    even better), soaked for 1 hour in water to cover,
    then drained; heavy-duty aluminum foil

1. Place the granulated sugar, brown sugar, salt, chile powder, cumin, onion powder, garlic powder, cayenne, cinnamon, and allspice in a bowl and mix well with your fingers, breaking up any lumps in the brown sugar. Place the rub in a jar with a shaker lid.

(This makes more rub than you'll need for the Princess Ribs; stored away from heat and light it will keep for several weeks.)

2. Prepare the ribs:

Place a rack of ribs meat side down on a baking sheet. Remove the thin, papery membrane from the back of the rack by inserting a slender implement, such as a butter knife or the tip of a meat thermometer, under it. The best place to start is on one of the middle bones. Using a dishcloth, paper towel, or pliers to gain a secure grip, peel off the membrane. Repeat with the remaining racks.

TIPS: *What's the secret to championship ribs? It starts with the raw materials, says Dianna, who handpicks her baby backs from Premium Standard Farms. She buys the herbs and spices from a specialty spice market, not a grocery store. She uses cherry wood, not hickory, which she feels imparts a bitter flavor. Above all, she says, "you've got to feel the love."*

Dianna does her smoking over cherry wood pellets in a old Jedmaster barbecue cooker. To achieve the proper texture and tenderness, you've got to cook at a really low temperature (225°F) for a really long time (4 to 6 hours). I've adapted this recipe to a charcoal grill, but you'll find smoker instructions in the variation on page 136. And note: As long as you're going to invest this much time, you might as well make at least four racks of ribs—enough to feed a crowd.

3. Sprinkle the rub over both sides of the ribs. Gently pat the seasonings onto the meat but do not rub vigorously (Dianna believes vigorous rubbing bruises the meat). You will need about 2 to 3 teaspoons of rub for each side.

4. Set up a charcoal grill for smoking (see page 33) and preheat to low (225° to 250°F), using half the number of coals you would normally grill with. Place a large drip pan in the center of the grill under the grate.

5. When ready to cook, brush and oil the grill grate. Place the ribs bone side down in the center of the grate over the drip pan and away from the heat. (If your grill has limited space, stand the racks of ribs upright in a rib rack; see page 52.) Toss $1/2$ cup of wood chips on each mound of coals, then cover the grill. Smoke the ribs until browned and partially cooked, about 3 hours, adding 1 cup of wood chips and replenishing the coals every hour.

6. Remove the ribs from the grill, leaving the fire burning. Place 2 large pieces of heavy-duty aluminum foil, one on top of the other, on a work surface, shiny side down. Place a rack of ribs on top, bone side down. Repeat with more aluminum foil and the remaining racks of ribs. Generously brush the ribs on both sides with Sweet and Seriously Hot Barbecue Sauce. Fold the edges of the foil over the ribs and pleat them together to make a tight seal.

7. Place the wrapped ribs in the center of the grate, re-cover the grill, and continue cooking the ribs until cooked through and tender, 1 to 2 hours longer, 4 to 5 hours in all. When the ribs are done, you will be able to pull them apart with your fingers and the meat will have shrunk back from the ends of the bones by about $1/4$ inch (take care to avoid the scalding steam when you open the foil to check the ribs). Replenish the coals as needed.

8. Unwrap the ribs and transfer them to a large platter or cutting board. Let the ribs rest for a few minutes, then cut the racks in half or into individual ribs. Serve at once with the remaining Sweet and Seriously Hot Barbecue Sauce on the side.

Variation

How to cook Princess Ribs in a smoker: Set up and light the smoker according to the manufacturer's instructions (for more on smokers, see page 43) and preheat to low (225° to 250°F). Place the ribs in the smoker bone side down and smoke for 3 to 4 hours, adding 1 cup of wood chips and replenishing the coals every hour. Remove the ribs from the smoker and follow the instructions in Step 6 for wrapping them. Place the wrapped ribs back in the smoker and continue cooking until done, 1 to 2 hours longer. Replenish the coals if needed.

"RIB TIP"

If you love what you're doing, you'll be able to taste it in the ribs.

—DIANNA FICK, PRINCESS OF BARBECUE BARBECUE TEAM

SWEET AND SERIOUSLY HOT BARBECUE SAUCE

Like most good Kansas City barbecue sauces, this one starts thick and sweet, with a shot of Jack Daniel's for gumption. What sets it apart is a tooth-rattling blast of cayenne. Dianna Fick and her business partner Philip ("Bubba") Fick serve it at their restaurant, Bubba's BBQ Fixens in Maryville, Missouri. I've given a range for the cayenne pepper. Start with a half teaspoon. Add more to taste gradually—remember, the sauce will get hotter with time. **MAKES ABOUT 2 CUPS**

$1^1/_2$ cups ketchup

$1/_4$ cup Jack Daniel's or other Tennessee whiskey

3 tablespoons Worcestershire sauce

1 tablespoon fresh lemon juice

2 teaspoons cider vinegar

$1^1/_2$ teaspoons prepared mustard, either Dijon or yellow

1 teaspoon pickled jalapeño pepper juice (see Note), or 1 more teaspoon cider vinegar

$3/_4$ cup firmly packed brown sugar

1 tablespoon chile powder

$1^1/_2$ teaspoons garlic powder

1 teaspoon celery salt

$1/_2$ to 3 teaspoons cayenne pepper

Place the ketchup, Jack Daniel's, Worcestershire sauce, lemon juice, cider vinegar, mustard, jalapeño pepper juice, brown sugar, chile powder, garlic powder, celery salt, and cayenne in a nonreactive saucepan and whisk to mix. Add 2 tablespoons of water. Taste for seasoning, adding more cayenne as necessary. Place the pan over medium heat and let the sauce simmer gently until thick and richly flavored, 10 to 15 minutes, stirring often. If the sauce thickens too much, add another tablespoon or so of water. The sauce can be refrigerated, covered, for several weeks. Let it return to room temperature before using.

Note: Jalapeño pepper juice is the tart, fiery liquid that comes in jars of pickled jalapeños.

PORKOSAURUS MEMPHIS IN MAY CHAMPIONSHIP RIBS

METHOD: Smoking in a charcoal grill
ADVANCE PREP: None
SERVES: 8

There are lots of ways to monitor the cooking progress of barbecued ribs: by the color of the crust, by the internal temperature of the meat, by the amount of shrinkage at the ends of the bones. . . . But the Memphis-based Porkosaurus is the only barbecue team I know of that actually listens to how the ribs "sing." Porkosaurus uses a three-step cooking process, first smoking spice-crusted ribs, then wrapping them in aluminum foil and sizzling them with fruit juice, and finally, "roasting" the racks on the grill. By listening to how the bones "sing" as they sizzle, team captain Joffre DiSabatino knows just how hot to crank up the smoker. Don't laugh; such unconventional measures fetched Porkosaurus a rib championship at the Memphis in May World Championship Barbecue Cooking Contest in 2005. (Ribs is the hardest category to win because it has the

most contestants.)
So what else does it
take to make these
championship ribs?
Well, there's no barbecue
sauce served on its own,
explains team member
Tom Wilson, just a
"finishing" sauce brushed
on the ribs during the last
hour of cooking. And, the
honey in the sauce comes
from the hives of team
member Chuck Brooks.

TIPS: *Porkosaurus believes in starting the ribs at a low temperature (175°F) and increasing the heat very gradually to 225°F. Their other secret is to smoke with a mixture of hickory and apple—the hickory for "backbone," the apple for finesse. If you have a smoker, this is a good recipe for using it; you'll find instructions in the variation on page 141. Sorry, propane fans— you won't get the requisite smoke flavor on a gas grill.*

4 racks baby back pork ribs (8 to 10 pounds total)

$^1/_3$ to $^1/_2$ cup of your favorite barbecue rub
    (for example, the Sweet Smoky Barbecue Rub, page 204)

$1^1/_2$ cups of your favorite barbecue sauce
    (for example, the Spicy Apple Barbecue Sauce, page 158,
    or Bunker Blaster Barbecue Sauce, page 176)

$^1/_2$ cup balsamic vinegar

$^1/_2$ cup yellow mustard, such as French's

$^1/_4$ cup honey

1 tablespoon Italian seasoning or herbes de Provence

$^1/_2$ cup apple juice or apple cider

$^1/_2$ cup canned pineapple juice

You'll also need:

3 to 4 cups wood chips or chunks (preferably 2 cups hickory
    and 2 cups apple), soaked for 1 hour in water to cover,
    then drained; heavy-duty aluminum foil

1. Prepare the ribs: Place a rack of ribs meat side
down on a baking sheet. Remove the thin, papery
membrane from the back of the rack by inserting a
slender implement, such as a butter knife or the tip of a
meat thermometer, under it. The best place to start is on
one of the middle bones. Using a dishcloth, paper towel,
or pliers to gain a secure grip, peel off the membrane.

Repeat with the remaining racks. Sprinkle the barbecue rub over both sides of the ribs, rubbing it onto the meat.

2. Place the barbecue sauce, balsamic vinegar, mustard, honey, and Italian seasoning in a nonreactive bowl and whisk to mix. Set the "finishing" sauce aside.

3. Set up a charcoal grill for smoking (see page 36) and preheat to low (225° to 250°F), using half the number of coals you would normally grill with. Place a large drip pan in the center of the grill under the grate.

4. When ready to cook, brush and oil the grill grate. Place the ribs bone side down in the center of the grate over the drip pan and away from the heat. (If your grill has limited space, stand the racks of ribs upright in a rib rack; see page 52.) Toss ¼ cup each of hickory and apple chips on each mound of coals, then cover the grill. Smoke the ribs until browned and partially cooked, about 3 hours, adding 1 cup of wood chips and replenishing the coals every hour.

5. Remove the ribs from the grill, leaving the fire burning. Place 2 large pieces of heavy-duty aluminum foil, one on top of the other, on a work surface, shiny side down. Place a rack of ribs on top, bone side down.

"RIB TIP"

Barbecue is a lifelong education.

— JOFFRE DISABATINO,
PORKOSAURUS BARBECUE TEAM

Fold up the edges of the foil high enough that liquid will not run out. Pour 2 tablespoons each of apple juice and pineapple juice over the ribs. Fold the edges of the foil over the ribs and pleat them together to make a tight seal. Repeat with the remaining racks of ribs.

6. Place the wrapped ribs in the center of the grate, re-cover the grill, and continue cooking the ribs until cooked through and tender, about 1 hour longer.

If necessary, raise the heat until you can hear the ribs "sing" (sizzle) in their foil wrapping. You can raise the heat in one of two ways: either by opening the vents or by adding lit coals. Light the coals in a chimney starter about 20 minutes before you think you'll need them.

TIP: *The recipe makes more "finishing" sauce than you'll need for the ribs. What's left over can be refrigerated, covered, for several weeks. It would be great with grilled or smoked pork, ham, or poultry.*

7. Unwrap the ribs. Generously brush each rack on both sides with some of the "finishing" sauce. Place the ribs in the center of the grate bone side down and re-cover the grill. Continue cooking the ribs until darkly browned and very tender, 30 minutes to 1 hour longer, $4\frac{1}{2}$ to 5 hours in all. When the ribs are done, you will be able to pull them apart with your fingers and the meat will have shrunk back from the ends of the bones by about $\frac{1}{4}$ inch.

8. Transfer the ribs to a large platter or cutting board. Let the ribs rest for a few minutes, then cut each rack in half or into individual ribs. Lightly brush the ribs again with "finishing" sauce and serve at once.

Variation

How to cook Porkosaurus ribs in a smoker: Set up and light the smoker according to the manufacturer's instructions (for more on smokers, see page 43) and preheat it to very low (175°F). Place the ribs in the smoker bone side down and smoke for about 3 hours, adding $\frac{1}{2}$ cup each of hickory and apple chips and replenishing the coals every hour. Gradually increase the heat to 225°F after the first 30 minutes of cooking.

Remove the ribs from the smoker and follow the instructions in Step 5 for wrapping them. Place the wrapped ribs back in the smoker and continue cooking until cooked through and tender, about 1 hour longer. Then, remove the ribs from the foil and brush them on both sides with some of the "finishing" sauce. Return the ribs to the smoker and continue cooking until done, 30 minutes to 1 hour longer.

BEYOND BABY BACKS:

PORK SPARERIBS, COUNTRY-STYLE RIBS, AND RIB TIPS

If baby back ribs offer love at first bite, the bones in this chapter require a bit more seduction. They're tougher and more ornery than baby backs, but if you take your time and treat them right, you'll wind up with ribs that are richly endowed with flavor and character. Case in point: the Jamaican Jerk Spareribs; the Milk and Honey Spareribs from the Piedmont in Italy; or the soy and vinegar spiced Chamorro spareribs, which come all the way from Guam. You'll also learn to smoke rib tips the way they do in Kansas City and to cook country-style ribs directly over the fire. From oregano-scented Greek-style ribs flambéed with ouzo to country-style ribs flavored with honey, mead, and lemongrass, this chapter is all about big bones and big flavors.

JAMAICAN JERK SPARERIBS

METHOD: Indirect grilling
ADVANCE PREP: At least 4 hours for marinating the ribs
SERVES: 6

What was the first barbecue in the Americas? To judge from the writings of the early European explorers of the Caribbean, I'd wager it was a version of Jamaica's jerk. The defining ingredients of jerk—Scotch bonnet chiles, allspice, and a green onionlike plant called escallion—are all native to the West Indies. (The region was also the birthplace of rum.) For that matter, this was the birthplace of a live-fire cooking method on a wooden grate, which the Taino Indians called a *barbacoa*—the origin of our word *barbecue*. The tradition lives on in fiery jerk—particularly well suited to a rich, fatty meat like spareribs.

2 to 6 Scotch bonnet chiles, stemmed and seeded
   (for a hotter jerk, leave the seeds in)
1 bunch scallions or escallions (West Indian green onions),
   both white and green parts, trimmed and coarsely chopped
3 cloves garlic, coarsely chopped
1 piece (1 inch) fresh ginger, peeled and thinly sliced
3 tablespoons chopped fresh cilantro
1 teaspoon fresh thyme, or 1 teaspoon dried thyme
1 tablespoon brown sugar
2 teaspoons coarse salt (kosher or sea)
1/2 teaspoon freshly ground black pepper
1/2 teaspoon ground allspice
1/2 teaspoon ground cinnamon
2 tablespoons vegetable oil
2 tablespoons dark rum
1 tablespoon soy sauce
2 racks spareribs (6 to 8 pounds total)
Lime wedges, for serving

You'll also need:

*1¹/₂ cups wood chips (see Note), soaked for
1 hour in water to cover, then drained*

1. Place the Scotch bonnets, scallions, garlic, ginger, cilantro, thyme, brown sugar, salt, pepper, allspice, and cinnamon in a food processor and process until a coarse paste forms. With the motor running, add the oil, rum, and soy sauce to obtain a thick but spreadable paste. Taste for seasoning, adding more soy sauce or rum as necessary; the jerk seasoning should be highly flavored.

TIPS: *While the jerk seasoning here contains a number of ingredients, it's quite simple to prepare, especially when you use a food processor. (In Boston Beach, Jamaica, jerk's hometown, they still grind the ingredients together by hand.)*

The Scotch bonnet is one of the world's most blistering chiles, but removing the seeds definitely blunts its ferocity. Don't use more chiles than you mean to. And it's a good idea to wear rubber or latex gloves when handling Scotch bonnets. Take care not to touch your eyes.

It's best to cook the jerk ribs on a charcoal grill or in a smoker (you'll find smoker instructions in the variation on page 146). You get the spice and heat from a gas grill but not the characteristic smoke flavor.

2. Prepare the ribs:
Place a rack of ribs meat side down on a baking sheet. Remove the thin, papery membrane from the back of the rack by inserting a slender implement, such as a butter knife or the tip of a meat thermometer, under it. The best place to start is on one of the middle bones. Using a dishcloth, paper towel, or pliers to gain a secure grip, peel off the membrane. Repeat with the remaining rack.

3. Using a rubber spatula, spread the jerk seasoning on both sides of the ribs. Cover the ribs with plastic wrap and let marinate in the refrigerator for at least 4 hours or as long as overnight, turning them 3 or 4 times. The longer the ribs marinate, the richer the flavor will be. (The ribs can also be marinated in large heavy resealable plastic bags.)

4. Set up the grill for indirect grilling (see page 33) and preheat to medium (325° to 350°F). Place a large drip pan in the center of the grill under the grate. (For instructions on smoking on a gas grill see page 36.)

5. When ready to cook, brush and oil the grill grate. Place the ribs bone side down in the center of the grate over the drip pan and away from the heat. (If your grill has limited space, stand the racks of ribs upright in a rib rack; see page 52.) If cooking on a charcoal grill, toss half of the wood chips on each mound of coals. Cover the grill and cook the ribs until well browned, cooked through, and tender enough to pull apart with your fingers, $1\frac{1}{2}$ to 2 hours. When the ribs are done, the meat will have shrunk back from the ends of the bones by about $\frac{1}{4}$ inch. If using a charcoal grill, replenish the coals as needed.

6. Transfer the ribs to a large platter or cutting board. Let the ribs rest for a few minutes, then cut the racks in half. Serve at once with lime wedges.

Note: The traditional wood for cooking jerk in Jamaica is pimento (allspice wood). A more readily available substitute in the United States would be a fruit wood, such as apple or cherry.

Variation
How to cook Jamaican Jerk Spareribs in a smoker: Set up and light the smoker according to the manufacturer's instructions (for more on smokers, see page 43) and preheat to low (225° to 250°F). Place the ribs in the smoker bone side down and smoke until cooked through, 4 to 5 hours. You'll need to replenish the wood chips or chunks after the first and second hours of smoking and to replenish the coals every hour.

BEPPE'S RIBS

METHOD: Indirect grilling
ADVANCE PREP: None
SERVES: 6

New York City is undergoing a barbecue renaissance, thanks to the opening of Dinosaur Bar-B-Que, Rib, R.U.B., and Daisy May's, all in addition to the landmark Blue Smoke and Virgil's. But the best ribs I ever had in the Big Apple came not from a smokehouse but from the kitchen of an Italian restaurant—the lively Beppe near Madison Square. One-time chef-owner Cesare Casella was their creator, and while he braised his ribs to a Caravaggio brown in the oven, his soulful flavorings come through loud and clear on the grill.

For the ribs:

2 racks spareribs (6 to 8 pounds total)

About 2 tablespoons extra-virgin olive oil

Coarse salt (kosher or sea) and freshly ground black pepper

4 cloves garlic, finely chopped

2 tablespoons finely chopped fresh rosemary

2 tablespoons finely chopped fresh sage

1 to 3 teaspoons hot red pepper flakes

For the tomato sauce:

2 tablespoons extra-virgin olive oil

2 cloves garlic, finely chopped

1 tablespoon chopped fresh rosemary

$1/2$ teaspoon hot red pepper flakes

$2/3$ cup dry white wine

1 can (28 ounces) peeled plum tomatoes
    (preferably imported), with their juices

2 tablespoons Worcestershire sauce

2 teaspoons Tabasco sauce, or more to taste

Coarse salt (kosher or sea; optional)

You'll also need:

A grill-proof roasting pan or large aluminum foil drip pan

1. Prepare the ribs: Place a rack of ribs meat side down on a work surface. Remove the thin, papery membrane from the back of the rack by inserting a slender implement, such as a butter knife or the tip of a meat thermometer, under it. The best place to start is on one of the middle bones. Using a dishcloth, paper towel, or pliers to gain a secure grip, peel off the membrane. Repeat with the remaining rack. Cut the ribs into 3-bone pieces.

2. Arrange the ribs in the roasting pan and brush or rub both sides with about 2 tablespoons of olive oil. Generously season both sides of the ribs with salt and pepper and sprinkle them with the 4 cloves of garlic, 2 tablespoons of rosemary, 2 tablespoons of sage, and 1 to 3 teaspoons of hot pepper flakes (depending on how hot you like your ribs). Let the ribs marinate in the refrigerator, covered, while you make the tomato sauce and light the grill.

3. Make the tomato sauce: Heat the 2 tablespoons of olive oil in a nonreactive saucepan over medium heat. Add the 2 cloves of garlic, 1 tablespoon of rosemary, and $1/2$ teaspoon of hot pepper flakes and cook until the garlic is just beginning to brown, about 3 minutes. Add the white wine. Increase the heat to high, bring to a boil, and cook until the liquid is reduced by about half, 3 to 5 minutes. Add the tomatoes, Worcestershire and Tabasco sauces, and $1/2$ cup of water. Bring to a boil, then reduce the heat and let the sauce simmer gently until richly flavored, 10 to 15 minutes. Cut the tomatoes into small pieces with 2 knives or break them apart with a whisk (you will have about $3^1/4$ cups of sauce). Taste for seasoning, adding salt and/or more Tabasco sauce as necessary. Set the tomato sauce aside.

4. Set up the grill for indirect grilling (see page 33) and preheat to medium (325° to 350°F). Place a large drip pan in the center of the grill under the grate.

5. When ready to cook, brush and oil the grill grate. Place the ribs bone side down in the center of the grate over the drip pan and away from the heat. (If your grill has limited space, stand the racks of ribs upright in a rib rack; see page 52.) Cover the grill and cook the ribs until most of the fat has cooked out, about 1 hour.

TIPS: *These ribs are cooked using a two-step process: First, they're grilled using the indirect method, which melts out some of the fat, then they're braised in tomato sauce in a roasting pan on the grill.*

Smoke is not part of the Italian rib "ethos," so these ribs are a good candidate for a gas grill. (You can certainly use charcoal, too—just skip the wood smoke.)

6. Leaving the fire burning, transfer the ribs to a clean roasting pan or aluminum foil drip pan. Pour the tomato sauce over the ribs and tightly cover the pan with aluminum foil. Place the roasting pan in the center of the grate and re-cover the grill. Cook the ribs until tender, 45 to 60 minutes longer. Uncover the roasting pan and continue cooking the ribs until they are darkly browned and most of the tomato sauce has been absorbed, about 15 to 30 minutes longer, about 2 to $2^{1}/_{2}$ hours in all. If using a charcoal grill, replenish the coals as needed.

7. Transfer the ribs to a platter or serve them right from the roasting pan.

CHAMORRO RIBS
(GUAMANIAN VINEGAR SOY SPARERIBS)

METHOD: Indirect grilling
ADVANCE PREP: At least 4 hours for marinating the ribs
SERVES: 4

"**G**uam—where the sun first rises over American barbecue" is the motto of the Guam Bar-B-Q Federation. OK, when it comes to meccas of American barbecue, this tiny island in the Pacific likely isn't the first place you think of, but Chamorros (as the locals are known) are obsessed with live-fire cooking. I have this firsthand from Steve Cruz, founder of Guam's Ultimate Grilling Competition, who traveled all the way to the Barbecue University in West Virginia. Guamanian barbecue is based on the Filipino triad of flavorings—soy sauce, vinegar, and onion—but there's a distinctly local tropical twist here in the musky ripe mango and a tart, salty barbecue sauce called *finadene*. Put them together and you get ribs with an Asian accent but that are an indisputable part of the American barbecue tradition.

2 racks spareribs (6 to 8 pounds total)

2 cups soy sauce

1 cup distilled white vinegar

$1/4$ cup honey

1 teaspoon garlic salt

1 teaspoon freshly ground black pepper

1 teaspoon dried thyme

1 medium-size yellow onion, thinly sliced

3 cloves garlic, minced

1 jalapeño pepper or other hot chile, thinly sliced,
    or $1/2$ teaspoon hot red pepper flakes

1 ripe mango, peeled, seeded, and cut into $1/4$-inch dice

Finadene Sauce (recipe follows)

Sticky Rice (page 256), for serving

1. Prepare the ribs: Place a rack of ribs meat side down on a work surface. Remove the thin, papery membrane from the back of the rack by inserting a slender implement, such as a butter knife or the tip of a meat thermometer, under it. The best place to start is on one of the middle bones. Using a dishcloth, paper towel, or pliers to gain a secure grip, peel off the membrane. Repeat with the remaining rack. Cut each rack of ribs in half and place them in a nonreactive roasting pan or baking dish or in a large resealable plastic bag.

2. Place the soy sauce, vinegar, honey, garlic salt, black pepper, and thyme in a nonreactive mixing bowl and whisk until the honey dissolves. Stir in the onion, garlic, jalapeño, and mango. Set $1/2$ cup of this marinade aside in small nonreactive bowl to use as a baste.

3. Pour the remaining marinade over the ribs, turning to coat both sides. Let the ribs marinate in the refrigerator, covered, for at least 4 hours or as long as overnight, turning them several times. The longer the ribs are left to marinate, the richer the flavor will be.

> **TIPS:** *The recipe calls for meaty spareribs, but you can also use baby backs. In that case, the cooking time will be $1^1/4$ to $1^1/2$ hours. The ribs are traditionally served with sticky white rice.*
>
> *Charcoal is very much a part of the Asian barbecue tradition; wood chips and smoke are not. So, you can cook these ribs on either a charcoal or gas grill.*

4. Set up the grill for indirect grilling (see page 33) and preheat to medium (325° to 350°F). Place a large drip pan in the center of the grill under the grate.

5. When ready to cook, brush and oil the grill grate. Drain the ribs well, then place them over the fire bone side down and cook until seared on both sides, 3 to 5 minutes per side. Transfer the ribs to the center of the grate over the drip pan and away from the heat. (If your grill has limited space, stand the racks of ribs upright in a rib rack; see page 52.) Cover the grill and cook the ribs until well browned, cooked through, and tender enough to pull apart with your fingers, $1\frac{1}{2}$ to 2 hours. When the ribs are done, the meat will have shrunk back from the ends of the bones by about $\frac{1}{4}$ inch. Start basting the ribs with the $\frac{1}{2}$ cup of reserved marinade after they have cooked for 45 minutes. If using a charcoal grill, replenish the coals as needed.

6. Transfer the ribs to a large platter or cutting board and let rest for a few minutes. Serve the ribs with the Finadene Sauce and sticky white rice on the side.

FINADENE SAUCE

This isn't your typical North American barbecue sauce—it's not thick, it's not sweet, it's not even red. But when it comes to offsetting the fatty richness of pork, *finadene* (pronounced fee-na-DEE-nee) is effective, not to mention exceedingly tasty. And it's great splashed over sticky rice. **MAKES ABOUT 1 CUP**

$\frac{1}{2}$ cup soy sauce
$\frac{1}{4}$ cup fresh lemon juice or distilled white vinegar
$\frac{1}{4}$ medium-size yellow or sweet onion, finely chopped (about $\frac{1}{4}$ cup)
1 scallion, both white and green parts, trimmed and very thinly sliced crosswise

1 to 3 Thai or other Asian peppers, thinly sliced crosswise, or $\frac{1}{2}$ teaspoon red pepper flakes

Combine the soy sauce, lemon juice, onion, scallion, and pepper(s) in an attractive serving bowl and stir to mix with a fork. The sauce can be made up to 3 hours ahead.

MILK AND HONEY SPARERIBS

METHOD: Direct grilling, followed by indirect grilling
ADVANCE PREP: None
SERVES: 6

Legions of celebrated chefs, from Ferran Adrià to Charlie Trotter, have made pilgrimages to Cesare Giaccone's tiny restaurant, Da Cesare. Located in the equally tiny hamlet of Albaretto della Torre, it's only a short drive from Italy's truffle capital, Alba, in the Piedmont. Just when you've taken one too many wrong turns amid the steep Barolo vineyards and you utterly despair of ever finding the chalet-style dining room, you round a curve and crest a hill and can follow your nose to Cesare's restaurant. That nose will be led by a cacophony of rich aromas: spit-roasted baby goat, magnificently odiferous Piedmont truffles, and most distinctive of all, a dish of spareribs roasted with milk and honey and porcini mushrooms.

How Cesare came up with this dish, I can't imagine. What I do know is that like many Italian rib dishes—and unlike most North American ribs—the dish isn't about spice or smoke or barbecue, it's about the pork. The milk and honey cook right into the ribs, which come out so rich, so meaty, so intensely flavorful, you'll feel like you're tasting spareribs for the first time.

TIPS: *These ribs are seared directly over the fire, then transferred to a roasting pan to grill using the indirect method.*

Cesare uses the meaty wild mushroom called porcini (Boletus edulis or cèpe), and if you're lucky enough to live in the Pacific Northwest—or handy with a mouse and the Internet—you can find fresh porcinis in the United States. (Beware, they don't come cheap.) If not, I've made highly credible renditions of this recipe with shiitake mushrooms and even button mushrooms.

The farmstead milk Cesare uses is very, very rich. Its nearest equivalent in the United States is light cream or half-and-half.

12 ounces fresh porcini, cremini, or
    button mushrooms

2 racks spareribs (6 to 8 pounds total)

Coarse salt (kosher or sea) and freshly ground
    black pepper

2 tablespoons salted butter

1 to 2 cups light cream

4 to 6 tablespoons honey

2 tablespoons finely chopped fresh flat-leaf
    parsley

You'll also need:

A grill-proof roasting pan or large aluminum foil
    drip pan

1. Trim the ends off the stems of the mushrooms. Wipe the mushroom caps and stems clean with moist paper towels. Cut the stems off flush with the caps and coarsely chop the stems. Set the mushroom stems aside. Cut any large mushroom caps in quarters; cut medium-size caps in half. Leave any small caps whole. Set the mushroom caps aside separately.

2. Prepare the ribs: Place a rack of ribs meat side down on a work surface. Remove the thin, papery membrane from the back of the rack by inserting a slender implement, such as a butter knife or the tip of a meat thermometer, under it. The best place to start is on one of the middle bones. Using a dishcloth, paper towel, or pliers to gain a secure grip, peel off the membrane. Repeat with the remaining rack.

3. Cut the ribs into 3-bone pieces. Very generously, and I mean generously, season the ribs on both sides with salt and pepper.

4. Set up the grill for indirect grilling (see page 33) and preheat to medium (325° to 350°F).

5. Place the butter in the roasting pan and place the roasting pan directly over the fire. When the butter is melted and sizzling, add the mushroom caps and cook until browned on all sides, 4 to 6 minutes, stirring with a spatula. Using a slotted spoon, transfer the mushroom caps to a bowl and set aside. Add the mushroom stems to the pan and cook until browned, 3 to 5 minutes, stirring with a spatula. Remove the roasting pan from the heat; leave the fire burning. Using the slotted spoon, transfer the mushroom stems to the bowl with the mushroom caps.

6. Brush and oil the grill grate. Arrange the ribs on the grill directly over the fire and cook until browned on both sides, 2 to 4 minutes per side. Move the ribs with tongs as needed to brown them evenly. Transfer the ribs to the roasting pan, arranging them bone side down. Pour 1 cup of the cream over the ribs. Generously drizzle honey over each rack.

7. Place the roasting pan on the grill away from the heat and cover the grill. Cook the ribs until nicely browned, cooked through, and very tender, $1^{1}/_{2}$ to 2 hours, stirring the ribs and moving them around so that they cook evenly, adding more cream as needed to keep them moist. Eventually, all of the cream will be absorbed. If using a charcoal grill, replenish the coals as needed. About 15 minutes before the ribs are done, stir the reserved mushrooms into the roasting pan.

8. Taste for seasoning, adding more salt and pepper as necessary. If you'd like the ribs to be sweeter, add a little more honey. Sprinkle the parsley on top and serve at once.

BB'S RIB TIPS

METHOD: Smoking in a charcoal grill
ADVANCE PREP: None
SERVES: 4

To paraphrase the late Frank Perdue, it takes a tough guy to make a tender rib tip. Rib tips are the cartilaginous ends of spareribs. Most pit masters discard them, but when properly seasoned and lengthily smoked, they make for a great gnaw at a barbecue. Lindsay Shannon knows what I mean. Lindsay is the proprietor of one of my favorite Kansas City rib joints, BB's Lawnside BarB-Q, a boisterous roadhouse specializing in the three Bs of the Kansas City good life: blues, beer, and barbecue. (Blues buffs will also recognize Lindsay as the host of *The Kansas City Blues Show* on KCFX.)

Why would you want to prepare rib tips instead of baby back ribs or spareribs? For starters, like all meats with abundant connective tissue, they reward you with tremendous flavor when properly cooked. Then there's the professional pride of being able to transform this tough, ornery cut into moist, tender bones of bliss. Bottom line: Rib tips are the true test of a pit master's mettle.

TIPS: *Just what exactly is meant by a rib tip depends on where you live. In Kansas City—and this book—rib tips refer to the small meaty pieces of the breast bone that are trimmed off spareribs. These can weigh as little as 5 ounces or as much as a pound apiece. (Elsewhere, rib tips can mean the triangular point or end of a rack of spareribs or baby backs or even a boneless end piece of baby back ribs.)*

Finding rib tips can be a challenge. It's easy if you come from a meatpacking town, like Kansas City or Cincinnati, and rather harder elsewhere. A good mail-order source can be found on page 305. If rib tips are unavailable, you could make this recipe with two racks of baby back ribs (4 to 5 pounds). The cooking time will be 4 to 5 hours.

BB's uses meat tenderizer to soften the tough connective tissue in the rib tips. One good commercial blend is Adolph's.

THE PIT AT BB'S

BB'S Lawnside BarB-Q pit is a smoke-blackened brick and granite edifice built in 1950. The granite holds the heat like nobody's business, says Lindsay Shannon. For fuel he uses 80 percent hickory and 20 percent oak. His pit is fired with wood and nothing else. Ideally, you'd use a smoker when making BB's Rib Tips; you'll find instructions in the variation on page 158.

1 tablespoon coarse salt (kosher or sea)

1 tablespoon freshly ground black pepper

1 tablespoon sugar

1 tablespoon sweet paprika

1 tablespoon garlic powder

1 tablespoon meat tenderizer

$1/4$ teaspoon cayenne pepper

4 to 5 pounds rib tips

Spicy Apple Barbecue Sauce (recipe follows)

You'll also need:

4 cups wood chips or chunks (preferably hickory; see Note), soaked for 1 hour in water to cover, then drained

1. Place the salt, black pepper, sugar, paprika, garlic powder, meat tenderizer, and cayenne in a small bowl and mix with your fingers, breaking up any lumps in the paprika and garlic powder.

2. Place the rib tips on a baking sheet. Sprinkle the rub over both sides of the rib tips, rubbing it onto the meat.

3. Set up a charcoal grill for indirect grilling (see page 33) and preheat to low (225° to 250°F), using half the number of coals you would normally grill with. Place a large drip pan in the center of the grill under the grate

4. When ready to cook, place the seasoned rib tips bone side down in the center of the grate over the drip

"RIB TIP"

Always have some blues music playing while you cook ribs. Preferably something really bluesy, like Muddy Waters or B.B. King. The sound wafts across the meat, making it tender.

—LINDSAY SHANNON,
BB's LAWNSIDE BARB-Q

pan and away from the heat. Toss $1/2$ cup of wood chips on each mound of coals, then cover the grill. Smoke the rib tips until nicely browned and very tender, 4 to 5 hours in all, turning the rib tips after $2^{1/2}$ hours. Add 1 cup of wood chips every hour for 3 hours and replenish the coals as needed.

5. Transfer the rib tips to a large platter or cutting board. Let the ribs rest for a few minutes, then cut them into $1^{1/2}$-inch pieces (figure on 7 or 8 pieces per serving). Spoon a little Spicy Apple Barbecue Sauce over the ribs and serve the remaining sauce on the side.

Note: To be strictly authentic here, use a 4-to-1 blend of hickory and oak chips or chunks.

Variation

How to cook BB's Rib Tips in a smoker: Set up and light the smoker according to the manufacturer's instructions (for more on smokers, see page 43) and preheat to low (225° to 250°F). Place the rib tips in the smoker bone side up and smoke until cooked through, 4 to 5 hours, adding 1 more cup of wood chips every hour for the first 3 hours.

SPICY APPLE BARBECUE SAUCE

I've always liked BB's barbecue sauce. Apple juice makes it sweet and ground cloves and cinnamon make it spicy—think of it as a sort of liquid apple pie. Leave yourself plenty of time to boil off most of the water in the apple juice. For ketchup, BB's prefers Hunt's. There are several options for the mild red pepper, including Anaheim chile powder and ancho chile powder. **MAKES ABOUT 2½ CUPS**

1 cup ketchup

2 cups apple juice

⅓ cup molasses

¼ cup cider vinegar

¼ cup firmly packed dark brown sugar

2 tablespoons granulated sugar

1½ teaspoons mild red pepper or chile powder

1 teaspoon ground cinnamon

½ teaspoon ground cloves

½ teaspoon celery seed

Coarse salt (kosher or sea) and freshly ground black pepper

1. Place the ketchup, apple juice, molasses, cider vinegar, brown sugar, granulated sugar, red pepper, cinnamon, cloves, and celery seed in a large heavy nonreactive saucepan and gradually bring to a boil over medium heat, whisking to mix.

2. Reduce the heat to low and let the sauce simmer until thick and richly flavored, about 40 minutes, whisking it often. When it's properly cooked down, you'll have about 2½ cups. Season the sauce with salt and black pepper to taste; it should be highly seasoned. The sauce can be refrigerated, covered, for several weeks. Let it return to room temperature before using.

COUNTRY-STYLE RIBS
WITH CHILEAN PEPPER SAUCE

METHOD: Direct grilling
ADVANCE PREP: None
SERVES: 4

The country-style rib is a rib that believes it's a pork chop. Cut from the shoulder, it does look like an elongated pork chop and its tender, well-marbled meat tastes better grilled directly over the heat rather than grilled using the indirect method or smoked. When Chileans cook ribs, they grill them right over the charcoal. Their seasonings are simple—salt, maybe pepper—but meat is always served with a tangy tomato, onion, and pepper salsa called *pebre*. If you're ready for a change of pace from the heavily smoked ribs of the American barbecue circuit, these spicy grilled ribs are your ticket.

> 1 large, luscious ripe red tomato (the sort that goes splat when you drop it)
>
> 1 small sweet white onion, finely chopped
>
> 1/4 green bell pepper, finely chopped
>
> 1 to 2 jalapeño peppers, seeded and minced (for a hotter pebre leave the seeds in)
>
> 1/4 cup chopped fresh cilantro
>
> 1 clove garlic, minced
>
> 1/4 cup extra-virgin olive oil
>
> 2 tablespoons red wine vinegar, or more to taste
>
> Coarse salt (kosher or sea) and freshly ground black pepper
>
> About 2 pounds country-style pork ribs (see Note)

1. Finely chop the tomato and place it with its juices and seeds in a nonreactive mixing bowl. Add the onion, bell pepper, jalapeño pepper(s), cilantro, garlic, olive oil, vinegar, 1/2 teaspoon salt, and 1/2 teaspoon black pepper, but do not mix. Cover the bowl until you are ready to serve the *pebre*.

2. Set up the grill for direct grilling, building a three-zone fire (see page 31), and preheat the hot zone to high; use the Mississippi test to check the heat (see page 35). If a flare-up occurs, you can move the ribs to the unlit part of the grill.

3. Generously season the ribs on both sides with salt and pepper.

4. When ready to cook, brush and oil the grill grate. Arrange the ribs on the grill over the hot zone and on a diagonal to the bars of the grate. Cook the ribs until nicely browned on both sides and cooked through, 3 to 5 minutes per side, giving each rib a quarter turn after 1½ minutes to create a handsome crosshatch of grill marks.

TIPS: *Country-style ribs are generally sold next to the pork chops in the supermarket meat department. You could certainly prepare baby back ribs this way, too. Grill them using the direct method over a medium-low heat (300°F), 15 to 20 minutes per side. To serve four, you'll need two racks.*

To be strictly authentic, you'd grill these country-style ribs over charcoal like the Chileans do, but since no smoke is involved, this is also a good recipe for a gas grill.

5. Transfer the ribs to a platter or plates and let rest for a few minutes. Stir the *pebre* well, adding more salt and/or vinegar as necessary; the mixture should be highly seasoned. Spoon the *pebre* over the ribs and serve at once.

Note: Country-style ribs come both bone-in and boneless. Either way you'll need about 2 pounds.

COUNTRY-STYLE RIBS
WITH OREGANO AND MINT

METHOD: Direct grilling
ADVANCE PREP: None
SERVES: 4

I'm not sure anyone in Greece has ever grilled a country-style rib, but a Peloponnesian influence is obvious here in the use of garlic, oregano, and mint. (Yes, there's more to Greek barbecue than lamb—pork, for example, is popular in Cyprus.) Remember to set

aside a portion of unused marinade for basting and
serving. And for a theatrical touch, you can flambé the
ribs with ouzo, an anise-flavored Greek liqueur that's
available at most liquor stores.

For the ribs:

About 2 pounds country-style pork ribs (see Note)
Coarse salt (kosher or sea) and freshly ground black pepper
2 cloves garlic, minced
1 tablespoon finely chopped fresh or dried oregano
1 tablespoon finely chopped fresh or dried mint

For the marinade and basting sauce:

1 clove garlic, minced
1 teaspoon coarse salt (kosher or sea)
$1/2$ teaspoon freshly ground black pepper
3 tablespoons red wine vinegar
$1/2$ cup extra-virgin olive oil (preferably Greek)
*1 tablespoon finely chopped fresh or dried oregano or
    mint, or a mixture of both*
$1/4$ cup ouzo (optional), for flambéing

1. Prepare the ribs: Arrange the ribs in a baking dish
and generously season both sides with salt and pepper.
Sprinkle the ribs on both sides with the 2 minced garlic
cloves and the 1 tablespoon each of oregano and mint,
patting the seasonings onto the meat.

2. Make the marinade and basting sauce: Place the
1 minced garlic clove, 1 teaspoon of salt, and $1/2$ teaspoon
of pepper in a nonreactive mixing bowl and mash with
the back of a wooden spoon. Whisk in the vinegar. Whisk
in the olive oil in a thin stream, then add the 1 tablespoon
of oregano. Pour half of this mixture over the ribs, turning
to coat both sides. Set the other half aside for basting.
Let the ribs marinate in the refrigerator, covered, while
you set up the grill.

3. Set up the grill for direct grilling, building a three-
zone fire (see page 31), and preheat the hot zone to high;

use the Mississippi test to check the heat (see page 35). If a flare-up occurs, you can move the ribs to the unlit part of the grill.

4. When ready to cook, brush and oil the grill grate. Arrange the ribs on the grill over the hot zone and on a diagonal to the bars of the grate. Cook the ribs until nicely browned on both sides and cooked through, 3 to 5 minutes per side, giving each rib a quarter turn after 1½ minutes to create a handsome crosshatch of grill marks. Once you have turned the ribs over, start brushing the cooked side with the basting sauce.

5. Transfer the ribs to a platter or plates and let rest for a few minutes, then spoon any remaining basting sauce over them. To flambé the ribs, warm the ouzo in a small saucepan on the grill or over low heat on the stove; do not let it boil. Remove the ouzo from the heat and, working away from anything flammable and making sure that your sleeves are rolled up and your hair is tied back, if necessary, touch a long kitchen match to the ouzo—it will ignite. Pour the flaming ouzo over the ribs and serve at once.

> **TIPS:** Greek oregano has a more pungent flavor than Italian, although you can use either in this dish. Look for the oregano at Greek markets and specialty food shops or see the Mail-Order Sources on page 305.
>
> Greeks would grill the ribs over charcoal, but since no smoke is involved, this is a good recipe for a gas grill. You could also prepare baby back ribs in this fashion. To serve four, you'll need two racks. You'll find instructions in the variation below.

Note: Country-style ribs come both bone-in and boneless. Either way you'll need about 2 pounds.

Variation

How to make baby back ribs with oregano and mint:
To prepare baby back ribs this way, grill them directly over medium-low heat (300°F), 15 to 20 minutes per side. Start basting the ribs once the outside is cooked. Or grill

them using the indirect method over medium heat (325°
to 350°F) for 1¼ to 1½ hours. You'll need 2 racks to feed
4 people.

HONEY MEAD COUNTRY-STYLE RIBS

METHOD: Direct grilling
ADVANCE PREP: At least 30 minutes for marinating
the ribs
SERVES: 4

"**S**ometimes I get tired of the typical tomato-based
barbecue sauces," writes Bill Knutson. I don't know if
Bill has Viking in his blood, but the recipe the San
Franciscan submitted to the Lip-Smackin' Rib Recipe
Contest featured ribs basted with a singular—
and succulent—sauce brewed from lemongrass, honey,
and mead. Mead is wine made from honey, the stuff the
Vikings quaffed during their legendary toasts and drinking
bouts in chambers appropriately named mead halls. Bill
uses the sauce on baby backs (which you can certainly
do; follow the direct grilling instructions and cooking time
in the variation on page 167). I've adapted his recipe to
the most "direct grillable" of all ribs, the country-style rib.

3 stalks lemongrass (see facing page)

About 2 pounds country-style ribs (see Notes)

Coarse salt (kosher or sea) and freshly ground black pepper

*4 cloves garlic; 2 finely chopped, 2 peeled and gently
    crushed with the side of a cleaver*

3 cups mead (honey wine)

¼ cup extra-virgin olive oil

¼ cup honey

*2 teaspoons Thai chile sauce or Chinese garlic chile sauce
    (see Notes)*

2 tablespoons (¼ stick) unsalted butter

LEMONGRASS

Native to Southeast Asia and essential to the cuisines of that region, lemongrass is a long, slender plant blessed with an aromatic grassy, lemony aroma and flavor, but with none of the lemon's acidity. Fresh lemongrass comes in stalks that are 15 to 18 inches long; the edible part is the bottom 4 to 6 inches of the bulbous cream-colored base.

Once available only at ethnic markets, lemongrass today can be found at many supermarkets. Look for stalks that feel heavy and moist. Because lemongrass is so fibrous, it's frequently used in large pieces to flavor marinades, rather than eaten in sauces. There's no real substitute, but strips of lemon zest (the yellow oil-rich outer rind of the fruit) will give you respectable results should fresh lemongrass not be available. Use a vegetable peeler to remove the zest.

1. Trim the lemongrass: Cut the top part off each lemongrass stalk, leaving about a 4-inch piece of the thick base. Do not discard the tops of the stalks. Using the side of a cleaver, gently crush the bases of the lemongrass and set them aside for making the mead sauce.

2. Place the lemongrass trimmings in a nonreactive baking dish. Place the ribs on top and generously season them on both sides with salt and pepper. Sprinkle the chopped garlic over the ribs. Pour 1 cup of the mead and the olive oil over the ribs and let marinate in the refrigerator, covered, for 30 minutes to 1 hour, turning once or twice.

3. Meanwhile, place the remaining 2 cups of mead and the honey, chile sauce, and crushed lemongrass and garlic in a heavy nonreactive saucepan and bring to a boil over medium-high heat. Cook the sauce until reduced by roughly half, 5 to 8 minutes; it should be thick and syrupy. Whisk in the butter and season the sauce with salt and pepper to taste, then strain it and set aside.

4. Set up the grill for direct grilling, building a three-zone fire (see page 31), and preheat the hot zone to high; use the Mississippi test to check the heat (see page 35). If a flare-up occurs, you can move the ribs to the unlit part of the grill.

TIPS: *Mead isn't exactly a staple these days at most wine shops, but a well-stocked liquor store should carry it. Two good brands are Redstone and Rabbit's Foot Meadery. For more information about mead, check out the websites: www.gotmead.com and www.solorb.com/mead. As an interesting variation, you could use a sweet Italian muscat (moscato) or sweet German riesling of the* spätlese *or* auslese *category.*

These ribs are grilled but not smoked, which is great if you happen to own a gas grill. You could certainly use a charcoal grill, or for even more flavor, light wood chunks and grill the ribs over a wood fire (see page 47).

5. When ready to cook, brush and oil the grill grate. Drain the ribs well, discarding the marinade, then arrange them on the grill over the hot zone and on a diagonal to the bars of the grate. Cook the ribs until nicely browned on both sides and cooked through, 3 to 5 minutes per side, giving each rib a quarter turn after $1^1/2$ minutes to create a handsome crosshatch of grill marks. Start basting the ribs with some of the mead sauce once you've turned them; baste both sides several times.

6. Transfer the ribs to a platter or plates and let rest for a few minutes. Spoon a little of the mead sauce on top of the ribs and serve the remaining sauce on the side.

Notes: Country-style ribs come both bone-in and boneless. Either way you'll need about 2 pounds.

There are a couple options for chile sauce here. You can use a sweet Thai chile sauce, like Mae Ploy or Mae Pranom, or a Chinese garlic chile sauce, like that made by Lee Kum Kee. Both are available in Asian markets, specialty food stores, and many supermarkets.

Variation

How to make honey mead baby back ribs: To prepare baby back ribs this way, grill them directly over medium-low heat (300°F), 15 to 20 minutes per side. Start basting them with the mead sauce once the outside is cooked. Or grill them using the indirect method over medium heat (325° to 350°F) for $1\frac{1}{4}$ to $1\frac{1}{2}$ hours. You'll need 2 racks to feed 4 people.

DEVILED COUNTRY-STYLE PORK RIBS

METHOD: Indirect grilling
ADVANCE PREP: At least 6 hours for brining the ribs
SERVES: 4

My assistant, Nancy Loseke, was born and raised in Iowa. When I asked her to contribute a rib recipe to this book, she responded with one inspired by the breaded pork chops she remembers her grandmother making for Sunday family dinners. Her grandmother was born in 1898 and lived on a farm in Iowa her whole life. "I can say with certainty there was no Dijon mustard in her pantry, no shallots in the root cellar, no Marsala on the sideboard," says Nancy. "There were few spices in her cupboard, but she could do amazing things with table salt and an orange can of Watkins pepper that was a fixture on the back of her stove. She was a great but simple cook who passed away before pork became 'the other white meat.' In spirit, I know she'd stand cheek by jowl with the farmers—many of them Iowans—who are bringing back heritage breeds of pork like Berkshire. She'd want her pork to taste like it used to taste."

$^1/_2$ *cup kosher salt*

$^1/_2$ *cup firmly packed brown sugar*

About 2 pounds country-style pork ribs (see Note),
preferably Berkshire pork

4 large shallots, quartered (about $^1/_2$ cup)

2 cloves garlic, coarsely chopped

1 tablespoon chopped fresh tarragon

2 tablespoons Marsala, dry white wine, or apple juice

1 cup Dijon mustard

1 teaspoon freshly ground black pepper

4 tablespoons ($^1/_2$ stick) salted butter

2 cups dry bread crumbs

1. Place the salt and brown sugar in a large mixing bowl or pan. Add 2 quarts of cold water and whisk until the salt and brown sugar dissolve. Add the ribs and refrigerate, covered, until brined, 6 to 8 hours.

2. Place the shallots, garlic, and tarragon in a food processor or blender and finely chop them. Add the Marsala, mustard, and pepper and pulse until blended. Transfer this wet rub to a small nonreactive mixing bowl. Cover and refrigerate if not using immediately.

3. Drain the ribs, discarding the brine. Pat the ribs thoroughly dry on all sides with paper towels. Melt the butter in a medium-size saucepan over low heat. Add the bread crumbs and stir to combine. Transfer the crumb mixture to a shallow plate (a pie plate works well) or bowl.

4. Place a large piece of aluminum foil on a work surface and put the ribs on it. Place a second piece of aluminum foil on a rimmed baking pan. Set the plate of bread crumbs between the ribs and the baking sheet. Using a spatula or your hands, slather the ribs on all sides with the wet rub. Dredge each rib in the bread crumbs and transfer it to the prepared baking sheet.

TIP: *When the National Pork Board compared different breeds of pork, it gave top marks to Berkshire pigs in nineteen out of twenty categories (you can read more about Berkshire pork, also known as Kurobuta, on page 170). But the meat is expensive, and you're unlikely to see it at your local supermarket. You can order Berkshire and other purebred pork from retailers like Berkshire Meats, Inc.; you'll need to ask specifically for country-style ribs (see Mail-Order Sources on page 305).*

5. Set up the grill for indirect grilling (see page 33) and preheat to medium (325° to 350°F). Place a large drip pan in the center of the grill under the grate.

6. When ready to cook, brush and oil the grill grate. Place the ribs in the center of the grate over the drip pan and away from the heat. Cover the grill and cook the ribs until the crust is golden brown, the meat is cooked through, and an instant-read meat thermometer inserted in the thickest part of a rib registers about 160°F, 30 to 40 minutes.

7. To avoid knocking off the bread crumbs, using a spatula, carefully transfer the ribs to a serving platter or plates. Let the ribs rest for a few minutes before serving.

Note: Country-style ribs come both bone-in and boneless. Either way you'll need about 2 pounds.

BERKSHIRE PORK

Progress doesn't always march forward. The last century witnessed the rise of mass-produced food, prized for its uniformity, long shelf life, and ability to be shipped halfway around the world. The price we paid has been the decimation of small farms, unique livestock breeds, and highly localized produce grown first and foremost for flavor. Fortunately, in recent years, unique micro varieties are beginning to be appreciated—oddball antique apples, for example, or heirloom tomatoes that may look funny, and have low yields and a short harvest time, but are bursting with character and taste.

And so we come, in a roundabout way, to the Berkshire hog, which is neither new, despite its recent and highly theatrical appearance (a whole one seemed to descend from the sky in an episode of the *Iron Chef*), nor connected to the mountains of western Massachusetts, although it's likely someone there raises them. No, the Berkshire hog dates back more than three hundred years to the time when Oliver Cromwell's army wintered in the shire of the Berks in England. One day, so the story goes, Cromwell's men came across a herd of feral pigs; these were quickly dispatched by the hungry soldiers. Such was the exceptional flavor and succulence of the hogs that local farmers took to breeding them with domestic pigs.

The result has been the hog of choice in England for a couple of centuries, a slow-growing black pig with short, fine muscle fibers (the secret to the pork's tenderness) and dark reddish pink flesh (the secret to its rich flavor). Berkshire pigs mature more slowly than typical commercial hogs. The additional period of feeding produces a high degree of marbling—fat equals lusciousness—and a rich meaty taste. In short, you get a hog that tastes like the farm-raised pork of yesteryear.

Berkshire pork is raised on a small but growing number of American farms, the descendants of a gift of hogs from the British government to the United States in 1875. A similar gift was delivered to Japan, where it was called Kurobuta, black pig. In Japan, Kurobuta enjoys a cachet similar to that of Kobe beef. Indeed, many American chefs list their pork as Kurobuta on the menu, although the meat actually comes from Berkshire hogs raised in the United States.

One thing's for sure: If you're a rib lover, you should definitely try to find Berkshire pork ribs. Use a simple preparation—salt and pepper or a light sprinkling of rub and the barest whiff of wood smoke. What's wondrous here is the flavor of the meat. (On page 305, you'll find mail-order sources for Berkshire pork.)

BEEF RIBS

Pork ribs likely outsell beef ribs ten to one, but when it came to the www.barbecuebible.com Lip-Smackin' Rib Recipe Contest, the first prize went to a beef rib—the barbecued "pastramied" short ribs on page 196. If you like your bones oversize and over the top, the recipes in this chapter are for you. You'll find both beef back or long ribs (aka "dinosaur bones") and beef short ribs. And, you'll enjoy them every which way—spice-rubbed and smoked as they do in Texas, marinated and grilled as in Argentina, or sliced paper-thin, charcoal grilled, and served with hot bean paste and pickled vegetables, just as you'd find in Korea. This chapter also covers some lesser-known, but no less delectable, ribs ranging from veal ribs prepared with a French flair to bison ribs (served with a cabernet sauvignon barbecue sauce). These ribs won't leave you asking, "Where's the beef?"

SALT AND PEPPER BEEF RIBS

METHOD: Indirect grilling
ADVANCE PREP: None
SERVES: 4 to 6

Salt and pepper ribs are a Texas tradition, based on the very simple notion that when the beef is top-notch and the pit is hot and smoky, you don't need a lot in the way of seasonings to make barbecue that is world-class. As a matter of fact, you don't need much more than salt and pepper—the only seasonings used here. Of course, if you're like most Americans, you probably like barbecue sauce with your ribs. The molasses-flavored Bunker Blaster Barbecue Sauce will hit the spot. (For another Texas classic, see the Lone Star Beef Ribs on page 177.)

> **TIP:** *This recipe calls for a rack of beef long ribs, which are available at many supermarkets. If you happen to be buying a rib roast at the same time, ask the butcher to leave a little more flesh on the bones than normal when he carves out the roast. That way, you'll get meatier ribs. (Most racks of beef long ribs have sufficient meat, but I've seen some cut so parsimoniously, the bones are actually shiny.*

2 racks beef long ribs (beef back ribs; 5 to 6 pounds total)
Coarse salt (kosher or sea)
Cracked black peppercorns (not finely ground)
Hot red pepper flakes (optional; for spicier ribs)
Bunker Blaster Barbecue Sauce (recipe follows)

You'll also need:

1¹/₂ cups wood chips or chunks (preferably oak),
soaked for 1 hour in water to cover, then drained

1. Prepare the ribs: Place a rack of ribs meat side down on a baking sheet. Remove the thin, papery membrane from the back of the rack by inserting a slender implement, such as a butter knife or the tip of a meat thermometer, under it. The best place to start is on one of the middle bones. Using a dishcloth, paper towel, or pliers to gain a secure grip, peel off the membrane. Repeat with the remaining racks.

2. Generously season the ribs on both sides with salt, cracked black pepper, and hot pepper flakes, if using. Cover the ribs with plastic wrap and refrigerate them while you set up the grill.

> **TIP:** *Indirect grilling is my first choice here; the higher heat renders the fat and crisps the meat. You can also smoke the ribs; they'll be delicious, but they won't be as crisp. The variation below has instructions.*

3. Set up the grill for indirect grilling (see page 33) and preheat to medium (325° to 350°F). Place a large drip pan in the center of the grill under the grate. (For instructions on smoking on a gas grill, see page 36.)

4. When ready to cook, brush and oil the grill grate. Place the ribs bone side down in the center of the grate over the drip pan and away from the heat. If cooking on a charcoal grill, toss half of the wood chips on each mound of coals. Cover the grill and cook the ribs until well browned, cooked through, and tender enough to pull apart with your fingers, $1\frac{1}{2}$ to 2 hours in all. When the ribs are done, the meat will have shrunk back from the ends of the bones by about $\frac{1}{4}$ inch. If using a charcoal grill, replenish the coals as needed.

5. Transfer the ribs to a large platter or cutting board and let them rest for a few minutes. Cut the racks in half, if you are serving 4, or into 1- or 2-rib pieces. Serve at once with the Bunker Blaster Barbecue Sauce.

Variation

How to cook Salt and Pepper Beef Ribs in a smoker:
Set up and light the smoker according to the manufacturer's instructions (for more on smokers, see

page 43) and preheat to low (225° to 250°F). Place the ribs in the smoker bone side down and smoke until cooked through, 4 to 5 hours.

BUNKER BLASTER BARBECUE SAUCE

This sauce was created at the Barbecue University by students "Skipper" Beck, Jeff Polep, and Ellie Lamore. It was the grand champion in a barbecue sauce contest judged by none other than KC Masterpiece barbecue sauce creator Rich Davis. The smoky, earthy flavor of the molasses complements the beef without overpowering it. The recipe makes more sauce than you'll likely need for two racks of beef long ribs, but it would also make a good accompaniment for chicken, pork, or even lamb ribs. **MAKES ABOUT 3 CUPS**

2¹/₂ cups ketchup
¹/₂ cup molasses
¹/₄ cup white wine vinegar
1¹/₂ teaspoons liquid smoke
2 tablespoons minced fresh onion
2 tablespoons brown sugar
¹/₄ teaspoon coarse salt (kosher or sea)
¹/₂ teaspoon chile powder
¹/₂ teaspoon onion powder
¹/₂ teaspoon garlic powder
¹/₈ teaspoon cayenne pepper

Place the ketchup, molasses, vinegar, liquid smoke, onion, brown sugar, salt, chile powder, onion and garlic powders, and cayenne in a heavy nonreactive saucepan and whisk to mix. Gradually bring the sauce to a boil over medium heat, whisking as needed. Reduce the heat slightly and let the sauce simmer gently until thick and richly flavored, about 10 minutes. The sauce can be refrigerated for several months in a clean jar; let it return to room temperature before using.

LONE STAR BEEF RIBS

METHOD: Indirect grilling on a charcoal grill
ADVANCE PREP: None
SERVES: 4 to 6

When it comes to ribs, Texas lies at the opposite end of the spectrum from Kansas City or Memphis. Texans prepare ribs with simple seasonings and an even simpler sauce. The typical Central Texas barbecue rub consists primarily of salt, pepper, and cayenne, with little or no sweetener. (Other permissible seasonings might include chile powder, garlic powder, or cumin, depending on the pit master.) As for the sauce, it's little more than meat drippings reddened with a squirt of ketchup. The focus is kept on what a Texan believes matters most: the marriage of meat and wood smoke.

For the Lone Star rib rub:

3 tablespoons coarse salt (kosher or sea)

3 tablespoons pure chile powder

1 tablespoon cracked black pepper

2 teaspoons garlic powder

2 teaspoons dried oregano

1 teaspoon cayenne pepper

1 teaspoon ground cumin

For the mop sauce:

1 bottle Lone Star beer or other lager-style beer

$1/2$ cup distilled white vinegar

$1/2$ cup brewed coffee

2 racks beef long ribs (beef back ribs; 5 to 6 pounds total)
Bare-Bones Barbecue Sauce (page 182)

You'll also need:

$1^1/2$ cups wood chips or chunks (preferably oak), soaked for
1 hour in water to cover, then drained; barbecue mop

1. Make the Lone Star rib rub: Place the salt, chile powder, cracked pepper, garlic powder, oregano, cayenne, and cumin in a small bowl and mix with your fingers. Set aside 1 tablespoon of the rub for the Bare-Bones Barbecue Sauce.

2. Make the mop sauce: Place the beer, vinegar, coffee, and $1\frac{1}{2}$ tablespoons of the Lone Star rib rub in a nonreactive bowl and whisk to mix. Set the mop sauce and remaining rub aside separately.

3. Prepare the ribs: Place a rack of ribs meat side down on a baking sheet. Remove the thin, papery membrane from the back of the rack by inserting a slender implement, such as a butter knife or the tip of a meat thermometer, under it. The best place to start is on one of the middle bones. Using a dishcloth, paper towel, or pliers to gain a secure grip, peel off the membrane. Repeat with the remaining rack.

4. Generously sprinkle the ribs on both sides with the remaining rub, using about 1 tablespoon per side and rubbing it onto the meat. (Any leftover rub will keep for several weeks in a sealed jar away from heat and light.) Cover the ribs with plastic wrap and refrigerate them while you set up the grill under the grate.

5. Set up a charcoal grill for indirect grilling (see page 33) and preheat to medium (325° to 350°F). Place a large drip pan in the center of the grill.

6. When ready to cook, brush and oil the grill grate. Place the ribs bone side down in the center of the grate over the drip pan and away from the heat. Toss half of the wood chips on each mound of coals. Cover the grill and cook the ribs for 45 minutes.

7. Mop the ribs on both sides with some of the mop sauce. Re-cover the grill and continue cooking the ribs until they are well browned, cooked through, and tender enough to pull apart with your fingers, 45 minutes to 1¼ hours longer, 1½ to 2 hours in all. When the ribs are done, the meat will have shrunk back from the ends of the bones by about ¼ inch. Mop the ribs once or twice more and replenish the coals as needed.

8. Transfer the ribs to a large platter or cutting board and let rest for a few minutes. If possible, save the drippings from the ribs for the Bare-Bones Barbecue Sauce (see Note). Cut the racks in half, if you are serving 4, or into 1- or 2-rib pieces. Serve at once with the barbecue sauce on the side.

Note: Drippings from the ribs will accumulate in the grill's drip pan. Wearing heatproof gloves, remove the pan and pour the drippings through a fine-mesh strainer into a heatproof bowl or measuring cup. Loosely cover the ribs with aluminum foil to keep them warm while you make the Bare-Bones Barbecue Sauce. Adding the drippings is optional, but it sure makes the sauce suave and rich.

> **TIPS:** *In keeping with Texas dimensions, I call for two racks of the largest ribs commercially available—beef long ribs.*
>
> *There are several options for the chile powder, including chipotle chile powder (made from smoked jalapeño peppers) and ancho chile powder, which has a sweet, earthy Southwestern flavor.*
>
> *Texans tend to cook hotter than pit masters elsewhere in the country. It's not uncommon to find a pit that burns at 400°F. The fuel of choice in Central Texas is post oak. To approximate this setup at home, use a wood-burning grill with a cover or a charcoal-burning grill with oak chips or chunks.*

Variation

How to cook Lone Star Beef Ribs in a smoker: Set up and light the smoker according to the manufacturer's instructions (for more on smokers, see page 43) and preheat to low (225° to 250°F). Place the ribs in the smoker bone side down and smoke until cooked through, 4 to 5 hours. Start mopping the ribs with the mop sauce after 1 hour, then mop the ribs again once every hour.

BARBECUE MOPS AND MOP SAUCES

Barbecue breeds ingenuity. How else can a pit master transform a tough, ornery cut of bone and meat into a smoky, tender, meaty stave of edible bliss? Ingenuity led pit masters away from the obvious muscle power of direct grilling to the subtle gentle heat of indirect grilling and smoking. Ingenuity is also responsible for one of the most distinctive American cooking utensils: the barbecue mop. Here's how I imagine it was invented.

Some time in the early days of barbecue, a pit master named Bubba faced the formidable task of cooking ribs for two hundred or so of his closest buddies. In order to keep the ribs from drying out and to add an extra layer of flavor, Bubba decided to baste them with a mixture of his favorite barbecue beverages—maybe beer, coffee, and apple cider. He dumped the ingredients in a clean bucket—at least we hope it was clean—and started to apply the mixture to the ribs with a basting brush. Realizing how inefficient this was, he looked around, and his eye settled on a clean cotton floor mop—at least we hope it was clean, too.

So Bubba dipped the mop in the bucket of liquid and began swabbing it over the ribs. The mop was a lot more efficient than a basting brush, and more important, it looked cool as all get out. Today, full-size floor mops are used to apply flavoring mixtures at competition barbecues and in large-volume smokehouses, like the Moonlite Bar-B-Q Inn, in Owensboro, Kentucky. This is all well and good if you're cooking ribs for one hundred, but overkill when you're preparing ribs for family or friends.

Enter the barbecue mop, a miniature version of the full-size floor mop. Barbecue mops are available at most barbecue and cookware shops. Some models even come with removable heads to facilitate cleaning. And, speaking of cleaning, this is the chief challenge in using a barbecue mop. I recommend soaking the mop in a bowl with several changes of hot soapy water for an hour or so. Then, if it's dishwasher safe, run it through the dishwasher. If not, soak it even longer and rinse it thoroughly.

Once you have a mop, you need to prepare your mop sauce. The ingredients can be as varied as beer, wine, coffee, apple cider, or other beverages; vinegar; pickle or sauerkraut juice; soy sauce, hot sauce, Worcestershire sauce; olive oil or vegetable oil; beef broth; mustard, ketchup, horseradish; onions, garlic, celery, jalapeño peppers; and all manner of herbs, spices, and barbecue rubs. Most pit masters use combinations of these ingredients. Somewhere, there just might be someone crazy enough to have used them all at once.

Conspicuously absent from the list (or present in only small quantities) are sweeteners, like brown sugar, molasses, or honey. The reason is simple—the sugar in these will burn with prolonged exposure to heat. The idea behind a mop sauce is that you apply it during the cooking process; you don't want it to burn before the meat is done. That's important because mop sauces not only add flavor and give you something to do during the three to four hours it takes to smoke ribs to perfection, they also keep the meat from drying out.

So what do you do if you don't have a mop? One alternative is to use a long-handled basting brush. Another is to place the liquid flavorings in a mister or spray bottle and spray them on the meat (obviously, this works only for thin mop sauces).

One final note of caution: Never use the mop on raw meat; this risks contaminating both the mop and the remaining mop sauce. Before mopping I always wait until the ribs have cooked for a half hour or so and the exterior of the meat is hot. Better safe than sorry.

BARE-BONES BARBECUE SAUCE

When it comes to serving the right sauce with Texas-style barbecue, Rick Schmidt, owner of the renowned Kreuz Market in Lockhart, Texas, puts it this way: Don't. For Schmidt, barbecue sauce is at best peripheral and, at worst, utterly superfluous with properly smoke-roasted meats. And you won't find a drop of it at his restaurant. Other Texas pit masters are more broad-minded, allowing for sauce, but keeping it simple. And this being the Lone Star State, jalapeño peppers are always welcome. If you tend to be a minimalist or don't like sweet barbecue sauces, this one's for you. **MAKES ABOUT 1 CUP**

1 tablespoon vegetable oil

1 small onion, finely chopped

1 clove garlic, minced

1 fresh jalapeño pepper, seeded and minced (for a hotter sauce, leave the seeds in)

1/2 cup Lone Star beer or other lager-style beer

About 1/4 cup beef stock (see Note)

1/2 cup ketchup

1 tablespoon steak sauce, such as A.1.

1 tablespoon Worcestershire sauce

1 1/2 teaspoons Lone Star rib rub (from the Lone Star Beef Ribs on page 177)

1. Heat the oil in a heavy nonreactive saucepan over medium heat. Add the onion, garlic, and jalapeño and cook until lightly browned, about 3 minutes, stirring with a wooden spoon. Add the beer, increase the heat to high, and boil until reduced by about half.

2. Add the beef stock, ketchup, steak sauce, Worcestershire sauce, and Lone Star rib rub, reduce the heat to medium-high, and slowly bring the sauce to a boil. Add 1 to 2 tablespoons of water or beef stock, enough to thin the sauce to a pourable consistency, and let simmer until the flavors meld, 3 to 5 minutes.

Note: If you've saved the rib drippings from the drip pan to make a richer sauce, add 1 to 2 tablespoons of them along with the beef stock.

DINOSAUR RIBS
(PINEAPPLE MARINATED SMOKED BEEF RIBS)

METHOD: Smoking in a charcoal grill
ADVANCE PREP: At least 8 hours for marinating the ribs
SERVES: 4 to 6

Rich Davis is a legend of American barbecue, not to mention a great guy, good friend, and lifetime supporter of the arts of smoke and fire. You may not know his name, but I'm sure you know his sauce, a thick, reddish brown elixir he spent a lifetime developing, a sauce that epitomizes Kansas City's love of spice and smoke—KC Masterpiece. Before I tell you about his ribs, let me tell you three other things about Dr. Davis. First, that he was a distinguished child psychiatrist (hence the title Dr.). Second, that he has been a medical school founder and dean. Finally, that he has advanced the understanding of the history of America by his unbelievably generous act of turning his archives over to me when I was writing *BBQ USA*.

TIPS: *The ribs of choice for this recipe are the long bones cut from the chuck end of the rib cage. Often sold as individual ribs, they have considerably more meat on them than the slender long bones sold in racks. Each rib can weigh up to 12 ounces. If they're not available in your supermarket, ask a butcher to cut them for you. Or use two racks of regular beef long ribs (follow the cooking instructions for the Lone Star Beef Ribs on page 177).*

You can cook these ribs on a charcoal grill or a smoker (see the variation on page 185). With gas, you'd get the fruit flavor, but not the smoke.

Now, let me tell you about his ribs. Rich calls them Dinosaur Bones, and these massive, meaty beef bones are so packed with flavor that one or two make a full serving. They're marinated in pineapple juice, then slowly smoked over hickory. A final basting of (what else?) KC Masterpiece gives the ribs the luster of an old master painting.

1 cup apple cider vinegar

$^1/_3$ cup sugar

$1^1/_2$ tablespoons dry mustard

2 teaspoons salt

1 quart canned pineapple juice

1 cup Worcestershire sauce

$^1/_2$ medium-size onion, finely chopped (about $^1/_2$ cup)

$^1/_4$ cup vegetable oil

$^1/_4$ cup sweet smoky barbecue sauce (such as KC Masterpiece Original), plus $^1/_2$ cup for serving

12 large beef ribs (meaty long ribs; each 9 to 12 ounces; 6 to 9 pounds total)

You'll also need:

$4^1/_2$ cups of wood chips or chunks (preferably hickory), soaked for 1 hour in water to cover, then drained

1. Place the vinegar in a large nonreactive saucepan and bring to a boil over medium heat. Add the sugar, mustard, and salt and let simmer until the sugar and salt dissolve completely, whisking well. Add the pineapple juice, Worcestershire sauce, onion, oil, and the $^1/_4$ cup of barbecue sauce and whisk to mix. Remove the saucepan from the heat and let the sauce cool to room temperature, then refrigerate it until the marinade is cold.

2. Meanwhile, prepare the ribs: If you want to remove the membranes, place a rib on a work surface meat side down. Remove the thin, papery membrane from the back of the rib by inserting a slender implement, such as a butter knife or the tip of a meat thermometer, under it. The best place to start is at the end of the bone. Using a dishcloth, paper towel, or pliers to gain a secure grip, peel off the membrane. Repeat with the remaining ribs.

3. Place the ribs in a nonreactive roasting pan or baking dish. Whisk the marinade once more, then pour it over the ribs, turning them to coat both sides. Let the ribs marinate, covered, in the refrigerator for 8 to 12 hours, turning them 3 or 4 times. The longer the ribs marinate, the richer the flavor will be. (The ribs can also be marinated in large heavy resealable plastic bags.)

4. Set up a charcoal grill for smoking (see page 33) and preheat to low (225° to 250°F), using half the number of coals you would normally grill with. Place a large drip pan in the center of the grill under the grate.

5. When ready to cook, brush and oil the grill grate. Drain the ribs, discarding the marinade. Place the ribs bone side down in the center of the grate over the drip pan and away from the heat. Toss ³⁄₄ cup of wood chips on each mound of coals, then cover the grill. Cook the ribs until darkly browned and very tender, 4 to 5 hours. When the ribs are done, the meat will have shrunk back from the ends of the bones by about ¹⁄₂ inch. Add 1¹⁄₂ cups of wood chips every hour and replenish the coals as needed; there is no need to add wood chips after the ribs have cooked for 3 hours.

6. Transfer the ribs to a large platter or plate and let rest for a few minutes. Brush the ribs with the remaining ¹⁄₂ cup of barbecue sauce, then serve at once.

Variation

How to cook Dinosaur Ribs in a smoker: Set up and light the smoker according to the manufacturer's instructions (for more on smokers, see page 43) and preheat to low (225° to 250°F). Place the ribs in the smoker bone side down and smoke until cooked through, 4 to 5 hours.

KOBE BEEF

I first tasted Kobe beef at Tokyo's landmark *robatayaki* (country-style grill) restaurant Inakaya. It was love (make that lust) at first bite. Imagine meat that combined the haunting flavor of aged prime beef with the tongue-coating richness of foie gras. Imagine beef fatty and tender enough to melt on your tongue like a snowflake, with the smoky charred flavor you associate with expertly grilled steak. Unfortunately, you'd better endow your imagination with deep pockets, for such mind-boggling richness, tenderness, and flavor don't come cheaply. And, like many gastronomic wonder foods, Kobe beef is surrounded by mystery, hype, and confusion.

First, there's the name: Kobe (pronounced KO-bay) is a cattle-raising center in the southern part of Japan's main island (it's just one of dozens of regions in Japan that boast extraordinary beef). But what makes the beef famous has less to do with its place of origin than the breed of cattle and the way it's raised. The breed is called *wagyu*. These are steers with bright red, supernaturally tender meat and an equally supernaturally generous marbling of white fat.

A Kobe steak looks like white lace laid atop a red tablecloth. The white is the fat; the red is the meat; and to the naked eye, it looks like they're in roughly equal proportion.

As for the mystique, you've probably heard tales of cows being nourished with beer and receiving daily massages. It's true that some of the cows are fed beer, but only during the hottest months to stimulate their appetites so they'll eat more of their regular diet, grain. As for the massage, it's a rubdown with sake, but the purpose is to make the cow's coat shine, not, as is often claimed, to redistribute the fat (if fat distribution were that easy, we wouldn't need liposuction).

In the 1970s, a few *wagyu* steers were brought to North America as breed stock, the origin of the "Kobe" beef (or more accurately Kobe-style beef) raised in the United States and Canada. Unfortunately, while some of this *wagyu* beef is delicious, much of it is overpriced and unremarkable. In my experience, even the best of it lacks the unctuous richness of the Japanese meat. Which is not to say you shouldn't try it—especially the Kobe-style beef from such quality purveyors as Snake River Farms and Lobel's of New York (see Mail-Order Sources on page 305).

This brings us to Kobe-style beef ribs. I've never seen them in Japan, but they are available in limited quantities in the United States. Forget about finding Kobe back ribs (beef long ribs). The meat from the rib roast is so expensive, every last shred is trimmed off the bones. Instead, look for Kobe-style short ribs and use them in any of the recipes on pages 188 through 204. They're especially well suited to Asian preparations, like the sake-grilled short ribs on page 188.

So, what's the connection—if any— between Kobe beef and the notorious basketball star, Kobe Bryant? Legend has it Kobe's father was so smitten by a Kobe beef dinner he had when he played for the 76ers that he named his son after the meat.

SAKE-GRILLED SHORT RIBS

METHOD: Indirect grilling, followed by direct grilling
ADVANCE PREP: None
SERVES: 6 as an appetizer, 4 as a main course

My rib book would not be complete without a recipe from my stepson, Jake Klein, chef at the restaurant Pulse in Manhattan. Jake did much of his training in Hong Kong and Japan, so Asian flavors are a running theme in his grilling. He's made these crusty, sweet-salty, garlicky, and gingery bones a signature dish at Pulse. The exotically flavored ribs are all the more remarkable in that they were developed in a kitchen without a grill. (Pulse is located in a historic Rockefeller Center building, where the safety code prohibits exposed flames.) Jake uses a panini machine to produce the grill marks and crust on his ribs, thus this is a good recipe for apartment or condo dwellers who have no choice but to grill indoors (you'll find instructions for doing this in the variation on page 190). Another cool thing about these ribs is that they're served yakitori style—on skewers.

1 bunch scallions, both white and green parts,
*   trimmed and coarsely chopped;*
*   finely chop 3 tablespoons scallion greens*
*   and set aside for serving*
6 cloves garlic, coarsely chopped
3 to 6 shallots, coarsely chopped (for $^1\!/_2$ cup)
1 piece (2 inches) fresh ginger, peeled and
*   coarsely chopped*
$^1\!/_2$ cup sake, or more as needed
Coarse salt (kosher or sea) and freshly ground
*   black pepper*
12 bone-in individual beef short ribs
*   (about 4 pounds total)*
Pac-Rim Barbecue Sauce (recipe follows)

You'll also need:

9 by 11–inch aluminum foil pan; 12 twelve-inch bamboo skewers (optional; see Note)

1. Place the scallions, garlic, shallots, and ginger in a food processor and finely chop. With the motor running, add $^1/_2$ cup sake, or enough to obtain a thick paste. Season this wet rub with salt and pepper to taste.

2. Generously season the ribs on all sides with salt and pepper.

3. Spread a third of the wet rub in the bottom of the aluminum foil pan. Arrange 6 ribs on top and spread half of the remaining wet rub over them, using a spatula. Arrange the remaining ribs on top and spread the remaining wet rub over them. Cover the pan with aluminum foil, crimping the edges to make a tight seal.

> **TIPS:** *Sake is Japanese rice wine—if it's unavailable, substitute dry sherry.*
>
> *This recipe involves a two-step grilling process. The ribs are grilled using the indirect method until they're tender, then grilled directly over the heat to sear the crust.*

4. Make the Pac-Rim Barbecue Sauce.

5. Set up the grill for indirect grilling (see page 33) and preheat to medium-low (300°F).

6. Place the pan with the ribs in the center of the grill away from the heat and cover the grill. Cook the ribs for 2 hours. Then, remove the aluminum foil, re-cover the grill, and cook the ribs until deep golden brown and very tender, 1 to 2 hours longer, 3 to 4 hours in all. When done, you should be able to pull the meat off the rib bones with a fork. If using a charcoal grill, replenish the coals as needed.

7. Just before serving, brush the ribs all over with Pac-Rim Barbecue Sauce and move them directly over the fire. Grill until sizzling and browned on all sides, 1 to 2 minutes per side, 4 to 8 minutes in all.

8. Transfer the ribs to a platter or plates and sprinkle the reserved scallion greens over them. Serve at once with the remaining Pac-Rim Barbecue Sauce on the side.

Note: To serve the ribs yakitori style, after they have been grilled in Step 6, pull out the bones. Squeeze the meat into compact rectangles, then insert a bamboo skewer lengthwise through each. Brush the ribs with the barbecue sauce and grill until sizzling, 1 to 2 minutes per side. To keep the exposed parts of the bamboo skewers from burning, slide a folded sheet of aluminum foil under them.

Variation

How to cook Sake-Grilled Short Ribs indoors:
Preheat the oven to 300°F. Prepare the ribs through Step 3, then bake them until very tender, 3 to 4 hours. Brush the ribs with Pac-Rim Barbecue Sauce and cook them on a preheated contact grill or in a grill pan until browned, 4 to 6 minutes total on a contact grill, 2 to 3 minutes per side in a grill pan.

PAC-RIM BARBECUE SAUCE

This sauce features a sort of yin and yang of Asian flavors—the briny tang of oyster sauce (a Chinese condiment made with soy beans and flavored to resemble oysters) plays against the sweetness of sugar and mirin (sweet rice wine). And there's enough garlic to ward off a posse of vampires. Oyster sauce (sometimes called oyster-flavored sauce) and mirin are available at Asian markets, natural foods stores, and many supermarkets. **MAKES ABOUT 1½ CUPS**

1 cup oyster sauce

1 cup chicken stock
(preferably homemade)

1 cup mirin (sweet rice wine)

3 to 6 shallots, coarsely
chopped (for $^1/_2$ cup)

6 cloves garlic, coarsely
chopped (about
2 tablespoons)

$^1/_2$ cup sugar

2 tablespoons black
peppercorns

1 teaspoon liquid smoke

1. Place the oyster sauce, chicken stock, mirin, shallots, garlic, sugar, peppercorns, and liquid smoke in a heavy nonreactive saucepan and whisk to mix. Bring the mixture to a boil over a medium-high heat.

2. Lower the heat to medium or medium-low and let the sauce simmer until thick, richly flavored, and reduced to about $1^1/_2$ cups, whisking as needed, 20 to 30 minutes. When the sauce is the proper consistency, it will thickly coat the back of a spoon.

3. Remove the sauce from the heat and pour it through a fine-mesh strainer into a bowl, pressing on the solids to extract the juices. The sauce can be refrigerated, covered, for at least 1 week. Let it return to room temperature before using.

KOREATOWN BEEF SHORT RIBS (KALBI KUI)

METHOD: Direct grilling
ADVANCE PREP: At least 2 hours for marinating the ribs
SERVES: 4

Visit Soot Bull Jeep between mealtimes and this is what you'll see: A squadron of cooks hunched over low worktables, cutting the generously marbled meat off a mountain of beef short ribs, slicing

TIPS: *This recipe may seem complicated, but actually it's a series of simple steps and most of it—like the dipping sauce and cucumber salad—can be prepared well in advance. By the time you add the rice, salad, grilled garlic and jalapeños, and garlic bean paste, you've got a whole meal. But, if you're pressed for time, you can certainly just make the short ribs.*

Korean-style short ribs can be grilled on a charcoal or a gas grill, but for the most authentic experience, use a hibachi. Place it in the center of the table (outdoors, of course, and on a fireproof pad or inverted baking sheet) and let your guests cook the short ribs to their taste.

each piece with surgical precision into paper-thin sheets. It's a task that goes on for hours, such is the popularity of *kalbi kui* (Korean-style grilled short ribs) in Los Angeles's Koreatown, and few places make better *kalbi kui* than Soot Bull Jeep. The restaurant's name— loosely translated as Natural Charcoal Restaurant—tells the story, as do the sparks and smoke rising from the brazier in the center of each of the ten tables.

Soot Bull Jeep is one of the few charcoal-burning Korean grill restaurants in Los Angeles, one where patrons cook the food themselves. "Meat tastes better grilled over charcoal," explains Pusan-born Boo Sang Park, who opened the popular restaurant in 1983. His Korean ribs provide the pyrotechnic pleasure of getting to grill your own dinner.

For the ribs and marinade:

3 pounds bone-in beef short ribs, preferably in strips

4 cloves garlic, minced

$1/4$ cup sugar

$1/2$ cup soy sauce

$1/4$ cup Asian (dark) sesame oil

1 teaspoon freshly ground black pepper

For the dipping sauce (yang-nyum jang):

1 clove garlic, minced

2 tablespoons sugar

$1/4$ cup soy sauce

$1/2$ teaspoon freshly ground black pepper

For serving:

6 cloves garlic, thinly sliced

2 jalapeño peppers, thinly sliced crosswise

2 medium-size heads romaine lettuce, broken into whole leaves, rinsed, and spun dry

$1/2$ cup Korean hot bean paste (optional; see Note)

Korean Cucumber Salad (recipe follows)

Sticky Rice (see page 256)

You'll also need:

A vegetable grate (sometimes called a grilling grid)

1. Prepare the short ribs: Place a short rib on a work surface meat side up. Cut the meat off the rib by running a sharp knife between the top of the bone and the fleshy

> **TIP:** *A vegetable grate is a rectangular wire grid. The closely spaced wires keep small pieces of food, like the garlic and pepper slices, from falling into the fire. Look for vegetable grates at stores that carry grill supplies or search online.*

part of the meat. You'll wind up with a rectangle of meat. Starting at a long end, thinly slice the meat sharply on the diagonal with the grain. The idea is to cut slices of meat that are $1\frac{1}{2}$ to 2 inches wide, 2 to 3 inches long, and about $\frac{1}{8}$ inch thick. Set aside the bone, which will have a little meat attached to each side. Repeat with the remaining short ribs.

2. Make the marinade: Place the 4 minced garlic cloves and $\frac{1}{4}$ cup of sugar in a mixing bowl and mash them together with the back of a wooden spoon. Add the $\frac{1}{2}$ cup of soy sauce and the sesame oil and 1 teaspoon of black pepper; stir to mix. Stir in the sliced short rib meat and the bones. Let the short ribs marinate, covered, in the refrigerator for 2 to 4 hours.

3. Meanwhile, make the dipping sauce: Place the remaining minced garlic clove and 2 tablespoons of sugar in a mixing bowl and mash together with the back of a wooden spoon. Stir in the $\frac{1}{4}$ cup of soy sauce, $\frac{1}{2}$ teaspoon of black pepper, and $\frac{1}{4}$ cup of

water. Divide the dipping sauce among 4 small bowls
for serving.

4. Shortly before you're ready to begin grilling,
place the sliced garlic and jalapeños in small bowls.
Arrange the lettuce leaves on a plate. Place the hot
bean paste, if using, and the cucumber salad and rice
in separate bowls, each with a serving spoon. Cover the
rice to keep it warm.

5. Set up the grill for direct grilling (see page 31; in
the best of all worlds, you'll be using a charcoal-burning
hibachi). Preheat the grill to high; use the Mississippi test
to check the heat (see page 35). Place the vegetable grate
on the grill grate and preheat it as well.

6. When ready to cook, lightly oil the vegetable grate,
using a folded paper towel dipped in vegetable oil and
holding it with tongs.

7. Arrange the beef bones and some of the slices of
beef on the vegetable grate. Grill until cooked to taste,
2 to 4 minutes per side for medium well (Koreans like
their beef ribs rather well done), or to taste, turning with
tongs or chopsticks. The bones will take a little longer;
they should be nicely browned, with sizzling meat on
the sides. After you turn the beef, arrange some of the
garlic and jalapeño slices on the vegetable grate and
cook until lightly browned, 1 minute per side. Serve the
grilled meat, garlic, and jalapeños, then continue cooking
more meat, garlic, and jalapeños.

8. To eat _kalbi kui,_ spread a lettuce leaf with a little
of the hot bean paste, if using, and top it with rice. Place
a few slices of grilled meat on the rice and top this with
some cucumber salad and grilled garlic and jalapeño
slices. Roll the lettuce leaf up like a taco, then dip it in
the bowl of dipping sauce. Serve the grilled bones
separately for gnawing on.

Note: Korean hot bean paste—*samjang*—is a spicy condiment made by blending fermented soybean paste and hot pepper paste. Sometimes called Soy Bean Paste Plus, it's available in Asian markets or see the Mail-Order Sources on page 305. Alternatively you can use a Chinese hot bean paste or sauce. But don't worry if you can't find either one—the ribs will still be terrific without them.

KOREAN CUCUMBER SALAP

Variations on this simple salad turn up throughout Asia, where the cool, crisp, tart cucumber is used to counterpoint hot, salty meat. Kirby cucumbers (also known as a pickling cucumber) are small cucumbers with a high ratio of flesh to seeds. In a pinch, you can use a regular cucumber—simply cut it in half lengthwise and scrape out the seeds with a spoon before slicing.

MAKES ABOUT 1 CUP

3 tablespoons rice vinegar or
    distilled white vinegar
1 tablespoon sugar
1/2 teaspoon coarse salt
    (kosher or sea)
2 Kirby (pickling) cucumbers,
    peeled and thinly sliced
1/4 medium-size onion, thinly
    sliced crosswise

1. Place the vinegar, sugar, and salt in a nonreactive mixing bowl and whisk until the sugar and salt dissolve.

2. Stir in the cucumber and onion. Let the salad marinate in the refrigerator, covered, for at least 10 minutes or as long as 4 hours before serving.

GRANDPA'S BARBECUED PASTRAMIED SHORT RIBS

METHOD: Indirect grilling on a charcoal grill
ADVANCE PREP: At least 12 hours for marinating the ribs
SERVES: 4

O K, here it is: the grand champion of the Lip-Smackin' Rib Recipe Contest we ran on www.barbecuebible.com. "These ribs were my grandfather's favorite," explains Jasmina Shane, from Bayside, New York. "They combine the best of two great smoked dishes, barbecued ribs and pastrami." (The food historian in me feels obliged to observe that the word *pastrami* comes from a Middle and Near East cured meat called *basturma;* although not smoked, it's still popular in Turkey and Syria.) What these ribs and traditional pastrami have in common is the spicing, an aromatic mixture of coriander, mustard seed, and garlic. Jasmina's grandpa lived to be almost one hundred years old— who knew ribs were a health food?

TIPS: *Beef chuck short ribs come from the underside of the steer. They're meatier but tougher than long ribs, so I recommend wrapping them in aluminum foil halfway through the cooking process to make them more tender. You can certainly prepare beef long ribs with these seasonings (follow the directions in the Lone Star Beef Ribs recipe on page 177). For that matter, the pastrami rub is pretty compelling on pork or lamb ribs.*

Star anise is a star-shaped Southeast Asian spice with a smoky licoricy flavor. Look for it in Chinese and Asian markets and in specialty food stores or see the Mail-Order Sources on page 305. In a pinch, you can use ground or whole aniseed. The easiest tool to use for crushing the spices is a large, heavy mortar and pestle.

This recipe calls for smoking the ribs on a charcoal grill using the indirect method. You can also cook them in a smoker following the instructions in the variation on page 198.

For the ribs and wet rub:

3 to 4 pounds bone-in beef short ribs

3 tablespoons coriander seeds

2½ tablespoons black peppercorns

2 whole star anise, broken in pieces, or
1 teaspoon aniseed or ground anise

2 tablespoons mustard seeds

3 tablespoons dark brown sugar

1 large head of garlic (8 to 10 cloves), broken into
individual cloves, peeled, and coarsely chopped

2 tablespoons coarse salt (kosher or sea)

1 to 2 tablespoons canola or other vegetable oil

For the mop sauce:

1 cup ginger ale

½ cup cider vinegar

1 teaspoon coarse salt (kosher or sea)

Your favorite barbecue sauce, for serving

You'll also need:

1½ cups wood chips or chunks, soaked for
1 hour in water to cover, then drained

1. Prepare the ribs: Using a sharp knife, deeply score the meaty top part of each rib in a crosshatch pattern. The cuts should be about ½ inch deep and ½ inch apart. Place the ribs in a nonreactive roasting pan.

2. Make the wet rub: Place the coriander seeds, peppercorns, anise, mustard seeds, and brown sugar in a mortar and, using a pestle, pound them until coarsely crushed. Or, you can crush them in a food processor fitted with a metal blade, running the machine in short bursts. Pound in or puree the garlic and the 2 tablespoons of salt. Add enough oil to obtain a thick paste.

3. Using a spatula, spread the wet rub over the ribs on all sides. Cover the ribs tightly with plastic wrap and let marinate in the refrigerator for at least 12 hours or overnight.

4. Just before you plan to grill, make the mop sauce: Place the ginger ale, vinegar, and 1 teaspoon of salt in a small nonreactive bowl and whisk until the salt dissolves. Set the mop sauce aside.

5. Set up a charcoal grill for indirect grilling (see page 33) and preheat to medium (325° to 350°F). Place a large drip pan in the center of the grill under the grate.

6. When ready to cook, brush and oil the grill grate. Place the ribs bone side down in the center of the grate over the drip pan and away from the heat. Toss the wood chips on the coals. Cover the grill and cook the ribs for 45 minutes.

7. Baste the ribs on both sides with the mop sauce. Re-cover the grill and continue cooking the ribs until cooked through and very tender, 45 minutes to 1¼ hours longer, 1½ to 2 hours in all. Mop the ribs once or twice more and, if they start to brown too much after 1½ hours, wrap them with aluminum foil. Replenish the coals as needed.

8. Transfer the ribs to a platter or plates and let rest for a few minutes. Serve the ribs with the barbecue sauce of your choice.

Variation

How to cook Grandpa's Barbecued Pastramied Short Ribs in a smoker: Set up and light the smoker according to the manufacturer's instructions (for more on smokers, see page 43) and preheat to low (225° to 250°F). Smoke the ribs until cooked through, 4 to 5 hours. You'll need to add 1 cup of soaked wood chips or chunks every hour for the first 3 hours. Replenish the coals as needed. Spray or baste the ribs with mop sauce once an hour.

ARGENTINEAN SHORT RIBS
WITH TWO CHIMICHURRIS

METHOD: Direct grilling
ADVANCE PREP: None
SERVES: 4

T he perfect ribs for steak fanatics, *tira de asado* are short ribs cut in long strips that literally hang off the plate. You'll find these unusual ribs at Argentinean steak houses, where butchers cut beef short ribs crosswise on band saws into thin "steaks." Once available only in South America, Argentinean short ribs are turning up at Latin-themed steak houses and multiethnic food markets all across America. The traditional accompaniment is *chimichurri,* an herb, oil, and vinegar based "steak sauce," but just what passes for *chimichurri* depends on where you're dining. In the pampas (grasslands) of Argentina, it's a simple affair— some salt, hot pepper flakes, and dried oregano moistened with vinegar and vegetable oil. In the cities, it might be a lush, emerald-green pestolike puree of fresh garlic, flat-leaf parsley, wine vinegar, and extra-virgin olive oil. These ribs feature the best of both: The spartan gaucho mixture is used to season the ribs, while the fresh herb *chimichurri* is served as a sauce.

TIP: *When I started in the barbecue business, if you wanted tira de asado, you had to order it custom cut. With the growing Latinization of the American diet, you can increasingly find this singular cut at a number of butcher shops and meat markets (my local supermarket in Miami carries tira de asado). If it's not available in your area, ask your butcher to cut beef short ribs crosswise into* $1/2$*-inch-wide strips on a band saw or order the ribs from one of the Mail-Order Sources on page 305.*

1 tablespoon coarse salt (kosher or sea)

1 tablespoon dried oregano

1 teaspoon freshly ground black pepper

1 teaspoon hot red pepper flakes

2 cloves garlic, minced

About 3 pounds bone-in beef short ribs,
   cut crosswise into long ¹/₂-inch-wide strips

1 to 2 tablespoons olive oil

Chimichurri Sauce (recipe follows)

TIP: As with most of the recipes in this book that use the direct grilling method, you can use a gas grill, charcoal grill, or hibachi. For a haunting smoke flavor, grill the short ribs on a wood fire (see Wood-Burning Grills on page 47).

1. Make the chimichurri rub:
Place the salt, oregano, black pepper, hot pepper flakes, and garlic in a small bowl and stir to mix.

2. Place the short ribs in a baking dish. Sprinkle the *chimichurri* rub on both sides of the ribs, rubbing it onto the meat. Lightly drizzle olive oil over the ribs on both sides, rubbing it onto the meat. Cover the ribs with plastic wrap and refrigerate them while you make the sauce and set up the grill.

3. Make the Chimichurri Sauce and set it aside.

4. Set up the grill for direct grilling (see page 31) and preheat to high; use the Mississippi test to check the heat (see page 35).

5. When ready to cook, brush and oil the grill grate. Place the short ribs on the grate and cook until sizzling and darkly browned on the outside and cooked to taste, 3 to 5 minutes per side for medium.

6. Transfer the ribs to a platter or plates and let rest for a couple of minutes. Serve the ribs with the Chimichurri Sauce spooned over them or on the side.

CHIMICHURRI SAUCE
(ARGENTINEAN "PESTO")

In a marked demonstration of human ingenuity, fresh herb *chimichurri* contains both a breath polluter—raw garlic—and a natural mouthwash—parsley. The net effect is the gutsy flavor of garlic without the price to pay at the moment of the goodnight kiss. A lot of ink has been spilled on the etymological origins of this curiously named sauce. The prevailing story centers on a British bartender working in Buenos Aires named Jimmy and his favorite seasoning, curry powder. By this reasoning, "Jimmy's curry" became *chimichurri*. There are two problems here: Curry powder is not an ingredient used in Argentinean cooking. And why would Argentina's national condiment come from an Englishman? Whatever its origins, the assertive blend makes a terrific sauce for beef ribs. **MAKES ABOUT 1 CUP**

1 bunch fresh flat-leaf parsley, rinsed, shaken dry, and stemmed

3 to 4 cloves garlic, coarsely chopped

1 teaspoon dried oregano

1 teaspoon hot red pepper flakes

$^1/_2$ cup extra-virgin olive oil

3 to 4 tablespoons red wine vinegar

Coarse salt (kosher or sea) and freshly ground black pepper

1. Place the parsley, garlic, oregano, and hot pepper flakes in a food processor and finely chop, running the machine in short bursts.

2. With the motor running, add the olive oil in a thin stream, followed by 3 tablespoons of the vinegar and 3 tablespoons of water. Taste the *chimichurri,* adding another tablespoon of vinegar to make it more sour, if desired. If necessary, add another tablespoon of water to thin the *chimichurri* to a pourable consistency. Season the *chimichurri* with salt and pepper to taste; it should be highly seasoned.

SWEET SOY-GRILLED SHORT RIBS

METHOD: Direct grilling
ADVANCE PREP: At least 1 hour for marinating the ribs
SERVES: 4

Meaty beef ribs, sweet with sugar, salty with soy and oyster sauce, pungent with that trinity of Asian flavorings (ginger, garlic, and scallion) and crustily charred on the grill—if this is your idea of paradise, heaven lies in China, where individual beef short ribs are sawed crosswise into smaller pieces and flash charred on the grill. This particular recipe was inspired by the Imperial restaurant in Denver, but similar versions are found across Asia, from Hong Kong to Seoul. It's perfect for the Type A grill jockey, who lacks the patience for low, slow traditional smoking.

> **TIP:** *The chief challenge here will be finding crosscut single-rib short ribs. If you live near an Asian market with a butcher shop, you may be able to purchase these ribs ready cut. Another option is to use Argentinean tira de asado (see page 199) and cut them into individual bones. Barring these options, make friends with a butcher and ask for individual short ribs cut crosswise on a band saw into 1/2-inch-wide pieces. In a pinch, you can use full-size short ribs; you'll find instructions for doing this in the variation on the facing page.*

1 cup sugar
3/4 cup Chinese oyster sauce (see Note)
1/2 cup soy sauce
1/2 cup sake (Japanese rice wine), Chinese rice wine, or dry sherry
3 cloves garlic, minced
1 piece (1 inch) peeled fresh ginger, minced
2 scallions, white parts minced, green parts thinly sliced
About 3 pounds bone-in individual beef short ribs, cut crosswise into 1/2-inch-wide pieces

1. Place the sugar, oyster sauce, soy sauce, sake, garlic, ginger, and scallion whites in a large, nonreactive mixing bowl and whisk to mix. Stir in the short ribs. Cover the bowl and let the ribs marinate in the refrigerator for 1 to 2 hours.

TIP: *Asians don't generally smoke their meats, so this is a perfect recipe for gas grillers. You could certainly also use a charcoal grill or hibachi.*

2. Set up the grill for direct grilling (see page 31) and preheat to high; use the Mississippi test to check the heat (see page 35).

3. When ready to cook, brush and oil the grill grate. Place the short ribs on the grate and grill until sizzling and darkly browned on the outside and cooked to taste, 3 to 4 minutes per side for medium.

4. Transfer the ribs to a platter or plates, sprinkle the scallion greens on top, and serve.

Note: Oyster sauce (sometimes called oyster-flavored sauce) is a thick brown condiment made from oyster extract, soybeans, sugar, and salt, but curiously, no fresh shellfish. It does, however, have a briny tang reminiscent of oysters.

Variation
How to cook full-size Sweet Soy-Grilled Short Ribs:
You'll need about 3 to 4 pounds of bone-in individual short ribs. Make the marinade following the directions in Step 1, then marinate the short ribs for 3 to 4 hours. Set up the grill for indirect grilling (see page 33) and preheat to medium (325° to 350°F). When ready to cook, brown the ribs on both sides directly over the fire before moving them to the center of the grate, over the drip pan and away from the heat, and covering the grill. The ribs will be tender and cooked through after $1\frac{1}{2}$ to 2 hours. If the ribs start to brown too much halfway through cooking, wrap them in aluminum foil.

SWEET SMOKY BARBECUE RUB

Here's a good all-purpose barbecue rub based on a classic American rub that you can customize by adding smoked paprika or smoked salt. These ingredients help deliver a smoky flavor, even if you're using a gas grill. If you're grilling with wood or charcoal, they reinforce the smoke flavor even more. Smoked paprika is a newly fashionable (but not new) ingredient from Spain, sold by the name of *pimentón de la Vera* (one good brand is La Chinata) and available in Spanish markets and specialty food stores (or see Mail-Order Sources on page 305). As for smoked salt, it comes in a wide range of flavors and prices, from the basic smoky salt sold in the supermarket spice rack to exotic Danish and Welsh smoked versions (also see Mail-Order Sources). If all this sounds too fussy, use regular kosher salt and sweet paprika. **MAKES ABOUT 1¹/₄ CUPS**

RABBI'S RIBS

METHOD: Smoking in a charcoal grill
ADVANCE PREP: None
SERVES: 4

Over the years, I've heard from numerous grill jockeys who don't eat pork for a variety of reasons. Well, these meaty beef bones are for you. The recipe features a technique not seen elsewhere in the book: brushing the ribs with fresh garlic oil to add an extra layer of flavor before applying the rub. Combine this with a pugnacious peach and horseradish

1/4 cup firmly packed
    dark brown sugar

1/4 cup sweet paprika

2 tablespoons coarse salt
    (kosher or sea)

2 tablespoons hickory-smoked
    salt, or more coarse salt

2 tablespoons freshly ground
    black pepper

1 tablespoon smoked paprika
    (see Note), or more sweet
    paprika

1 tablespoon garlic powder

1 tablespoon onion powder

1 tablespoon dry mustard

1 teaspoon celery seed

Place the brown sugar, sweet paprika, coarse salt, smoked salt, pepper, smoked paprika, garlic powder, onion powder, mustard, and celery seed in a bowl and mix with your fingers, breaking up any lumps in the brown sugar, garlic powder, or mustard with your fingers. Store the rub in an airtight jar away from heat or light; it will keep for several weeks. Plan on using 1 1/2 to 2 tablespoons of rub per rack of baby backs; more for larger racks of ribs.

Note: *Pimentón de la Vera* comes in sweet, semisweet, and hot versions. All will work in this rub—choose the one that suits your taste best.

barbecue sauce and you've got ribs designed to give anyone a religious experience.

2 cloves garlic, peeled and pureed in a garlic press

1 1/2 tablespoons vegetable oil

3 to 4 pounds bone-in beef short ribs

2 to 3 tablespoons Sweet Smoky Barbecue Rub (above)

1 can (12 ounces) Cel-Ray soda or cream soda (optional)

Peach Horseradish Barbecue Sauce (recipe follows)

You'll also need:

4 cups wood chips or chunks (preferably hickory or oak),
    soaked for 1 hour in water to cover, then drained;
    barbecue mop or spray bottle (optional)

1. Place the garlic and oil in a small bowl and whisk to mix. Brush this garlic oil on both sides of the ribs. Sprinkle both sides of the ribs with Sweet Smoky Barbecue Rub, patting the garlic and spices onto the meat. Cover the ribs with plastic wrap and refrigerate them while you set up the grill.

TIPS: *I call for meaty beef short ribs here, but you could also use plate-burying beef long ribs. In that case, you'll want a $2^1/2$- to 3-pound rack of long ribs. These can be smoked low and slow at 225° to 250°F for 4 to 5 hours or grilled using the indirect method at 325° to 350°F for $1^1/2$ to 2 hours. In either case, if the ribs start to dry out before they're done, wrap them in aluminum foil halfway through.*

Served at Jewish-style delicatessens, Dr. Brown's Cel-Ray is a celery-flavored soda. It's available at many delis. If you can't find it or cream soda, you can also substitute Sprite or ginger ale.

The recipe calls for smoking the ribs in a charcoal grill, but the ribs can also be cooked in a smoker. You'll find instructions in the variation on the facing page.

2. Place the Cel-Ray soda, if using, in a bucket or bowl for mopping or pour it in a spray bottle.

3. Set up a charcoal grill for smoking (see page 33) and preheat to low (225° to 250°F), using half of the number of coals you would normally grill with. Place a large drip pan in the center of the grill under the grate.

4. When ready to cook, brush and oil the grill grate. Place the ribs bone side down in the center of the grate over the drip pan and away from the heat. Toss $1/2$ cup of wood chips on each mound of coals. Cover the grill and cook the ribs for 1 hour.

5. Mop or spray the ribs on both sides with the Cel-Ray soda, if using. Re-cover the grill and continue cooking the ribs until well browned, cooked through, and tender, 3 to 4 hours longer, 4 to 5 hours in all. If using the Cel-Ray soda, mop the ribs once an hour. Add 1 cup of wood chips after each of the first three hours of cooking and replenish the coals every hour.

6. Transfer the ribs to a large platter or cutting board and let rest for a few minutes. Serve the ribs at once with the Peach Horseradish Barbecue Sauce on the side.

Variation

To cook the Rabbi's Ribs in a smoker: Set up and light the smoker according to the manufacturer's instructions (for more on smokers, see page 43) and preheat to low (225° to 250°F). Place the ribs in the smoker bone side down and smoke until cooked through, 4 to 5 hours. Start mopping the ribs with the Cel-Ray soda, if using, after 3 hours, then mop them again once every hour. You'll need to replenish the wood chips or chunks after each of the first three hours of smoking and to replenish the coals every hour.

PEACH HORSERADISH BARBECUE SAUCE

This sauce owes its brassy fruit flavor to peach preserves and its heat to freshly grated horseradish. And freshly grated horseradish owes its heat to a sulfuric compound that is released when the root is cut and comes in contact with the air. Thus, the finer you grate the horseradish, the hotter the sauce. If necessary, you could use prepared horseradish, but the sauce won't have quite as much bite. **MAKES ABOUT 1 CUP**

¹/₄ cup peach preserves

¹/₄ cup Dijon mustard

¹/₄ cup bourbon

3 tablespoons cider vinegar

3 tablespoons Worcestershire sauce

1 tablespoon soy sauce, or more to taste

1 piece (2 inches) fresh horseradish, peeled

(for about 2 tablespoons finely chopped)

Coarse salt (kosher or sea) and freshly ground black pepper

1. Place the peach preserves, mustard, bourbon, cider vinegar, Worcestershire sauce, and soy sauce in a heavy nonreactive saucepan over medium-high heat. Gradually bring to a boil, whisking the ingredients until smooth. Lower the heat to medium and let the sauce simmer gently until thick and richly flavored, 3 to 5 minutes.

2. Meanwhile, finely grate the horseradish on a box grater or finely chop it in a food processor.

3. Remove the sauce from the heat and let cool until warm, then stir in the horseradish. Season the sauce with salt and pepper to taste and more soy sauce if necessary. The sauce can be refrigerated, covered, for up to 1 week. Let it return to room temperature before using.

ROTISSERIE VEAL RIBS
WITH HERBES DE PROVENCE

METHOD: Spit roasting
ADVANCE PREP: None
SERVES: 2

A mericans and Europeans take different approaches to ribs. On our side of the Atlantic, ribs are a blank canvas on which the pit master paints a smoky masterpiece. For Europeans, ribs are about the meat—pork should taste like pork, beef like beef, and so on. French and Italian rib men keep the seasonings simple—salt, pepper, maybe some dried herbs—shying away from the extravagant spicing and smoking characteristic of American barbecue.

TIP: Herbes de Provence *is a mixture of dried basil, oregano, thyme, lavender, and other Mediterranean herbs. You can find good commercial blends at specialty food stores or natural foods stores. Or, you'll find a recipe in* How to Grill *and* The Barbecue! Bible.

If ever there was a rib suited to this approach, it's the delicately flavored veal rib. Save this recipe for an intimate dinner; only two racks of veal ribs will fit on the rotisserie, although you may have some welcome leftovers.

> 2 racks veal ribs (2 to 3 pounds total;
>   see box on page 210)
> 2 tablespoons extra-virgin olive oil
> Coarse salt (kosher or sea) and freshly ground
>   black pepper
> 3 cloves garlic, finely chopped
> 3 to 4 tablespoons herbes de Provence
> Tomato Caper Vinaigrette (recipe follows)
> Lemon wedges, for serving

1. Prepare the ribs:
Place a rack of ribs meat side down on a baking sheet. Remove the thin, papery membrane from the back of the rack by inserting a slender implement, such as a butter knife or the tip of a meat thermometer, under it. The best place to start is on one of the middle bones. Using a dishcloth, paper towel, or pliers to gain a secure grip, peel off the membrane. Repeat with the remaining rack.

TIP: This recipe would also be good prepared with "true" pork baby back, those diminutive racks that weigh not more than $3/4$ to $1^{1}/_{4}$ pounds each (see page 88). The cooking time will be thirty-five minutes to one hour.

2. Drizzle the olive oil on both sides of the ribs, rubbing the oil over the meat with a basting brush or your fingertips. Season both sides of the ribs with salt and pepper and generously sprinkle garlic and *herbes de Provence* over them.

3. Thread the ribs onto the rotisserie spit: Place a rack of ribs bone side up on a work surface. Using a sharp, slender knife, make starter holes in the center of the meat between every two ribs. Twist the knife blade to widen the holes; this will make it easier to insert the spit.

SHOPPING FOR VEAL RIBS

Finding veal ribs may present a bit of a challenge. My local supermarket sometimes carries them, so keep an eye on the meat counter. Or, make friends with a butcher and ask to have veal ribs set aside or special ordered for you.

Repeat with the remaining rack of ribs. Use an over and under weaving motion to thread the spit through the holes in the racks of ribs.

4. Set up the grill for spit roasting following the manufacturer's instructions and preheat to high. If you are cooking on a charcoal grill, use the Mississippi test to check the heat (see page 35). Place a large drip pan in the center of the grill directly under the spit.

5. When ready to cook, attach the spit to the rotisserie mechanism, turn on the motor, and cover the grill. Cook the ribs until they are golden brown, tender, and cooked through, 35 minutes to 1 hour, depending on their size. When the ribs are done, the meat will have shrunk back from the ends of the bones by about 1/4 inch.

6. Transfer the spit with the ribs to a cutting board. Carefully remove the spit, then let the ribs rest for a few minutes. Cut each rack of ribs into 2-bone segments. Serve the ribs with a little Tomato Caper Vinaigrette spooned over them. Serve the remaining vinaigrette on the side with the lemon wedges.

Variation

How to cook Veal Ribs with Herbes de Provence using the indirect method: Set up the grill for indirect grilling (see page 33) and preheat it to medium-high (400°F). Place the ribs bone side down in the center of the grill. The ribs will be cooked through and tender after 35 minutes to 1 hour. There's no need to use wood chips, as wood smoke is not part of Mediterranean tradition.

TOMATO CAPER VINAIGRETTE

Normally, I wouldn't serve an oil-based condiment with a fatty meat like ribs. But veal ribs are relatively lean and the robust flavors of tomato, caper, and olives continue the Mediterranean theme of the *herbes de Provence*. **MAKES ABOUT 1 CUP**

**1 small clove garlic,
   minced**
**¹/₂ teaspoon coarse salt
   (kosher or sea),
   or more to taste**
**2 tablespoons
   red wine vinegar**
**¹/₂ cup extra-virgin
   olive oil**
**1 medium-size ripe tomato,
   peeled, seeded, and
   cut into ¹/₄-inch dice**
**1 tablespoon capers,
   drained**
**4 pitted black olives,
   finely chopped**
**2 fresh basil leaves
   (optional), thinly slivered**
**Freshly ground black
   pepper**

Place the garlic and salt in a nonreactive mixing bowl and mash with the back of a wooden spoon.

Add the vinegar and whisk to mix. Whisk in the olive oil in a thin stream. Add the tomato, capers, olives, and basil, if using. Season the vinaigrette with salt and pepper to taste; it should be highly seasoned. You can also place the vinaigrette ingredients in a blender and puree them until smooth, but you'll lose the chunky texture. The vinaigrette can be prepared up to 2 hours ahead.

FISH (OR VEAL) RIBS
WITH GASTRIQUE BARBECUE SAUCE

METHOD: Indirect grilling, followed by direct grilling
ADVANCE PREP: None
SERVES: 4

In a field rife with strange flavor combinations (I've seen rib recipes made with pickle juice, watermelon, even chocolate syrup), these ribs are surely the most singular. Had they not been served by one of the most accomplished seafood chefs in the country, Rick Moonen of the restaurant rm seafood in Las Vegas, I might have dismissed the very notion of a fish rib as pure fantasy. But it turns out that there's an Amazonian fish called *tambaqui* with ribs so large, they can actually be braised or barbecued. They were a specialty of Rick's at Oceana, in New York City.

Tambaqui's a bit hard to track down. But, I've also made Rick's recipe with veal ribs, which are delicate like the fish, and that's what this recipe calls for. In either case, you'll enjoy a complex sweet/sour barbecue sauce based on a classic French preparation called a *gastrique*—basically caramel (burnt sugar) deglazed with vinegar. Sweet. Sour. Garlicky. Caramelized. Whether fish or veal, these ribs have oceans of flavor.

> **TIPS:** According to Rick Moonen, tambaqui is a "huge fish that eats nuts from rubber trees in the Amazon and Orinoco river basin and actually has molar-type teeth to chew the hard nuts that fall into the water. The ribs are large and thick." If you can get a hold of tambaqui ribs, you can cook them the same way as the veal. They are likely to take 40 minutes to 1 hour.
>
> For even more flavor, add 1 1/2 cups of fruit wood—such as apple or cherry—chips or chunks to the fire, following the instructions on page 47.

For the ribs:

4 racks veal ribs (4 to 6 pounds total; see box on page 210)

Coarse salt (kosher or sea) and freshly ground black pepper

2 cloves garlic, chopped

1 tablespoon stemmed fresh thyme leaves

For the gastrique barbecue sauce:

2 tablespoons extra-virgin olive oil

1 medium-size onion, finely chopped (about 1 cup)

3 cloves garlic, minced

2 teaspoons stemmed fresh thyme leaves

1 cup sugar

$1/4$ cup red wine vinegar

2 cups ketchup

1 cup veal or chicken stock (preferably homemade),
  or more as needed

$1^1/2$ teaspoons Tabasco sauce

$1^1/2$ teaspoons Worcestershire sauce

Coarse salt (kosher or sea) and freshly ground
  black pepper

1. Prepare the ribs: Place a rack of ribs meat side down on a baking sheet. Remove the thin, papery membrane from the back of the rack by inserting a slender implement, such as a butter knife or the tip of a meat thermometer, under it. The best place to start is on one of the middle bones. Using a dishcloth, paper towel, or pliers to gain a secure grip, peel off the membrane. Repeat with the remaining racks.

2. Season the ribs on both sides with salt and pepper and sprinkle both sides with the chopped garlic and 1 tablespoon of thyme. Cover the ribs with plastic wrap and refrigerate them while you make the sauce and set up the grill.

3. Make the gastrique barbecue sauce: Heat the olive oil in a heavy nonreactive saucepan over medium heat. Add the onion, minced garlic, and 2 teaspoons of thyme and cook until the onion is soft but not brown,

3 to 4 minutes, stirring with a wooden spoon. Set the cooked onion mixture aside in the saucepan.

4. Place the sugar in a separate heavy nonreactive saucepan. Add $1/2$ cup of water, cover the pan, and cook over high heat for 1 minute. Uncover the pan and continue cooking until the sugar caramelizes (turns a deep golden brown), 5 to 8 minutes more. Do not let the sugar burn.

5. Remove the saucepan with the caramelized sugar from the heat and immediately add the vinegar. It will hiss and sputter; take care to avoid the fumes. Return the pan to the heat and bring the vinegar mixture to a boil, whisking with a metal whisk until the vinegar is fully incorporated.

6. Add the vinegar mixture to the onion mixture, along with the ketchup, veal stock, Tabasco sauce, and Worcestershire sauce, place over medium-low heat, and let the sauce simmer gently until thick and richly flavored, 15 to 20 minutes. Taste for seasoning, adding salt and pepper as necessary; the sauce should be highly seasoned. If the sauce is too thick, thin it with a little more stock. Remove the pan from the heat.

7. Set up the grill for indirect grilling (see page 33) and preheat to medium (325° to 350°F). Place a large drip pan in the center of the grill under the grate.

8. When ready to cook, brush and oil the grill grate. Place the ribs bone side down in the center of the grate over the drip pan and away from the heat. (If your grill has limited space, stand the racks of ribs upright in a rib rack; see page 52.) Cover the grill and cook the ribs until cooked through and tender, 1 to $1\frac{1}{4}$ hours. When the ribs are done, the meat will have shrunk back from the ends of the bones by about $1/4$ inch. Start basting the ribs with the *gastrique* barbecue sauce after 30 minutes and baste them every 15 minutes after that. If using a charcoal grill, replenish the coals as needed.

9. Just before serving, brush the ribs once more on both sides with some of the *gastrique* sauce. Move the ribs directly over the fire and grill until the sauce is sizzling, 1 to 3 minutes per side.

10. Transfer the ribs to a large platter or cutting board and let them rest for a few minutes. Then, serve the ribs at once as whole racks or cut them into individual ribs. Serve the remaining *gastrique* barbecue sauce on the side.

Variation

How to cook fish or veal ribs in a smoker: Set up and light the smoker according to the manufacturer's instructions (for more on smokers, see page 43) and preheat it to low (225° to 250°F). Place the ribs in the smoker bone side down and smoke until cooked through, 3 to 4 hours, lightly basting them with the *gastrique* barbecue sauce during the last 1½ hours.

BISON RIBS
WITH CABERNET SAUVIGNON BARBECUE SAUCE

METHOD: Indirect grilling, followed by direct grilling
ADVANCE PREP: At least 1 hour for marinating the ribs
SERVES: 4 to 6

The bison (aka, buffalo; the terms are interchangeable) is the largest land mammal to be found in North America since the last Ice Age. According to the National Bison Association, a herd of seventy million of these splendid creatures roamed the American plains prior to the seventeenth century. (To get an idea of just how large the herds were, rent the movie *Dances with Wolves* with Kevin Costner.) But by the late nineteenth century, these mammoth herds had been hunted to the verge of extinction.

Today, the bison is making a comeback, and there are at least four compelling reasons you should try cooking some on the grill. First, bison meat has the rich flavor of beef—indeed, many people say it tastes a little sweeter than beef. Second, it contains only a fraction of the fat found in beef or pork—as little as 25 percent, depending on the cut. Third, bison are raised in free-range conditions, grazing largely on grass without being fed growth hormones, antibiotics, or animal by-products. Finally, by cooking and eating bison, you're participating in a culinary tradition that literally goes back to the Ice Age. A rosemary-scented cabernet sauvignon barbecue sauce rounds out the dish, uniting vine and rib.

1 cup dry red wine

$1/2$ cup extra-virgin olive oil

2 shallots, finely chopped

1 carrot, finely chopped

2 cloves garlic, crushed with the side of a knife

2 bay leaves

1 teaspoon dried thyme leaves

3 to 4 juniper berries, crushed with the side of a knife,
*   or 2 tablespoons gin*

2 racks bison (buffalo) ribs (about 6 pounds total;
*   see Note)*

Coarse salt (kosher or sea) and freshly ground
*   black pepper*

Garlic powder

Cabernet Sauvignon Barbecue Sauce
*   (recipe follows)*

You'll also need:

$1^1/2$ cups wood chips or chunks (optional; preferably oak),
*   soaked for 1 hour in water to cover, then drained;*
*   heavy-duty aluminum foil*

1. Place the wine,

olive oil, shallots, carrot, garlic, bay leaves, thyme, and juniper berries in a nonreactive mixing bowl and whisk to mix. Set this marinade aside.

2. Prepare the ribs:

Place a rack of ribs meat side down on a work surface. Remove the thin, papery membrane from the back of the rack by inserting a slender implement, such as a butter knife or the tip of a meat thermometer, under it. The best place to start is on one of the middle bones. Using a dishcloth, paper towel, or pliers to gain a secure grip, peel off the membrane. Repeat with the remaining rack.

TIPS: *Because bison ribs tend to be leaner than beef ribs, I like to give them an extra shot of moistness in the form of a marinade. The one here plays the earthy acidity of red wine against the piney freshness of juniper berries. If you don't have juniper berries, you can use a shot of their namesake spirit, gin.*

Bison is so much leaner than beef, I suggest using a two-step cooking process. First, grill the ribs using the indirect method and wood smoke. Halfway through, wrap the ribs in aluminum foil so they can cook in their own juices and without drying out.

I like to flavor the ribs with smoke, so I suggest using a charcoal grill or smoker. If you're using a gas grill, consider basting the ribs with Steve's Smoky Butter Baste on page 28.

3. Generously season the ribs on both sides

with salt, pepper, and garlic powder. Place the ribs in a large nonreactive roasting pan or baking dish and let sit for 5 minutes. Pour the marinade over them, turning the racks to coat both sides. Let the ribs marinate, covered, in the refrigerator for 1 to 2 hours. The longer the ribs marinate, the richer the flavor will be. (The ribs can also be marinated in large heavy resealable plastic bags.)

4. Set up the grill for indirect grilling (see page 33)

and preheat to medium (325° to 350°F). Place a large drip pan in the center of the grill under the grate. (For instructions on smoking on a gas grill, see page 36.)

5. When ready to cook, brush and oil the grill grate. Place the ribs bone side down in the center of the grate over the drip pan and away from the heat. If cooking on a charcoal grill and using wood chips, toss half of them on each mound of coals. Cover the grill and cook the ribs for about $1\frac{1}{2}$ hours. If using a charcoal grill, replenish the coals as needed.

6. Lightly brush the ribs on both sides with some of the Cabernet Sauvignon Barbecue Sauce. Tightly wrap each rack in heavy-duty aluminum foil. Re-cover the grill and continue cooking the ribs until they are cooked through and tender enough to pull apart with your fingers, 30 minutes to 1 hour longer, 2 to $2\frac{1}{2}$ hours in all. When the ribs are done, the meat will have shrunk back from the ends of the bones by about $\frac{1}{2}$ inch.

7. Just before serving, unwrap the ribs and brush them once more on both sides with the Cabernet Sauvignon Barbecue Sauce. Move the ribs directly over the fire and grill until the sauce is sizzling and browned, 1 to 3 minutes per side.

8. Transfer the ribs to a large platter or cutting board. Let the ribs rest for a few minutes, then cut the racks in half. Serve at once with any remaining Cabernet Sauvignon Barbecue Sauce on the side.

Note: You may be able to find or order bison ribs at a butcher shop that specializes in game. Otherwise, see Mail-Order Sources on page 305. Each rack should weigh between $2\frac{1}{2}$ and 3 pounds.

CABERNET SAUVIGNON BARBECUE SAUCE

R ed wine may seem like an odd ingredient for barbecue sauce, especially for ribs. Of course, many American pit masters spice their sauces with beer, bourbon, or rum. In Europe, on the other hand, there is a long tradition of saucing meats with the wine you plan to serve with them.

Cabernet sauvignon is a terrific wine for pairing with buffalo. The red berry flavors in the wine make a spot-on match for the sweet, rich meat. The wine's acidity keeps the sauce from being too sweet. **MAKES ABOUT 1 1/4 CUPS**

2 tablespoons butter

2 to 3 shallots, finely chopped (for about 1/4 cup)

2 teaspoons finely chopped fresh rosemary

1 cup cabernet sauvignon or other full-flavored red wine

1/2 cup tomato sauce

1/4 cup firmly packed brown sugar

2 tablespoons Worcestershire sauce

1 tablespoon fresh lemon juice

1 to 2 teaspoons hot sauce, such as Texas Pete or Tabasco

1 teaspoon liquid smoke

2 teaspoons dry mustard

1/4 teaspoon ground mace or nutmeg

Coarse salt (kosher or sea) and freshly ground black pepper

1. Melt 1 tablespoon of the butter in a heavy nonreactive saucepan over medium heat. Add the shallots and rosemary and cook until just beginning to brown, about 3 minutes, stirring with a whisk. Add the cabernet sauvignon, increase the heat to high, and let boil until reduced by about half, 4 to 6 minutes.

2. Add the tomato sauce, brown sugar, Worcestershire sauce, lemon juice, hot sauce, liquid smoke, mustard, and mace and whisk to mix. Let the sauce simmer gently until thick and richly flavored, 6 to 8 minutes. Season the sauce with salt and pepper to taste, then whisk in the remaining 1 tablespoon of butter. Let the sauce cool to room temperature before serving. The sauce can be refrigerated, covered, for at least 1 week. Let it return to room temperature before using. (You may need to reheat and whisk the sauce to blend in the butter.)

LAMB RIBS

Pork and beef may be America's most popular ribs, but on any given day, more people on the world's barbecue trail are probably grilling lamb. The lamb-eating sector of Planet Barbecue begins in Mauretania and extends across Africa and the eastern Mediterranean, through the Near and Middle East, Central Asia, India, and Indonesia, all the way to Australia and New Zealand.

Which brings us to this chapter and to bones you may have never known existed—smoked Aussie lamb ribs with a ginger, rum, and pineapple barbecue sauce; Mediterranean-influenced garlic and mint ribs grilled directly over the flames; yogurt-marinated, tandoori-style ribs in the Indian tradition; even *méchoui*-style (spice-stung, spit-roasted) ribs from Morocco. And, if you happen to have known and loved a rowdy barbecue joint called Hoodoo Barbecue in Boston's Kenmore Square back in the 1980s, you'll find a reconstruction of their famous lamb ribs with vanilla barbecue sauce—plus the true story of just how the vanilla found its way into the recipe.

GRILLED LAMB RIBS
WITH GARLIC AND MINT

METHOD: Indirect grilling
ADVANCE PREP: At least 4 hours for marinating the ribs
SERVES: 4

N orth Americans are so obsessed with pork and beef ribs that we lose sight of the fact that on any given night, the barbecue meat of choice for half the world is lamb. Robustly scented with garlic and mint, these lamb ribs are grilled until audibly crisp. The recipe was inspired by one of our Lip-Smackin' Rib Recipe Contest winners, Jacob Esbo, but similar recipes can be found as far away as New Zealand. If you're used to the sweet, smoky flavor of American ribs, the forthright simplicity of this grilled lamb will come as a revelation. In keeping with the Mediterranean overtones of the recipe, the lamb is served with garlic-spiked Middle Eastern–style grilled vegetables. The Minted Yogurt Drink on page 274 would make an appropriate accompaniment.

4 racks Denver lamb ribs (trimmed lamb breast;
    4 to 5 pounds total)
Coarse salt (kosher or sea) and coarsely ground
    black pepper or cracked black peppercorns
6 cloves garlic, minced
1/4 cup finely chopped fresh mint, or 1/4 cup dried mint
1 lemon, cut in half and seeded, plus 1 lemon,
    cut into wedges, for serving
1 cup extra-virgin olive oil
1/2 cup red wine vinegar
Middle Eastern Grilled Vegetables
    (recipe follows), for serving

1. Prepare the ribs:

Place a rack of ribs meat side down on a work surface. Remove the thin, papery membrane from the back of the rack by inserting a slender implement, such as a butter knife or the tip of a meat thermometer, under it. The best place to start is on one of the middle bones. Using a dishcloth, paper towel, or pliers to gain a secure grip, peel off the membrane. Repeat with the remaining racks.

2. Place the ribs in a

nonreactive roasting pan. Generously season each rack on both sides with salt and pepper. Sprinkle the garlic and mint over both sides of the racks, patting them onto the meat. Let the ribs sit for 5 minutes. Squeeze the juice from the lemon halves over both sides of the ribs. Pour the olive oil and vinegar over the ribs, turning them several times to coat both sides. Cover the roasting pan and let the ribs marinate in the refrigerator for at least 4 hours, or as long as overnight, turning them once or twice. The longer the ribs marinate, the richer the flavor will be. (The ribs can also be marinated in large heavy resealable plastic bags.)

3. Set up the grill for indirect grilling (see page 33) and preheat to medium (350°F). Place a large drip pan in the center of the grill under the grate.

4. When ready to cook, brush and oil the grill grate. Place the ribs bone side down in the center of the grate over the drip pan and away from the heat. (If your grill

FINDING LAMB RIBS

Almost every recipe in this chapter calls for Denver ribs—breast meat that has been trimmed to form roughly the lamb version of spareribs. These are the smallest and fastest cooking of all the ribs in this book. Finding lamb ribs can be a challenge. Greek or Middle Eastern butcher shops or markets specializing in halal meats (the Muslim equivalent of kosher) are good sources. Given a few days' notice, most supermarket meat departments can order lamb ribs, if they don't already stock them. Or, see the Mail-Order Sources on page 305.

TIP: *Baby back pork ribs would be quite delicious prepared in this fashion. Grilled using the indirect method, they'll be done after cooking 1¼ to 1½ hours.*

has limited space, stand the racks of ribs upright in a rib rack; see page 52.) Cover the grill and cook the ribs until well browned, cooked through, and tender enough to pull apart with your fingers, 40 minutes to 1 hour. When the ribs are done, the meat will have shrunk back from the ends of the bones by about ¼ inch.

5. Transfer the ribs to a large platter or cutting board and let them rest for a few minutes. Serve the racks, whole or cut into individual ribs, along with the grilled vegetables and lemon wedges.

Variation

How to grill lamb ribs using the direct method: In most of the lamb-eating world, ribs are grilled directly over the fire. To do this at home, build a three-zone fire, preheating one zone to medium, one zone to low, and leaving the safety zone unlit (see page 31). Start grilling the ribs bone side down over the medium zone. If the ribs begin to brown too much, move them over the low zone. If there are flare-ups from dripping lamb fat, you can transfer the ribs to the safety zone. The cooking time will be 12 to 18 minutes per side.

MIDDLE EASTERN GRILLED VEGETABLES

METHOD: Direct grilling
ADVANCE PREP: None
SERVES: 4

Throughout the Middle and Near East, lamb is served with grilled tomatoes, onions, eggplant, and other vegetables. Naturally, you can grill the vegetables at the same time you cook the lamb, but grilled vegetables are also good served at room temperature. For convenience and so as to not overcrowd your grill, you may wish to grill the vegetables ahead of time—or right before you put on the lamb.

4 plum tomatoes,
cut in half lengthwise
1 bunch scallions, root end
trimmed, top 2 inches
cut off
1 eggplant (about 1 pound),
cut crosswise into ³/4-inch-
thick slices
¹/4 cup extra-virgin olive oil,
or more as needed
Coarse salt (kosher or sea)
and freshly ground black
pepper
3 cloves fresh garlic, minced

1. Set up the grill for direct grilling (see page 31) and preheat to medium-high (400°F; use the Mississippi test to check the heat (see page 35).

2. Using a pastry brush, brush the tomatoes, scallions, and eggplant on all sides with olive oil. Generously season the vegetables with salt and pepper. Sprinkle the garlic over the tomatoes and eggplant.

3. When ready to cook, brush and oil the grill grate. Place the vegetables on the grate and cook until well browned on all sides, 3 to 6 minutes per side, turning them with tongs.

4. Arrange the grilled vegetables on a platter to serve with the Grilled Lamb Ribs with Garlic and Mint (page 222), either hot or at room temperature.

A GAZETTEER OF SOME OF THE WORLD'S MORE EXOTIC RIBS

CHAR SIU

Chinese sweet pork spareribs, marinated and basted with a sauce made from sweet hoisin sauce, rice wine, and Chinese five-spice powder, then roasted in an oven and sometimes deep-fried. (For a grilled baby back version, see page 77.)

COSTILLAS ADOBADAS

Mexican pork ribs marinated overnight in a potent puree of chiles, garlic, and spices. After baking in the marinade until tender, the ribs are glazed with pureed chiles and sweetened with honey.

FLANKEN

Eastern European Jewish-style boiled beef short ribs. Cooked along with carrots, cabbage, and other vegetables, the ribs are served with their broth.

GEWURZTE SCHWEINSRIPPCHEN

German braised, spicy spareribs. Dusted with flour and browned in fat, the bones are braised in a flavorful liquid spiced up with onion, garlic, allspice, cloves, and cayenne. Spaetzle is the traditional accompaniment.

KALBI KUI

Korean beef short ribs. Typically, the meat is butterflied thinly or sliced and grilled over charcoal. *Kalbi kui* is served with a variety of *panchan* (pickles and salted vegetables) and wrapped up in romaine lettuce leaves. (For a recipe, see page 191.)

MUU THOT

Thai pork spareribs marinated in a paste of coriander roots, garlic, fish sauce, oyster sauce, and white pepper and then deep-fried until golden brown. Served with *nam prik jim* (sweet chile sauce).

NYAMA CHOMA

Kenyan charcoal-grilled goat or beef short ribs. Served with *kachumbari,* a robust relish of onions, tomatoes, and chile peppers, and always with oceans of beer. According to Nairobi journalist Okoth Fred Mudhai, *nyama choma* "seems to carry a spirit of its own, in that it cannot be as enjoyable when one eats it by oneself as it is when enjoyed in a group."

PAI GWAT

Small bites of sparerib stewed with Chinese salted black bean sauce and chiles—a popular dim sum.

PINNEKJØTT

Norwegian salted lamb ribs. They're steamed and served with mashed rutabagas. A traditional Christmas dish, the ribs taste a lot better than they sound.

SPUNTATURE AL SUGO

One Italian contribution to the pantheon of ribs, *spuntature al sugo* are spareribs in a simple tomato sauce with garlic and red wine vinegar (for a similar recipe, see page 147).

TABAK MAAZ

Kashmiri lamb ribs that are subjected to a two-step cooking process. First, they are braised in a mixture of milk and water spiked with cardamom, ginger, aniseed, cinnamon, cloves, turmeric, and asafetida. Once the ribs are tender, they are sizzled with garlic in ghee (clarified butter).

TIRA DE ASADO

Argentinean crosscut beef short ribs, grilled and served like steak with *chimichurri* sauce. (For a recipe, see page 199.)

TANDOORI LAMB RIBS

METHOD: Indirect grilling
ADVANCE PREP: At least 12 hours for marinating the ribs
SERVES: 4

When it comes to ribs, you don't normally think of India. But flame-roasted lamb is an ancient Indian tradition. (How ancient? The tandoor, India's barbecue pit, has been around for at least five millennia.) So, here's a dish you've probably never had in an Indian restaurant, but one that explodes with the yogurt, ginger, garlic, and spice flavors of the subcontinent—tandoori lamb ribs.

> 4 cloves garlic, coarsely chopped
>
> 1 piece (2 inches) fresh ginger, peeled and coarsely chopped
>
> 2 teaspoons coarse salt (kosher or sea)
>
> 2 teaspoons dry mustard
>
> 1 teaspoon freshly ground black pepper
>
> 1 teaspoon ground cumin
>
> 1 teaspoon ground coriander
>
> $1/2$ teaspoon ground mace or nutmeg
>
> $1/2$ teaspoon ground cardamom
>
> $1/2$ teaspoon ground turmeric
>
> $1/4$ to 1 teaspoon cayenne pepper
>
> $1/4$ cup vegetable oil
>
> $1/4$ cup fresh lemon juice
>
> $1/2$ teaspoon red food coloring (optional)
>
> 2 cups whole-milk yogurt
>
> 4 racks Denver lamb ribs (trimmed lamb breast; 4 to 5 pounds total)
>
> 3 tablespoons salted butter, melted
>
> 8 to 12 cilantro sprigs (optional), for serving
>
> Lemon wedges, for serving

1. Place the garlic, ginger, salt, mustard, black pepper, cumin, coriander, mace, cardamom, turmeric, and cayenne in a food processor and finely chop. With the motor running, add the oil in a thin stream, then process until a coarse paste forms. With the motor running, add the lemon juice and food coloring, if using. Stop the motor and add the yogurt. Run the processor in short bursts just to mix. Do not overprocess or the marinade may separate.

2. Prepare the ribs: Place a rack of ribs meat side down on a rimmed baking sheet. Remove the thin, papery membrane from the back of the rack by inserting a slender implement, such as a butter knife or the tip of a meat thermometer, under it. The best place to start is on one of the middle bones. Using a dishcloth, paper towel, or pliers to gain a secure grip, peel off the membrane. Repeat with the remaining racks of lamb.

TIPS: *Like many Asian barbecuers, Indians like the taste of flame-seared foods but not wood smoke. So gas grillers, take comfort: This is a great recipe for a gas grill. Of course, if you have a charcoal grill, you'll feel right at home, as most Indian tandoors burn charcoal.*

Indian tandoori comes tinted an electric orange color, the result of adding food coloring to the marinade. I've made this optional— I don't bother with it at home—but to be authentic you'd add it.

3. Spoon the marinade over the ribs, turning them several times to coat on all sides. Cover the ribs with plastic wrap and let marinate in the refrigerator for 12 to 24 hours, turning them 2 or 3 times. The longer the ribs marinate, the richer the flavor will be. (The ribs can also be marinated in large heavy resealable plastic bags.)

4. Set up the grill for indirect grilling (see page 33) and preheat to medium-high (400°F). Place a large drip pan in the center of the grill under the grate.

5. When ready to cook, brush and oil the grill grate. Place the ribs bone side down in the center of the grate over the drip pan and away from the heat. (If your grill has limited space, stand the racks of ribs upright in a rib rack; see page 52.) Cover the grill and cook the ribs until well browned, cooked through, and tender enough to pull apart with your fingers, 40 minutes to 1 hour. When the ribs are done, the meat will have shrunk back from the ends of the bones by about ¼ inch.

6. Transfer the ribs to a large platter or cutting board and let them rest for a few minutes. Cut the ribs into 2- or 3-rib sections and brush them with the melted butter (this may seem like overkill, but it's one of the hallmarks of Indian grilling). Sprinkle the cilantro sprigs, if using, on top and serve with the lemon wedges.

AUSSIE LAMB RIBS
WITH GINGER, RUM, AND PINEAPPLE BARBECUE SAUCE

METHOD: Indirect grilling, followed by direct grilling
ADVANCE PREP: None
SERVES: 4

We have a saying at www.barbecuebible.com: There's no such thing as strangers in barbecue, just friends who haven't met. Thanks to the BBQ Board, I've corresponded with hundreds of pit masters around the world and sampled their food, virtually at least, through descriptions and photos. These lamb ribs are the creation of an Australian grill master named Peter Lee, who lives in Brisbane, Queensland (he has a website, www.bbqblue.com.au).

Peter claims to have used my Memphis-style ribs in *The Barbecue! Bible* as his starting point. He substituted lamb breast (as Australians call lamb ribs) for the baby backs and a pungent cinnamon, fennel, and caraway rub for the Memphis spice mix. And he concocted his barbecue

sauce from three typical Queensland ingredients—fresh
pineapple, dark rum, and ginger marmalade. If you already
love lamb, this recipe is a surefire home run, and if you
have mixed feelings about the richly flavored meat, it just
might turn you into a convert.

1 cup pineapple juice

2 tablespoons brown sugar

1 tablespoon sweet paprika

2 teaspoons coarse salt (kosher or sea)

1 teaspoon ground cinnamon

1 teaspoon fennel seed

1 teaspoon granulated onion or onion powder

$^1/_2$ teaspoon granulated garlic or garlic powder

$^1/_2$ teaspoon caraway seed

$^1/_2$ teaspoon ground ginger

$^1/_2$ teaspoon freshly ground black pepper

$^1/_8$ teaspoon ground cloves

4 racks Denver lamb ribs (trimmed lamb breast;
    4 to 5 pounds total)

Ginger, Rum, and Pineapple Barbecue Sauce
    (recipe follows)

You'll also need:

Spray bottle (optional); $1^1/_2$ cups wood chips or
    chunks (optional; preferably pecan or hickory),
    soaked for 1 hour in water to cover, then
    drained

1. Place the pineapple juice in a spray bottle or in
a bowl and set it aside (you'll use it for basting the ribs).

2. Place the brown sugar, paprika, salt, cinnamon,
fennel seed, granulated onion and garlic, caraway
seed, ginger, pepper, and cloves in a small bowl and
mix with your fingers, breaking up any lumps in the
brown sugar.

3. Prepare the ribs: Place a rack of ribs meat side
down on a baking sheet. Remove the thin, papery

TIP: *Peter gives two options for cooking the ribs—indirect grilling at a moderate heat in a charcoal grill and slow smoking in a smoker. The indirect method gives you ribs with a delectable chew (and of course it's much quicker). A smoker produces a softer, smokier rib in the style of Kansas City. (Instructions for cooking the lamb ribs in a smoker appear in the variation on the facing page.)*

For the very best results with the indirect method, use a charcoal grill and wood chips. I've also had good results using a gas grill—according to Peter, very few Australians are into smoking.

membrane from the back of the rack by inserting a slender implement, such as a butter knife or the tip of a meat thermometer, under it. The best place to start is on one of the middle bones. Using a dishcloth, paper towel, or pliers to gain a secure grip, peel off the membrane. Repeat with the remaining racks.

4. Sprinkle the rub over both sides of the ribs, rubbing it onto the meat. Cover the ribs with plastic wrap and refrigerate them while you set up the grill.

5. Set up the grill for indirect grilling (see page 33) and preheat to medium (350°F). Place a large drip pan in the center of the grill under the grate. (For instructions on smoking on a gas grill, see page 36.)

6. When ready to cook, brush and oil the grill grate. Place the ribs bone side down in the center of the grate over the drip pan and away from the heat. (If your grill has limited space, stand the racks of ribs upright in a rib rack; see page 52.) If cooking on a charcoal grill and using wood chips, toss half of them on each mound of coals. Cover the grill and cook the ribs for 20 minutes.

7. Spray or baste the ribs on both sides with some of the pineapple juice. Re-cover the grill and continue cooking the ribs until well browned, cooked through, and tender enough to pull apart with your fingers, 20 to 40 minutes longer, 40 minutes to 1 hour in all. When the ribs are done, the meat will have shrunk back from the ends of the bones by about $1/4$ inch. Spray or baste the ribs again every 15 minutes.

8. Just before serving, brush the ribs on both sides with a little of the Ginger, Rum, and Pineapple Barbecue Sauce and move them directly over the fire. Grill the ribs until the sauce is sizzling and browned, 2 to 3 minutes per side.

9. Transfer the ribs to a large platter or cutting board and let them rest for a few minutes. Serve the racks, whole or cut into individual ribs, with the remaining barbecue sauce on the side.

Variation

How to cook lamb ribs in a smoker: Set up and light the smoker according to the manufacturer's instructions (for more on smokers, see page 43) and preheat to low (225° to 250°F). Place the ribs in the smoker bone side down and smoke until cooked through, 3 to 4 hours. Spray or baste the lamb with pineapple juice once an hour.

GINGER, RUM, AND PINEAPPLE BARBECUE SAUCE

This sauce combines the best of Asia and the British Commonwealth: ripe pineapple, dark rum, and ginger marmalade—all grown or made Down Under—plus one ingredient from nearby Southeast Asia, *kejap manis,* sweet soy sauce. *Kejap manis,* the etymological descendant of the Malaysian pickled fish sauce that also gave us the word *ketchup,* is a thick sweet soy sauce available in Asian markets and specialty food stores. In a pinch, you can substitute equal parts regular soy sauce and molasses. One flavorful variation is to substitute Thai chile sauce for

TIP: *If you don't have ginger marmalade, you can still make a delectable—though completely different— sauce by substituting pineapple preserves and a 2-inch piece of fresh ginger that has been peeled and chopped. Puree the ginger with the pineapple in Step 1.*

the *kejap manis.* As for ginger marmalade, you'll find it at specialty food stores or via the Internet (see Mail-Order Sources on page 305).

MAKES ABOUT 2 ½ CUPS

2 cups diced ripe pineapple (see Note)

1 cup ginger marmalade

2 tablespoons kejap manis (sweet soy sauce) or Thai chile sauce, or more to taste

½ cup dark rum

Coarse salt (kosher or sea) and freshly ground black pepper

1. Puree the pineapple in a food processor or blender. Pour it into a heavy nonreactive saucepan and bring to a boil over medium heat. Add the ginger marmalade and *kejap manis.* Let simmer until the marmalade melts, whisking to blend.

2. Increase the heat to high and whisk in the rum. Let the sauce boil until thick and richly flavored, 3 to 5 minutes. Taste the sauce for seasoning, adding more *kejap manis* as necessary and salt and pepper to taste (you may not need much salt on account of the soy sauce). Let the sauce cool to room temperature before serving. It can be refrigerated, covered, for several weeks. Let the sauce return to room temperature before using.

Note: Ideally the sauce should be made with fresh pineapple, but in a pinch you can use unsweetened canned pineapple.

"MECHOUI" OF LAMB RIBS

METHOD: Spit roasting
ADVANCE PREP: At least 2 hours for marinating the ribs (optional)
SERVES: 2

Méchoui is the North African version, in spirit at least, of a Carolina pig pickin'—a community feast centered around a whole lamb seasoned with a paste of pungent spices, then roasted crackling crisp in a fire pit or on a spit. That's the inspiration for the ribs here, although I'm not sure this exact recipe has ever been served in Morocco. In keeping with the North African theme, the lamb is served with harissa, a spicy hot sauce.

> 1 small onion, peeled and quartered
>
> 3 cloves garlic, peeled and cut in half
>
> 1 piece (1 inch) fresh ginger, peeled and cut into 1/4-inch slices
>
> 3 tablespoons sweet paprika
>
> 2 teaspoons coarse salt (kosher or sea), or more to taste
>
> 1 teaspoon freshly ground black pepper
>
> 1 teaspoon ground coriander
>
> 1/2 teaspoon ground cinnamon
>
> 1/4 teaspoon ground cardamom
>
> 1 teaspoon grated lemon zest
>
> 3 tablespoons fresh lemon juice (from 1 medium-size lemon), or more to taste
>
> 2 to 3 tablespoons extra-virgin olive oil, or as needed
>
> 2 racks Denver lamb ribs (trimmed lamb breast; about 2 pounds total)
>
> Harissa (recipe follows), for serving
>
> Lemon, for serving

1. Place the onion, garlic, ginger, paprika, salt, pepper, coriander, cinnamon, and cardamom in a food processor fitted with a metal chopping blade. Run the

TIP: *If you don't have a rotisserie, you can grill the ribs on a gas or charcoal grill using the indirect method. The cooking time will be 40 minutes to an hour at medium-high (400°F).*

machine in short bursts until a coarse paste forms. With the motor running, add the lemon zest, lemon juice, and enough olive oil to obtain a paste the consistency of mayonnaise. Taste for seasoning, adding more salt and/or lemon juice as necessary; the spice paste should be highly seasoned (you'll have about 1 cup).

2. Prepare the ribs: Place a rack of ribs meat side down on a baking sheet. Remove the thin, papery membrane from the back of the rack by inserting a slender implement, such as a butter knife or the tip of a meat thermometer, under it. The best place to start is on one of the middle bones. Using a dishcloth, paper towel, or pliers to gain a secure grip, peel off the membrane. Repeat with the remaining rack.

3. Using a rubber spatula, spread each side of the ribs with the spice paste. Cover the ribs with plastic wrap and refrigerate until ready to grill. The ribs will be good cooked right away, better if marinated for 2 hours, and spectacular if marinated overnight.

4. Thread the ribs onto the rotisserie spit: Place a rack of ribs bone side up on a work surface. Using a sharp, slender knife, make starter holes in the center of the meat between every 4 or 5 ribs. Twist the knife blade to widen the holes; this will make it easier to insert the spit. Repeat with the remaining rack of ribs. Use an over and under weaving motion to thread the spit through the holes in the racks of ribs.

5. Set up the grill for spit roasting following the manufacturer's instructions and preheat to high. If you are cooking on a charcoal grill, use the Mississippi test to check the heat (see page 35). Place a large drip pan in the center of the grill directly under the spit.

6. When ready to cook, attach the spit to the rotisserie mechanism, turn on the motor, and cover the grill. Cook the ribs until they are golden brown and cooked through, 30 to 45 minutes. When the ribs are done, the meat will have shrunk back from the ends of the bones by about 1/4 inch.

7. Transfer the spit with the ribs to a cutting board. Carefully remove the skewer, then let the ribs rest for a few minutes. Serve the racks, whole or cut into individual ribs, with the Harissa and lemon wedges.

HARISSA
(NORTH AFRICAN HOT SAUCE)

arissa is to North Africa what Tabasco sauce is to Louisiana—a fiery red elixir as essential to human happiness as barbecue itself. Harissa is popular from Tunis to Marrakech, and the formulas vary as much as the foods for which the sauce is destined. Most versions call for some sort of dried hot red chile to be fortified with garlic, coriander, and cumin. Here's a quick version made with hot paprika (or you can use red chile powder). Be sure to use only very fresh paprika. **MAKES ABOUT 3/4 CUP**

2 tablespoons hot paprika

3 cloves garlic, coarsely chopped

2 teaspoons coarse salt (kosher or sea), or more to taste

1 teaspoon ground coriander

1/2 teaspoon ground cumin

1/2 cup extra-virgin olive oil

1 tablespoon fresh lemon juice, or more to taste

Place the paprika, garlic, salt, coriander, cumin, olive oil, lemon juice, and 2 tablespoons of hot water in a blender. Puree until a smooth sauce forms. Taste for seasoning, adding more salt and/or lemon juice as desired. The harissa can be refrigerated, covered, for at least 1 week. Let it return to room temperature before using.

HOODOO BARBECUE LAMB RIBLETS
WITH VANILLA BARBECUE SAUCE

METHOD: Indirect grilling, followed by direct grilling
ADVANCE PREP: None
SERVES: 4

'Que heads of a certain age may remember a rough-and-tumble Boston barbecue joint called Hoodoo Barbecue, located in an equally rough-and-tumble punk rock bar called the Rathskeller in pregentrified Kenmore Square. Despite the grubby surroundings (or perhaps because of them), pit master James Ryan dished up some of the best ribs in Beantown. The Hoodoo once even made the list of hundred top American restaurants in *Esquire* magazine, and gastronomically minded executives would take a cab there from Logan airport to sample the ribs.

Ryan could grill beef and baby back ribs with the best of them, but what set his menu apart were the lamb ribs—crusty and succulent, with the rich meaty flavor that makes lamb the preferred meat of the Middle East and Mediterranean. The ribs were served with white bread to help soak up the distinctive sauce. And I say this with affection:

TIPS: Lamb riblets are individual ribs cut from lamb spareribs. They're bigger, tougher, and fattier than Denver ribs, but when properly cooked, they reward you with larger-than-life flavor. Lamb riblets come both bone-in and boneless (when I have a choice in the matter, I get bone-in). Normally they run about five riblets to a pound. If you can't find them, you can use Denver lamb ribs. In that case, you'll need four racks (4 to 5 pounds total). The cooking time will be 40 minutes to 1 hour.

Ryan grilled ribs directly over a medium flame—a process you can certainly try. It's a lot less work to cook the ribs by the indirect method, moving them directly over the fire at the end to sizzle the sauce into the meat.

These ribs are more about spice than smoke, so you can use either a gas or charcoal grill.

They were greasy enough to plaster your goatee to your chin. Twenty years later, I still dream of Hoodoo's lamb ribs. Here's how I imagine they were made.

4 pounds lamb riblets
Garlic salt
Lemon pepper
Freshly ground black pepper
Sweet paprika
Vanilla Barbecue Sauce (recipe follows)
Sliced white bread, for serving

1. Generously season the ribs on both sides with garlic salt, lemon pepper, black pepper, and paprika. Cover the ribs with plastic wrap and refrigerate them while you set up the grill.

2. Set up the grill for indirect grilling (see page 33) and preheat to medium (325° to 350°F). Place a large drip pan in the center of the grill under the grate.

3. When ready to cook, brush and oil the grill grate. Place the ribs bone side down in the center of the grate over the drip pan and away from the heat. Cover the grill and cook the ribs until well browned, cooked through, and tender, 40 minutes to 1 hour. When the ribs are done, the meat will have shrunk back from the ends of the bones by about $1/4$ inch.

4. Just before serving, brush the ribs on both sides with a little of the Vanilla Barbecue Sauce and move them directly over the fire. Grill the ribs until the sauce is browned and bubbling, 2 to 3 minutes per side.

5. Transfer the ribs to a large platter or cutting board. Let the ribs rest for a few minutes. Then, serve the ribs with sliced white bread and the remaining Vanilla Barbecue Sauce on the side.

VANILLA BARBECUE SAUCE

Almost as remarkable as Hoodoo's caveman atmosphere was its barbecue sauce, which was sweet, sour, and fiery. Yet there was something about the sauce I couldn't quite put my finger on—a haunting, perfumed quality—that turned out to be a shot of vanilla extract. Ryan confided that the addition of this unexpected ingredient was an accident: An open bottle of vanilla fell off a shelf into a batch of sauce one day. Before he tossed the sauce, he decided to taste it. The vanilla turned out to be just what his sauce was missing.

MAKES 1 3/4 CUPS

> **TIP:** *For an even richer sauce, add a tablespoon or two of lamb drippings collected from the drip pan once you've taken the riblets off the grill.*

1 cup tomato sauce
1/4 cup molasses
1/4 cup distilled white vinegar
2 tablespoons Worcestershire sauce
2 tablespoons brown sugar
2 tablespoons Dijon mustard
1 to 2 teaspoons Tabasco sauce
1 1/2 teaspoons liquid smoke, or more to taste
1 1/2 teaspoons vanilla extract, or more to taste
Coarse salt (kosher or sea) and freshly ground black pepper

Combine the tomato sauce, molasses, vinegar, Worcestershire sauce, brown sugar, mustard, Tabasco sauce, liquid smoke, vanilla extract, and 1/4 teaspoon each of salt and pepper in a nonreactive saucepan and slowly bring to a boil over medium-high heat. Reduce the heat to medium and let the sauce simmer gently until dark, thick, richly flavored, and slightly reduced, 6 to 10 minutes. Taste for seasoning, adding more liquid smoke, vanilla, salt, and/or pepper as necessary. Let the sauce cool to room temperature before serving. Any extra will keep well in a sealed jar in the refrigerator for several weeks. The sauce goes great not just with lamb, but with poultry, beef, and even salmon.

SIDE DISHES

Man does not live on ribs alone (although there are probably some 'que heads out there who have tried)—which brings us to this slim but essential chapter on side dishes to serve at your next rib fest. Try the vegetarian "ribs" for starters—celery stalks stuffed with smoked blue cheese and smoked almonds. You'll notice a theme of smoke and fire running throughout the American barbecue staples here: potato salad made with smoke-roasted potatoes; baked beans enriched by smoked ribs; mac and cheese smoke roasted on the grill; barbecued corn. And of course, there are coleslaw recipes—here one made with fennel and one made with chayote squash.

You'll also discover some of the side dishes relished by rib masters elsewhere on Planet Barbecue, including a christophene (chayote squash) slaw enjoyed in the Caribbean and the sticky rice served with barbecued ribs in Asia. These may be side dishes, but you won't want to keep them on the sidelines.

CELERY "RIBS"
WITH SMOKED CHEESE

ADVANCE PREP: None
MAKES: 24 "ribs"; serves 8 to 12

A vegetarian dish may be the last recipe you'd expect to find in a rib cookbook. I couldn't resist the wordplay—the "ribs" in question are celery ribs (stalks). In keeping with the theme of smoke and spice running throughout, they're stuffed with smoked blue cheese and topped with smoked almonds. Serve these "ribs" as an appetizer—prelude to the real bones.

> 1 large bunch celery, trimmed
>
> 8 ounces cream cheese, at room temperature
>
> 4 ounces smoked blue cheese or regular blue cheese, crumbled (1 cup), at room temperature
>
> 1/4 teaspoon liquid smoke
> (optional; add to unsmoked blue cheese)
>
> 1 scallion, trimmed and finely chopped
>
> 1 to 2 teaspoons of your favorite hot sauce
>
> 1 to 2 tablespoons of your favorite beer
>
> Coarse salt (kosher or sea) and freshly ground black pepper
>
> 1/2 cup finely chopped smoked almonds
>
> 1/2 teaspoon pimentón de la Vera
> (Spanish smoked paprika; optional)

1. Break off 6 large unblemished celery ribs; set the remaining celery aside for another use. Rinse and pat dry the celery ribs, then cut each crosswise into roughly 3-inch pieces.

2. Place the cream cheese, blue cheese, liquid smoke, if using, scallion, and hot sauce in a food processor fitted with a metal blade and process until smooth. Add enough beer to make the mixture spreadable. Season the filling with salt and pepper to taste (you won't need much salt as blue cheese is already quite salty).

3. Using a spatula or butter knife (or a piping bag fitted with a star tip if you're feeling fancy), fill the hollow of the celery ribs with the cheese mixture. Sprinkle the chopped almonds and smoked paprika, if using, on top and serve. The celery ribs can be stuffed and refrigerated, covered, up to 6 hours before serving. Let them warm to room temperature and add the almonds and paprika just before serving.

> **TIP:** *We tested the stuffed celery recipe with a lot of different smoked cheeses and the champ was Smokey Blue, an award-winning smoked blue cheese made by the Rogue Creamery in Oregon. The cheese owes its haunting flavor to a sixteen-hour cold smoke over hazelnut shells. It's amazing stuff.*
>
> *Or, you can use an unsmoked blue cheese, like Roquefort or Gorgonzola, and add a few drops of liquid smoke. Chopped smoked almonds and, if you like, a dusting of pimentón de la Vera (Spanish smoked paprika, available at specialty food stores and Spanish markets), bring the dish to a smoky apotheosis.*

GRILLED CORN
WITH BARBECUE BUTTER

METHOD: Direct grilling
ADVANCE PREP: None
MAKES: 4 ears

No rib cookbook would be complete without the other dish you eat with your fingers hot off the grill (other than ribs, that is)—grilled corn. I've said it before and I'll say it again: There's nothing like the intense dry heat of the grill for caramelizing the sugars found in the corn. Grilling brings out the natural sweetness while imparting an irresistible touch of smoke. The ears here receive a double blast of barbecue flavor, from fire roasting the corn kernels and from a sprinkling of spice rub. So what's with the folded-back cornhusk? It makes a nifty handle for eating.

   4 ears sweet corn, in the husk
   4 tablespoons (¹/₂ stick) unsalted butter, melted,
      or 4 tablespoons extra-virgin olive oil
   1 to 2 tablespoons Sweet Smoky Barbecue Rub
      (page 204) or your favorite store-bought rub

You'll also need:
String (optional); an aluminum foil shield,
   made by folding a 12 by 18–inch piece
   of aluminum foil in thirds like a
   business letter

TIP: *I've got a marked preference for grilling corn sans husks. If you're used to corn grilled in the husk (an act I liken to showering with your socks on), I'm sure the smoky caramel flavors achieved by grilling corn without the husk will take your breath away.*

1. Cut the top ¼ inch off each ear of corn. Shuck an ear, stripping back the husk from the top but leaving it attached at the bottom (the action is a bit like peeling a banana). Remove and discard the corn silk. Gather the husk together so that it covers the stem and makes a sort of handle, then tie it together with string or strips of corn husk. Repeat with the remaining ears of corn.

2. Set up the grill for direct grilling (see page 31) and preheat to high; use the Mississippi test to check the heat (see page 35).

3. When ready to cook, brush and oil the grill grate. Lightly brush each ear of corn all over with some of the butter and sprinkle it with a little barbecue rub. Arrange the corn on the hot grate so that all the ears are pointed in the same direction, then slide the aluminum foil shield under the husks to keep them from burning. Grill the corn until the kernels are handsomely browned on all sides, 2 to 3 minutes per side, 8 to 12 minutes in all, turning it with tongs. As the corn grills, baste it with the remaining butter and sprinkle it with more barbecue rub.

4. Transfer the grilled corn to a platter or plates and serve at once.

OAXACAN GRILLED CORN BOATS

METHOD: Direct grilling, followed by indirect grilling
ADVANCE PREP: None
SERVES: 4

I ate—no, devoured—some of the tastiest grilled corn on the planet at the central food market in Oaxaca, Mexico. It was charred over charcoal, slathered with mayonnaise, and dusted with grated sharp Cotija cheese and chile powder. This recipe reprises those flavors in a unique side dish called a corn boat. The corn is first grilled directly over the fire to impart a smoke flavor. Then the kernels are cut off the cob, tossed with mayonnaise and Mexican melting cheese, and stuffed in a corn husk that's tied into a canoe shape before being grilled using the indirect method. The flavors are explosive and the result looks cool as all get out. Too lazy to make corn husk boats? Simply grill the corn and cheese mixture in an aluminum foil pan.

6 ears sweet corn, in the husk

About 2 tablespoons extra-virgin olive oil

Coarse salt (kosher or sea) and freshly ground
black pepper to taste

$1/4$ cup mayonnaise (preferably Hellmann's)

2 tablespoons salted butter, melted

$3/4$ cup (about 3 ounces) grated Oaxaca cheese or
Monterey Jack

1 to $1^1/2$ teaspoons ancho chile powder

2 teaspoons fresh lime juice

1 tablespoon chopped fresh cilantro

1. Cut the top $1/4$ inch off each ear of corn. Shuck an ear, carefully stripping the husk back as though you were peeling a banana and leaving it attached to the corn. Remove and discard the corn silk. Hold the ear in one hand and gently snap off the husk and stem end, keeping them attached together. Set the corn and husk aside, then repeat with the remaining ears of corn.

2. Set up the grill for direct grilling (see page 31) and preheat to high; use the Mississippi test to check the heat (see page 35).

3. When ready to cook, lightly brush the corn on all sides with olive oil and season with salt and pepper. Brush and oil the grill grate. Arrange the corn on the hot grate so that the ears are parallel to the bars of the grate (this makes turning easier). Grill the corn until golden brown on all sides, 2 to 3 minutes per side, 8 to 12 minutes in all.

4. Transfer the grilled corn to a platter or plate and let cool (the corn and reserved husks can be refrigerated, covered, for up to 48 hours). Cut the kernels off the grilled corn. The easiest way to do this is to place an ear of corn flat on a cutting board and slice the kernels off the cob, using broad strokes of a chef's knife held parallel to the ear.

5. Transfer the corn kernels to a mixing bowl. Add the mayonnaise, butter, cheese, chile powder, lime juice, and cilantro and stir to mix. Season with salt and pepper to taste; the corn mixture should be highly seasoned.

TIPS: *Grilled corn is one of those ingredients I always try to keep on hand. It's great for adding to corn bread and corn sticks (see the recipe on page 248), salads, and even mashed or baked potatoes. You can grill it ahead of time; the corn will keep for a couple of days in the refrigerator.*

Oaxaca cheese, also known as asadero, is a mild, white melting cheese similar in flavor to Monterey Jack. It's sold in disk-shaped rounds. Look for it in Mexican markets or substitute Jack cheese.

6. To make the corn boats, select 4 of the most attractive husks from those you have reserved. Discard the rest. Remove 2 to 3 leaves from one section of each husk, enough to form a 1$\frac{1}{2}$- to 2-inch gap. Keep the rest of the husk connected at the stem end. Arrange the loose leaves in the bottom of the husk boats to reinforce them. Using butcher's string, tie the loose end of each husk together. The result should look something like a corn husk canoe.

7. Spoon the corn mixture into the husk boats, dividing it evenly among them and mounding it slightly in the center. The corn boats can be filled up to 3 hours ahead; refrigerate them, covered, until ready to grill.

8. Set up the grill for indirect grilling (see page 33) and preheat to medium-high (400°F).

9. When ready to cook, arrange the corn boats on the grate away from fire and cover the grill. Cook the boats until the corn mixture is hot and sizzling and the cheese has melted, about 20 minutes. Serve the corn boats at once.

CORN STICKS ON THE GRILL

METHOD: Indirect grilling
ADVANCE PREP: None
MAKES: 14 corn sticks

C orn sticks are long, slender corn breads just large enough to consume in two or three bites. They're a snap to cook on the grill—all you need are cast-iron corn stick pans. To boost the corn and smoke flavor, I suggest adding some grilled corn kernels to the batter. The pepper Jack cheese provides even more fire power.

About 5 tablespoons butter, melted

About $1^1/_4$ cups yellow cornmeal

1 cup unbleached all-purpose white flour

3 tablespoons sugar

1 teaspoon baking powder

1 teaspoon baking soda

1 teaspoon salt

1 cup buttermilk or whole milk

1 large egg, lightly beaten with a fork

1 cup (about 4 ounces) coarsely grated pepper Jack cheese

$^1/_2$ cup grilled corn kernels (about 1 ear: optional; see Note)

You'll also need:
Two 7-stick corn stick pans

1. Set up the grill for indirect grilling (see page 33) and preheat to medium-high (400°F).

2. Using a pastry brush, lightly butter the corn stick pans with melted butter. Place the pans in the freezer for 5 minutes, then brush them with a second coat of butter (the freezing and double buttering process greatly reduces the chances that the corn sticks will stick to the pans). Sprinkle ¼ cup of the cornmeal over the indentations in the pans, shaking them to coat well. Dump out any excess cornmeal.

3. Make the batter: Place the remaining 1 cup of cornmeal and the flour, sugar, baking powder, baking soda, and salt in a mixing bowl and whisk to mix. Add the buttermilk, egg, and 3 tablespoons of butter and whisk just to mix. Using a rubber spatula, fold in the cheese and corn kernels, if using. Spoon the batter into the prepared corn stick pans (or, transfer the batter to a large measuring cup with a spout and pour it into the pans). Tap the pans on a work surface a few times to eliminate any air bubbles.

> **TIP:** *Corn stick pans are available at cookware shops and specialty food stores. Lodge makes thick cast-iron ones, which are great because they heat evenly.*

4. When ready to cook, place the corn stick pans in the center of the grate away from the heat and cover the grill. Cook the corn sticks until they are puffed, golden brown, and cooked through, 12 to 15 minutes. When done, a toothpick inserted in the center of a corn stick will come out clean.

5. Transfer the pans to a heatproof surface and let the corn sticks cool for 3 minutes, then invert them onto a baking sheet. Place the corn sticks in a cloth-lined basket or on a platter, or just hand them to people.

Note: To grill corn, first shuck it and remove the corn silk. Preheat the grill to high, then grill the corn directly over the heat, brushing with melted butter or olive oil, until golden brown on all sides, 2 to 3 minutes per side (8 to 12 minutes in all). The grilled corn can be refrigerated, covered, for up to 48 hours.

SMOKE-ROASTED SWEET POTATOES

METHOD: Indirect grilling
ADVANCE PREP: None
SERVES: 4 to 8

Barbecue was a New World invention. And sweet potatoes and maple syrup are indigenous New World foods. Put them together and you get a smoky, crisp-crusted side dish that just might take center stage. Of course, once you understand the principle of indirect grilling, you can smoke-roast just about anything, from the sweet potatoes here to the apples on page 275.

4 large sweet potatoes (6 to 8 ounces each)

4 tablespoons ($^1/_2$ stick) salted butter, melted

Coarse salt (kosher or sea) and freshly ground black pepper

2 tablespoons maple syrup

2 tablespoons brown sugar, for serving

You'll also need:

$1^1/_2$ cups wood chips or chunks (preferably maple or apple), soaked for 1 hour in water to cover, then drained

TIP: *My favorite sweet potato for this recipe is the succulent, supernaturally orange, and richly flavorful garnet yam. (Despite the name, the garnet is a sweet potato, not a true yam.)*

1. Scrub the sweet potatoes well all over with a stiff-bristled brush, then blot them dry with paper towels. Place the potatoes in an aluminum foil drip pan or large bowl. Pour 2 tablespoons of the butter over the potatoes and toss to coat on all sides. Season the potatoes *very* generously all over with salt and pepper.

SMOKY SWEET POTATO MASH

Depending on your tolerance for richness, ribs with mashed potatoes may sound like overkill—or heaven on earth. I'm of the latter opinion, especially when the spuds in question are sweet potatoes smoke-roasted on the grill.

For a smoky mash, prepare the Smoke-Roasted Sweet Potatoes at left, then scoop out the flesh and place it in a heavy saucepan. Using a potato masher or wooden spoon, mash the sweet orange flesh. Work in two tablespoons of melted butter, two tablespoons of maple syrup, two tablespoons of brown sugar, and two to four tablespoons of heavy cream. Season the potatoes with a little freshly grated nutmeg and salt and pepper to taste. Adding a splash of Tennessee whiskey would make a great dish even better.

2. Set up the grill for indirect grilling (see page 33) and preheat to medium-high (400°F). Place a large drip pan in the center of the grill under the grate. (For instructions on smoking on a gas grill, see page 36.)

3. When ready to cook, brush and oil the grill grate. Arrange the potatoes in the center of the grill over the drip pan and away from the heat. If cooking on a charcoal grill, toss half of the wood chips on each mound of coals. Cover the grill and cook the sweet potatoes until the skins are nicely browned and the flesh is very tender, 40 minutes to 1 hour. Use the "Charmin test" to check for doneness; squeeze a potato between your thumb and forefinger (carefully; it's hot). When it is done it will feel "squeezably soft."

4. Cut the sweet potatoes in half lengthwise and place on a platter or plates. Drizzle some of the remaining 2 tablespoons of butter and the maple syrup over the cut side of each potato. Sprinkle the brown sugar on top, then season the potatoes with salt and pepper to taste. The sweet potatoes can be eaten skin and all.

MOLASSES MUSTARD BAKED BEANS WITH RIBS

METHOD: Indirect grilling
ADVANCE PREP: None
SERVES: 6

Beans were one of the mainstays of the pre-Columbian New World diet. And so, of course, was barbecue. Which, perhaps, is why some sort of baked beans turn up virtually every time Americans grill. In Memphis and Kansas City baked beans are sweet, while in Texas and the Southwest they may contain not a lick of sugar. But no matter what, all beans benefit from a heady whiff of wood smoke. Usually this is supplied by a chunk of bacon or a shot of liquid smoke. In this recipe, the smoke flavor comes from the ribs you may have left over from when you make one of the other recipes in this book.

> 2 cans (each 15 ounces) navy beans, drained
>
> 2 cans (each 15 ounces) red beans or kidney beans, drained
>
> 1 medium-size onion, finely chopped
>
> 1 poblano pepper, or $^1/_2$ green bell pepper, seeded and finely chopped
>
> $^1/_2$ red bell pepper, seeded and finely chopped
>
> 2 cloves garlic, finely chopped
>
> $^1/_2$ cup molasses
>
> $^1/_2$ cup sweet smoky barbecue sauce, such as the Spicy Apple Barbecue Sauce (page 158)
>
> $^1/_2$ cup firmly packed dark brown sugar
>
> $^1/_4$ cup Dijon mustard
>
> $^1/_4$ cup of your favorite beer, or more if needed
>
> 2 tablespoons Worcestershire sauce
>
> 1 teaspoon liquid smoke (optional; see Note)
>
> Coarse salt (kosher or sea) and freshly ground black pepper
>
> $^1/_2$ to 1 rack smoky cooked pork or beef ribs, cut into individual ribs

You'll also need:

A large aluminum foil drip pan, about 9 by 11 inches;

1¹/₂ cups wood chips or chunks (optional),

soaked for 1 hour in water to cover, then drained

1. Place all of the beans in a large mixing bowl. Add the onion, poblano pepper, red bell pepper, garlic, molasses, barbecue sauce, brown sugar, mustard, beer, Worcestershire sauce, and liquid smoke, if using. Stir to mix, then season with salt and black pepper to taste; the beans should be very flavorful.

2. Spoon half of the bean mixture into the aluminum foil pan. Arrange the ribs on top and spoon the remaining beans over them.

3. Set up the grill for indirect grilling (see page 33) and preheat to medium (325° to 350°F). (For instructions on smoking on a gas grill, see page 36.)

4. When ready to cook, place the beans in the center of the grate away from the heat. If cooking on a charcoal grill and using wood chips, toss half of them on each mound of coals. Cover the grill and cook the beans until bubbling, browned, and richly flavored, 1 to 1¹/₂ hours. If the beans start to dry out, add a little more beer and/or cover them with aluminum foil. If using a charcoal grill, replenish the coals as needed.

TIP: *The beans can be cooked in a charcoal grill, gas grill, or smoker. Charcoal or a smoker give you the opportunity to add more smoke flavor, but thanks to the optional liquid smoke, even gas-grilled baked beans will be plenty smoky. You'll find instructions for baking the beans in a smoker on page 254.*

5. To serve, if you are feeling fastidious, remove the ribs, cut the meat off them, and add it back to the beans. If you're feeling more rustic, serve 1 or 2 ribs, bone and all, with each portion of beans.

Note: If you are not using wood chips or chunks, for a smokier flavor you can add liquid smoke to the beans.

Variation

How to bake beans in a smoker: Set up and light the smoker according to the manufacturer's instructions (for more on smokers, see page 43) and preheat to low (225° to 250°F). Place the beans in the smoker and smoke until bubbling and richly flavored, 2 to 3 hours. You'll need to replenish the wood chips or chunks after the first hour of smoking and to replenish the coals every hour.

SMOKY MAC AND CHEESE

METHOD: Indirect grilling
ADVANCE PREP: None
SERVES: 4

TIPS: *There are a lot of options for smoked cheese, including smoked cheddar or provolone, which have a sharp flavor, or smoked Gruyère or scamorza (a mozzarella-like cheese), which are milder.*

If your grill is tied up, you can certainly bake the macaroni and cheese in a preheated 400°F oven. Thanks to the bacon and smoked cheese, you'll still get a rich smoky flavor.

If you come from north of the Mason–Dixon Line or west of the Mississippi, mac and cheese may seem like a bizarre dish to serve at a barbecue. But if you come from the Deep South, no rib feast would seem complete without it. Not all macaroni and cheese is created equal, though, and this one owes its evocative smoke flavors to the addition of bacon and smoked cheese instead of the conventional cheddar.

Coarse salt (kosher or sea)

2 cups (about 8 ounces) elbow macaroni

1 teaspoon vegetable oil

4 tablespoons butter

1 slice bacon, cut into $1/4$-inch slivers

2 shallots, or 1 small onion, peeled and
    finely chopped

3 tablespoons all-purpose flour

1 cup whole milk

1 cup light cream or half-and-half

1 tablespoon Dijon mustard

2 cups (about 8 ounces) coarsely grated
    smoked cheese

$1/4$ teaspoon freshly grated or ground nutmeg
    (optional)

Freshly ground black pepper

$1/3$ cup toasted bread crumbs
    (preferably homemade)

You'll also need:

An aluminum foil drip pan or grill-proof roasting pan
    or baking dish (about 9 by 12 inches), sprayed or
    brushed with oil

1. Place 8 quarts of lightly salted water in a large
pot and bring to a rolling boil over high heat. Add the
macaroni and cook until al dente, about 8 minutes. Drain
the macaroni in a large colander, rinse it with cold water
until cool, and drain again. Toss the macaroni with the oil
to prevent clumping.

2. Make the sauce: Melt 2 tablespoons of the butter
in a large heavy saucepan over medium heat. Add the
bacon and shallots and cook until lightly browned,
3 to 4 minutes. Stir in the flour and cook for 1 minute.
Remove the pan from the heat and whisk in the milk
and cream. Return the pan to the heat, increasing it to
high. Let the sauce boil until thickened, about 3 minutes,
whisking well.

3. Remove the pan from the heat and stir in the mustard and drained macaroni, followed by the cheese. Add the nutmeg, if using, and season the macaroni with salt and pepper to taste; the macaroni should be highly seasoned. Spoon the macaroni and cheese into the oiled aluminum foil drip pan. The recipe can be prepared to this stage up to 48 hours ahead; let the macaroni and cheese cool to room temperature before covering and refrigerating it.

4. Melt the remaining 2 tablespoons of butter in a saucepan and stir in the bread crumbs. Spoon the bread crumb mixture over the top of the macaroni.

5. Set up the grill for indirect grilling (see page 33) and preheat to medium-high (400°F).

6. When ready to cook, place the macaroni and cheese in the center of the grate away from the heat. Cover the grill and cook the macaroni until the sauce is bubbly and the top is crusty and brown, 30 to 40 minutes. Serve at once.

STICKY RICE

ADVANCE PREP: None
SERVES: 4

For those of us who grew up eating corn bread, coleslaw, or baked beans with barbecue, white rice might seem downright bizarre as an accompaniment. But ribs without rice would be unthinkable for millions of barbecue buffs from Seoul to Tokyo, from Manila to Kuala Lumpur. Sticky rice is particularly good at absorbing the soy-based barbecue sauces that are so popular in the Far East. It would be good with the Guamanian ribs on page 150, the Koreatown short ribs on page 191, or for that matter, any Asian-style ribs.

2 cups medium-grain rice

1. Rinse the rice: Place it in a large bowl and add water to cover by 2 inches. Swirl the rice with your fingers, then pour off the cloudy water. Continue adding water and swirling the rice until the water remains clear, 4 to 6 rinsings. Drain the rice well in a colander for 30 minutes.

2. Place the rice in a large heavy saucepan with a tight-fitting lid, add 3 cups of water, and cover the saucepan. Cook the rice over medium-high heat until you can hear the water begin to boil. Increase the heat to high and let the rice boil for 2 minutes. Lower the heat to low and cook the rice until all the water is absorbed, 15 to 20 minutes. Do not uncover the rice until the end.

TIP: *It's sometimes said you can see the difference between Western and Asian cultures in the way they prepare rice. Just as Westerners value personal freedom and individuality, we tend to prepare long grain rice in such a way that each grain remains distinct. Asians put a high price on cohesion and community welfare, and they like their rice sticky and clumped together. (Sticky rice is easier to eat with chopsticks; long-grain rice, with a fork.)*

You'll need a medium-grain rice for this recipe. Good options include the Japanese-style CalRose and Kokuho Rose rices from California.

3. Remove the pan from the heat, stretch a clean dish towel over the top of the pot, put the lid back on, and let the rice stand for 15 minutes. Gently fluff the rice with a fork before serving.

Note: Electric rice steamers take all the guesswork and effort out of making sticky rice. If you eat a lot of it, these machines are definitely worth the investment. Simply follow the manufacturer's instructions.

CHRISTOPHENE (CHAYOTE) SLAW

ADVANCE PREP: None
MAKES: About 2 cups; serves 4

I first tasted this slaw at a restaurant called Indigo at the Guanahani resort on St. Barts in the French West Indies. It's a perfect example of how pit masters adapt barbecue classics to the ingredients they have on hand. Christophene (chayote) is a hard, pale green, avocado-shaped squash that serves as a sort of cabbage of the tropics. It's got more texture (moistly crunchy) than taste, but it's very pleasing and different from the traditional North American cabbage.

1¹/₂ pounds chayote squash (3 to 4 squash)

1 tablespoon poppy seeds

1 tablespoon finely chopped chives or scallion greens

3 tablespoons fresh lime juice, or more to taste

3 tablespoons extra-virgin olive oil

*Coarse salt (kosher or sea) and freshly ground
  black pepper*

TIP: *In the United States christophene is usually sold by its Spanish name, chayote. You can find it at many supermarkets. In Louisiana, it would be called mirliton. In a pinch, you could use shredded green cabbage or green papaya.*

1. Peel the chayote and cut it in half lengthwise through the flat side. Remove the seed. Cut the chayote into fine julienne. The best way to do this is with a mandoline but take care to protect your hands, as chayotes are very hard and mandoline blades are very sharp. You can also use the julienne disc of a food processor or the coarse side of a box grater, grating the chayote by hand.

2. Place the julienned chayote in a nonreactive mixing bowl and stir in the poppy seed, chives, lime juice, and olive oil. Season the slaw with salt and pepper to taste. It can be prepared up to 2 hours ahead and refrigerated, covered, until ready to serve. Be sure to taste the slaw for seasoning before serving, adding more salt and/or lime juice as necessary.

FENNEL SLAW

ADVANCE PREP: None
MAKES: About 2 cups; serves 4

I f you like licorice—or the anise-flavored French aperitif Pernod—this offbeat slaw is right up your alley. It's made with fresh fennel, the bulbous, pale green vegetable that tastes like licorice and crunches like celery. Add fresh orange sections and juice and you get a slaw that explodes with Mediterranean flavors.

1 small clove garlic, minced
$1/2$ teaspoon coarse salt (kosher or sea),
*   or more to taste*
2 to 3 fennel bulbs (about 1 pound)
1 large orange
1 tablespoon fresh lime juice, or more to taste
3 tablespoons extra-virgin olive oil
2 tablespoons toasted pine nuts (see page 281)
Freshly ground black pepper

1. Place the garlic and salt in a large nonreactive mixing bowl and mash with the back of a wooden spoon.

2. If the fennel bulbs come with stalks and fronds, finely chop about 1 tablespoon of the fronds. Set the remaining fronds aside for another use. Cut the fennel

TIP: *Fennel is available at most supermarkets. It grows wild along many central California roadsides. Trim off the stalks and feathery fronds; you can toss them on the coals for their smoke or tie them up with butcher's string to make a fennel-scented basting brush.*

bulbs lengthwise through the narrow end into paper-thin slices on a mandoline, in a food processor fitted with a slicing disc, or if you're feeling particularly venturesome, by hand. Add the fennel and leaves, if using, to the mixing bowl with the mashed garlic.

3. Peel the orange, taking care to remove all of the bitter white pith. Working over the mixing bowl with the fennel, make V-shape cuts between the membranes to remove the orange segments. Add them to the fennel. Squeeze the membranes over the fennel to extract any remaining juice.

4. Add the lime juice, olive oil, and pine nuts to the fennel and orange and toss to mix. Taste for seasoning, adding pepper to taste and more salt and/or lime juice as necessary; the slaw should be highly seasoned.

SMOKED POTATO SALAD

METHOD: Indirect grilling
ADVANCE PREP: About 15 minutes for hard-cooking the eggs
SERVES: 4 to 6

A barbecue feast just isn't complete without potato salad, and this one plays every smoke card in the deck. The spuds and garlic are both smoke-roasted on the grill. You can certainly do all this the day you plan to serve the salad, but you may find it easier to smoke these ingredients a day or two ahead.

1½ pounds small new potatoes, rinsed and
    scrubbed with a stiff brush
2 to 3 tablespoons extra-virgin olive oil
Coarse salt (kosher or sea) and freshly ground
    black pepper
6 cloves garlic, peeled
½ cup mayonnaise (preferably Hellmann's)
2 tablespoons Dijon mustard
1 tablespoon red wine vinegar, or more to taste
1 scallion, trimmed, white part minced, green parts
    thinly sliced
1 tablespoon drained
    capers
1 tablespoon drained,
    finely chopped pitted
    green olives or
    pimiento-stuffed olives
1 tablespoon finely
    chopped cornichons
    (tiny tart French
    pickles) or dill pickles
    (optional)
2 hard-cooked eggs, peeled
Sweet or smoked paprika (optional), for garnish

> **TIPS:** Don't be dismayed by the
> seemingly large quantity of garlic—
> smoke roasting blunts its pungency
> and nose-jarring bite.
>
> To hard-cook the eggs, place
> them in a large pot with water to
> cover. Bring to a boil over high heat
> and count eleven minutes from the
> time the water comes to a boil.
> Remove the shells while the eggs
> are still warm, working under cold
> running water.

You'll also need:
An 8 by 12–inch aluminum foil pan; 1½ cups
    wood chips (preferably oak or hickory),
    soaked for 1 hour in water to cover,
    then drained

1. Cut any large potatoes in quarters; cut medium-size potatoes in half; leave small ones whole. All the pieces should be bite size (about 1 inch across). Place the potatoes in the aluminum foil pan. Add 2 tablespoons of the olive oil and stir to coat. Season the potatoes generously with salt and pepper and stir to mix.

2. Set up the grill for indirect grilling (see page 33) and preheat to medium-high (400°F). (For instructions on smoking on a gas grill, see page 36.)

3. When ready to cook, place the pan with the potatoes in the center of the grate away from the heat. If cooking on a charcoal grill, toss half of the wood chips on each mound of coals. Cover the grill and cook the potatoes for 15 minutes.

4. Add the garlic to the pan with the potatoes and stir in 1 tablespoon of olive oil if the potatoes look dry. Re-cover the grill and continue cooking the potatoes until they are browned and tender (they should be easy to pierce with a skewer) and the garlic is soft, 30 to 45 minutes more, stirring once or twice so they cook evenly. Remove the pan from the heat and let cool to room temperature.

5. Meanwhile, make the dressing: Place the mayonnaise, mustard, and vinegar in a large nonreactive mixing bowl and whisk until smooth. Chop the garlic and add it to the dressing. Add the scallion white, capers, olives, and cornichons, if using, and whisk to mix.

6. Coarsely chop the hard-cooked eggs, then add them and the cooled potatoes to the dressing. Stir to mix. Taste for seasoning, adding salt and/or more vinegar to taste; the salad should be highly seasoned. You can serve it right away or refrigerate it, covered, for several hours to let the flavors blend. If you refrigerate the salad, taste for seasoning just before serving, adding more salt and/or vinegar as necessary.

7. Transfer the potato salad to a bowl, platter, or plates for serving. Sprinkle the scallion greens and paprika, if using, on top and serve at once.

DRINKS AND DESSERTS

What do you need to round out a rib feast? Drinks, of course, and dessert—the latter hot off the grill. And if you're looking for something other than the usual beer, try filling your glass with Spanish sangria (here, an unusual white one). Or, a potent French West Indian rum punch, fortified with cinnamon, vanilla, and ginger. Or still more unusual, an alcohol-free yogurt and mint drink from the Middle East. If you'd prefer a drink from closer to home, you'll find lemonade, mint juleps, and the South's beloved sweet iced tea.

No feast is complete without dessert. As far as I'm concerned, there are a lot of desserts that taste best grilled—from peach sundaes or fruit-and-pound-cake kebabs to smoke-roasted rum and brown sugar–stuffed "baked apples." Exercise a little imagination and you'll even find a rack of dessert ribs in this chapter—spice-crusted grilled banana "bones" drizzled with chocolate "barbecue" sauce. It's high time to make dessert part of your barbecue repertoire.

Drinks

When it comes to drinks, Bahamian pit masters ask, "Leaded or unleaded?" Whether or not you want alcohol with your 'que, the world of ribs has just the thing to quench your thirst. In the pages that follow, you'll find some of my favorites—both novel and traditional—to pour at your next rib fest.

DARK AND STORMY

ADVANCE PREP: None
SERVES: 2 (can be multiplied as desired)

It's a shame this vintage American cocktail has fallen out of fashion in recent years, because its two simple ingredients (dark rum and ginger beer) give you an uncommonly refreshing and complex-tasting beverage. It's possible to drink one as a cocktail. And it's possible to drink three or four throughout dinner and not have your grilling abilities too seriously impaired. The Dark and Stormy has become something of the official drink at Barbecue University TV shoots—a warm-up the night before we start shooting and our celebration libation when we wrap. So, why is it called a Dark and Stormy? The idea is to float the rum in the ginger beer so it creates an ominous cloud in the glass.

TIPS: *A Dark and Stormy is easy to make, containing only two primary ingredients, but unless you use real ginger beer (two good brands are Reed's Original Ginger Brew and Barritts Bermuda Stone Ginger Beer) and a very fine dark rum—like Appleton or Myers's, both from Jamaica—you won't get the full effect. Do not substitute ginger ale.*

Long cinnamon sticks at least 8 inches, are available at specialty food stores and spice shops (see Mail-Order Sources on page 305). If you have any left over, they're great used as skewers for cinnamon-grilled shrimp.

2 bottles (each 12 ounces) ginger beer, chilled

3 ounces (6 tablespoons) dark rum

2 long cinnamon sticks

2 lime wedges, for serving

Pour 1 bottle of ginger beer into each of 2 chilled beer mugs or tall glasses, tilting the glass and gently pouring the ginger beer down the side to minimize foaming. Gradually add 1$\frac{1}{2}$ ounces (3 tablespoons) of dark rum to each glass, so that it floats in the ginger beer. The best way to do this is to pour it over a spoon held at the surface of the ginger beer. Add a cinnamon stick, stir gently, and serve at once, garnished with a lime wedge.

GUADELOUPEAN RUM PUNCH
WITH VANILLA, CINNAMON, AND GINGER

ADVANCE PREP: At least 24 hours for the punch to stand

MAKES: 1 bottle

No French West Indian barbecue would be complete without some sort of rum punch, served before dinner as a cocktail or afterward as a digestif. The best rum punch I ever tasted came from a Guadeloupean vegetable seller at the tiny open-air market in Gustavia, St. Barts. It was obviously

TIPS: *No need to use a prime, barrel-aged rum for this punch—a strong (100 proof) white rum will do the trick. If possible, use a rum from Guadeloupe or Martinique. For sugar, I like the light brown lumps of cassonade (or Demerara) sugar sold at specialty food stores and many supermarkets. You could also use turbinado sugar (frequently sold under the name Sugar In The Raw), granulated sugar, or light brown sugar.*

homemade, requiring little more than a bottle of rum, some aromatics, and a paring knife. The punch tastes good after twenty-four hours, great after five days, and goes down like velvet after two weeks of aging.

> **1 bottle (1 fifth) white rum**
> **1 piece (2 inches) fresh ginger, peeled and**
> **   cut into ¹/₄-inch sticks or dice**
> **1 vanilla bean, cut into 1-inch pieces**
> **1 cinnamon stick (3 inches)**
> **6 lumps of light brown sugar or sugar cubes, or**
> **   2 tablespoons turbinado sugar, or more to taste**
> **Ice (optional), for serving**

1. Measure 1 cup of rum. Add the ginger, vanilla bean, cinnamon stick, and sugar to the rum in the bottle. Pour as much of the 1 cup of rum back into the bottle as you can, setting the rest aside for another use. Tightly screw on the cap, then shake the bottle a few times.

2. Let the rum punch stand for at least 24 hours or as long as 2 weeks. Shake the bottle several times each day to dissolve and blend the sugar. After 24 hours, taste the punch for sweetness, adding more sugar as necessary.

3. Serve the rum punch straight up (the way I like it) or over ice.

MINT JULEPS

ADVANCE PREP: 2 hours for the mint syrup to cool
SERVES: 8

The mint julep is, perhaps, America's most underappreciated cocktail—revered in Kentucky and consumed just about nowhere else. Its popularity pales next to that of the trendy mojito (a Cuban rum, lime, mint spritzer), for example, although they contain similar ingredients. Even in the South, outside of Kentucky you're hard-pressed to find a decent mint julep. I say it's time to rehabilitate a beverage that's synonymous with the Kentucky Derby and has enough backbone to stand up to barbecue.

TIPS: *The mint julep is traditionally served in a silver tumbler. Here's a mail-order source: http://www.silversuperstore.com/holloware/barware.html*

At The Greenbrier, former home of Barbecue University, when they make mint juleps, the bartenders dust the mint sprigs with confectioners' sugar.

For the mint syrup:

$^1/_2$ cup granulated sugar

8 large fresh mint leaves

For the mint julep:

Shaved or crushed ice

16 ounces (2 cups) bourbon

Confectioners' sugar (optional), for garnish

1 bunch fresh mint, separated into 8 sprigs

8 straws

1. Make the mint syrup: Place the granulated sugar, mint leaves, and $^1/_2$ cup of water in a saucepan and gradually bring to a boil over medium heat. Reduce the heat and let the syrup simmer gently until clear, about 3 minutes. Remove the pan from the heat and let the syrup cool to room temperature. Strain the mint syrup into a clean jar and store in the refrigerator until ready to use; it should chill for at least 2 hours. The mint syrup can be refrigerated for several weeks.

2. Make the mint juleps: Fill 8 silver tumblers or bar glasses three quarters full with shaved or crushed ice. Add 1 tablespoon of the mint syrup, or more to taste, and 2 ounces (4 tablespoons) of bourbon to each. Briskly stir the ingredients with a long-handled spoon.

3. Place the confectioners' sugar, if using, in a shaker or strainer and dust the mint sprigs with it. Garnish each julep with a mint sprig, add a straw, and serve at once.

WHITE SANGRIA

ADVANCE PREP: At least 2 hours for the flavor of the sangria to develop (optional)
SERVES: 6 to 8

Sangria, Spanish wine and fruit punch, is the ultimate summer refresher. A good one will preserve the quality of the wine while enhancing it with fruit; a bad one will taste like a wine-sodden fruit cocktail. The most familiar sangria is made with red wine and red fruit, but there are some fantastic white sangrias. Serve this one the next time you want to transcend the predictable.

> 2 bottles (750 milliliters each) semidry white wine
> $^1/_2$ cup Cointreau, triple sec, or other clear
>   orange liqueur
> 2 lemons, rinsed
> 4 cloves
> 2 oranges, rinsed
> 8 ounces cherries, rinsed and stemmed
> 1 bunch green seedless grapes (about 8 ounces),
>   stemmed, each grape cut in half lengthwise
> 1 apple, cored and cut into $^1/_2$-inch dice
> 2 cinnamon sticks (each 3 inches)
> 2 tablespoons sugar or honey, or more to taste

1. Pour the wine and Cointreau into a large pitcher.

2. Using a vegetable peeler, remove four $1^1/_2$ by $^1/_2$-inch strips of lemon zest (the oil-rich yellow outer rind) from 1 lemon. Insert 1 clove in each of the strips of zest and add them to the wine mixture (this prevents anyone from choking on a loose clove). Cut the remaining rind off the lemon and discard it. Thinly slice the peeled lemon, removing and discarding the seeds. Add the lemon slices to the wine mixture. Juice the other lemon and add the juice to the wine mixture.

3. Cut 1 orange crosswise into ½-inch slices, rind and all. Cut each slice in quarters, removing and discarding the seeds, if any. Add the orange quarters to the wine mixture. Juice the other orange and add the juice to the wine mixture.

4. Pit the cherries, using a cherry pitter, or cut them in half and removed the pits. Add the cherries, grapes, apple, and cinnamon sticks to the pitcher and stir to mix. Add the sugar or honey and stir to mix; you can always add more later if the sangria is not sweet enough. You can serve the sangria right away, but it will taste even better if you refrigerate it and let the flavors blend for 2 to 4 hours.

> **TIP:** *I recommend using a German Rhine or Mosel wine of at least spätlese sweetness for this sangria. German wines are graded by the degree of sweetness: Kabinett is the driest, followed by spätlese (slightly sweet), auslese (semisweet), beerenauslese (quite sweet), and trockenbeerenauslese (the sweetest). The categories refer to the natural sweetness of the wine—not added sugar. The greater the natural sweetness, the more expensive the wine. A spätlese makes a good compromise between sweetness and affordable price, but if you go with a drier wine, you can always add more sugar or honey.*

5. Just before serving, taste the sangria for sweetness, adding more sugar or honey if necessary. Serve the sangria in wine glasses and be sure to provide spoons for the fruit.

PANACHE
(BEER AND LEMON SODA)

ADVANCE PREP: None
SERVES: 2 (can be multiplied as desired)

The *panaché* (pronounced pan-a-SHAY) is one of the most refreshing beverages ever to be served at a barbecue. OK, you do have to overcome the initial reluctance most Americans will feel to the idea of mixing lemon soda and beer. Will it help any to tell you that this curious drink originated in France and that grown men there—even seasoned grill masters—drink it without embarrassment?

> **1 can (12 ounces) lemon soda, such as Sprite,**
>   **or 12 ounces of one of those fancy imported**
>   **European lemon sodas, chilled**
> **1 bottle (12 ounces) lager- or pilsner-style beer,**
>   **chilled**

Pour half of the lemon soda into each of 2 tall glasses, tilting the glass and gently pouring the soda down the side to minimize foaming. Fill each glass with beer, pouring it down the side also. Gently stir with a long-handled spoon and serve at once.

MINTED LEMONADE

ADVANCE PREP: At least 30 minutes for the lemonade to cool
SERVES: 4

If you hang out at typical barbecue joints, I bet it's been a while since you've had lemonade made from scratch. But fresh lemonade is one of the glories of American mixology. This lemonade delivers a triple dose of flavor—from the acerbic juice of the lemon, from the aromatic rind, and from the refreshing pungency of the fresh mint. Making it may be a little more complicated than dumping lemon juice and sugar in water, but cooking the lemon zest with the sugar and then adding the juice is the best way I know to extract the maximum flavor from a lemon.

4 lemons, rinsed

1 bunch fresh mint, rinsed and shaken dry

$^1/_3$ cup sugar, or more to taste

Ice, for serving

1. Using a vegetable peeler, remove eight $1^1/_2$ by $^1/_2$–inch strips of zest (the oil-rich yellow outer rind) from 2 lemons. Set the lemons aside. Place the lemon zest in a large nonreactive saucepan. Add the mint, setting aside 4 large sprigs for serving. Add the sugar and 5 cups of water. Bring the mixture to a boil over high heat, stirring with a wooden spoon until the sugar dissolves. Reduce the heat to medium and let the lemon mixture simmer for 5 minutes, then remove the pan from the heat and let cool for 5 minutes.

2. Strain the lemon mixture into a pitcher, pressing on the mint with the back of a spoon to extract all the liquid. If you're using a glass pitcher, place a large metal spoon in it before adding the hot liquid. The spoon will absorb some of the heat and keep the glass from cracking. Let the lemon mixture cool to room temperature, 30 minutes to 1 hour.

3. Meanwhile, cut one of the unzested lemons in half and cut 1 half lemon crosswise into four $^1/_4$ inch–thick slices, discarding the end of the lemon. Make a cut in each lemon slice running from the edge to the center and set the slices aside for garnish. Juice the remaining lemon half and the rest of the lemons. Strain the lemon juice into the lemon and mint mixture. Taste for sweetness, adding more sugar if necessary. Refrigerate the lemonade until ready to serve.

4. To serve, pour the lemonade into 4 tall ice-filled glasses. Stick a mint sprig in each and press a lemon slice over the rim of the glass. Serve at once.

SWEET TEA MY WAY
WITH BERGAMOT AND GINGER

ADVANCE PREP: At least 30 minutes for the tea to cool
SERVES: 4

Sweet tea is an indispensable accompaniment to barbecue in the American South—and an anathema just about everywhere else. Not that iced tea isn't supremely refreshing. It's just that to a Southerner, the tea isn't properly sweetened until it contains enough sugar to send you into hypoglycemic shock. My version adds a whiff of the exotic in the form of bergamot oil (the flavoring in Earl Grey tea) and fresh ginger.

TIPS: *To be strictly authentic, you'd use an ordinary supermarket variety of black tea or breakfast tea, but I like Earl Grey's musky flavor.*

The wide range in the amount of sugar called for takes into consideration individual sweet tooths.

4 bags Earl Grey tea or your favorite tea

4 slices (¹/₄ inch thick) peeled fresh ginger, gently crushed with the side of a cleaver

4 strips (each 1¹/₂ by ¹/₂ inch) lemon zest (the oil-rich yellow outer rind of the lemon)

2 to 8 tablespoons sugar, or more to taste

2 to 4 tablespoons fresh lemon juice (optional)

Ice, for serving

4 lemon wedges, for serving

1. Bring 5 cups of water to a boil in a large nonreactive saucepan. Remove the pan from the heat, add the tea bags, ginger, and lemon zest, and let steep for 3 minutes. Add sugar to taste—2 tablespoons if you like the taste of iced tea, the full 8 tablespoons if you come from south of the Mason–Dixon Line and like the taste of tea-flavored sugar. Let the tea steep for 5 minutes longer.

2. Strain the tea into a pitcher, pressing on the tea bags with the back of a spoon to extract all the liquid. If you're using a glass pitcher, place a large metal spoon in it before adding the hot tea. The spoon will absorb some of the heat and keep the glass from cracking. Let the tea cool to room temperature, 30 minutes to 1 hour, then refrigerate it until ready to serve.

3. Just before serving, stir the lemon juice, if using, into the tea. Taste for sweetness, adding more sugar if necessary. Pour the tea into 4 tall ice-filled glasses and garnish each with a lemon wedge. Yes, if you're serving Southerners, have extra sugar on the table.

HALF-AND-HALFS

ADVANCE PREP: None
SERVES: 4

The world of mixed drinks is filled with half-and-halfs—the equal part mixture of ale and stout or porter known in the United Kingdom as a black and tan, for example, or the half-and-half mixture of lemon soda and beer called a *panaché* and enjoyed in France (see page 269 for a recipe). Here's a half-and-half of nonalcoholic persuasion from the American South. For the best results, use homemade lemonade, such as the one on page 270, and homemade sweet tea, like the one on the facing page.

2 cups lemonade
2 cups sweet tea or iced tea
Sugar (optional)
Ice, for serving
4 lemon wedges, for serving

Combine the lemonade and sweet tea in a pitcher and stir to mix. Taste for sweetness, adding additional sugar if desired. Serve the Half-and-Halfs in tall ice-filled glasses, garnishing each with a lemon wedge.

Note: To give the Half-and-Half a tropical twist, use half mango tea and half limeade and garnish the glasses with lime wedges.

MINTED YOGURT DRINK

ADVANCE PREP: None
SERVES: 4

G iven the popularity and general excellence of yogurt in the Middle East—not to mention the Muslim proscription of alcohol—it's not surprising that the beer traditionally served at North American barbecues is replaced in that part of the world by a minted yogurt drink called *doogh* in Iran, *dug* in Afghanistan, and *lassi* in India. A drink made of salted yogurt may seem strange to American palates, but I wager you'll find it bizarrely refreshing.

> **TIP:** *There's also a sweet version of the yogurt drink made by substituting sugar to taste for the salt and adding an optional shot of rosewater (about 2 teaspoons).*

1¹/₂ cups plain yogurt

1 tablespoon dried mint

1 teaspoon coarse salt (kosher or sea), or more to taste

2¹/₂ to 3 cups club soda

Ice, for serving

Place the yogurt, mint, and salt in a large pitcher and stir to mix. Stir in club soda to taste; the mixture should have a consistency somewhere between that of half-and-half and a thin milkshake. Taste for seasoning, adding more salt if necessary. Serve the yogurt drink in tall ice-filled glasses.

Desserts

Y ou know Raichlen's rule: If something tastes good baked, sautéed, or fried, it probably tastes better grilled. Even dessert. *Especially* dessert. And so we come to the sweet conclusion. If you've never served a grilled dessert before, you're about to seriously boost your pit-masterly reputation.

A NEW "BAKED" APPLE

METHOD: Indirect grilling
ADVANCE PREP: None
SERVES: 6

O ne summer, I spent time touring prehistoric sites in the Dordogne in southwest France, and among the remarkable things I saw was a Neolithic hearth with the dark fossilized remains of flame-roasted crab apples. That gave me the idea for a remake of a classic American dessert: smoke-roasted apples stuffed with cream cheese, brown sugar, and rum.

6 sweet crisp apples, such as Braeburn or Fuji

4 tablespoons whipped cream cheese

4 tablespoons brown sugar

2 tablespoons rum or brandy

4 tablespoons unsalted butter

Ground cinnamon

2 marshmallows, each cut crosswise into 3 pieces

Vanilla or cinnamon ice cream (optional), for serving

You'll also need:

6 grilling rings or aluminum foil "doughnuts" (see Note);

$1^1/_2$ cups wood chips or chunks (optional; preferably apple), soaked for 1 hour in water to cover, then drained

1. Using a small melon baller, core the apples from the top. The idea is to remove the stem end and seeds, creating a cavity in the apple while leaving the bottom intact to hold in the filling. Place 1 apple on each stainless steel or aluminum foil ring, cavity side up.

2. Place 2 teaspoons of cream cheese in the cavity of each apple. Top with 2 teaspoons of brown sugar, 1 teaspoon of rum, and 2 teaspoons of butter, in that order. Sprinkle a little cinnamon over the filling and place a piece of marshmallow on top.

3. Set up the grill for indirect grilling (see page 33) and preheat to medium (325° to 350°F). Place a large drip pan in the center of the grill under the grate. (For instructions on smoking on a gas grill, see page 36.)

4. When ready to cook, carefully place the apples on their rings in the center of the grate over the drip pan and away from the heat. If cooking on a charcoal grill and using wood chips, toss half of them on each mound of coals. Cover the grill and cook the apples until they are golden brown and tender, 40 minutes to 1 hour. To test for doneness, squeeze the side of an apple; it should be quite soft.

TIP: *I've made smoking the apples optional. Obviously, you'll get more flavor if you toss some wood chips on the fire.*

5. Transfer the apples to a platter or plates for serving (if you leave them on the stainless steel rings, warn everyone that these may be hot). A scoop of ice cream would take this dessert over the top.

Note: In order to hold the apples so they cook upright, I like to use either stainless steel grilling rings or aluminum foil "doughnuts." Grilling rings are available at grill shops or online. The "doughnuts" can be made by crumpling and twisting 2 by 8–inch pieces of aluminum foil into $2\frac{1}{2}$ inch–wide rings.

DESSERT "RIBS"
(MOLASSES AND SPICE GRILLED BANANAS)

METHOD: Indirect grilling
ADVANCE PREP: None
SERVES: 4

O K, I know—you can't really eat ribs for dessert (that's not to say some diehard 'que head out there hasn't tried). But the notion of a dessert "rib" set me to thinking about how bananas are roughly shaped like ribs, and that a plate of grilled bananas could be arranged to look like a rack of ribs. The ones here even come with a brown sugar "rub" and a dark, sweet molasses, chocolate, rum, and butter "barbecue" sauce.

> **TIP:** *You want bananas that are just shy of ripe for grilling. The peels should be greenish yellow to yellow and completely free of any browning or brown "sugar" spots. Best to err on the side of underripeness.*

For the rub:
3/4 cup turbinado sugar (see Note)
1 teaspoon ground cinnamon
1/8 teaspoon ground nutmeg
1/8 teaspoon ground cloves

For the bananas:
4 bananas
2 to 3 tablespoons molasses
Molasses Rum Barbecue Sauce (recipe follows)
1/2 cup chopped toasted pecans (optional; see tip on page 281)

1. Make the rub: Place the turbinado sugar, cinnamon, nutmeg, and cloves in a small bowl and mix with your fingers, breaking up any lumps in the sugar. Set the rub aside.

2. Set up the grill for indirect grilling (see page 33) and preheat to high (450°F). Place a drip pan in the center of the grill under the grate.

3. Just before grilling, cut off and discard the ends the bananas. Place the bananas flat on a work surface and cut each in half lengthwise. Leave the skins on. Lightly brush the cut sides of the bananas with molasses, then generously sprinkle the rub on top.

4. When ready to cook, brush and oil the grill grate. Arrange the bananas on the grill, skin side down, in the center of the grill over the drip pan and away from the heat. Cover the grill and cook the bananas until the cut side is browned and bubbling and the flesh starts to shrink back from the skin, 12 to 20 minutes. Transfer the bananas to a platter, lining the halves up, skin side down, side by side in a row, so they look like a rack of ribs.

5. Drizzle some of the Molasses Rum Barbecue Sauce over the bananas, serving the remainder in a bowl on the side. If you want to gild the lily, as it were, sprinkle the chopped toasted pecans on top. You eat the bananas by scooping them out of their skins.

Note: Turbinado sugar (often sold under the brand name Sugar In The Raw) is a partially refined sugar with a coarsely granulated texture. Its brownish color comes from the molasses that has not been completely rinsed off. It's available in most supermarkets.

MOLASSES RUM BARBECUE SAUCE

N o, you're not misreading the recipe. This sauce really does call for a tablespoon of tomato paste. Remember, botanically speaking, tomatoes are fruits, not vegetables. And, the tomato paste helps to both offset the sweetness of the molasses and brown sugar and thicken the sauce. Of course, there's also a more conventional dessert ingredient here, too—chocolate.

MAKES ABOUT 1 CUP

3 tablespoons salted butter

1 ounce unsweetened chocolate, coarsely chopped

3 tablespoons molasses

3 to 4 tablespoons dark brown sugar

3 tablespoons dark rum

1 tablespoon tomato paste

1 teaspoon vanilla extract

$1/2$ teaspoon ground cinnamon

$1/8$ teaspoon ground cloves

1. Place the butter and chocolate in a heavy saucepan over medium heat and cook until melted, stirring with a whisk.

2. Add the molasses, brown sugar, rum, tomato paste, vanilla, cinnamon, and cloves and whisk to mix. Increase the heat to high and cook the sauce until it is thick and richly flavored, 3 to 5 minutes, whisking steadily. Let the sauce cool to room temperature before serving. The sauce can be refrigerated, covered, for several weeks (not that this is the sort of sauce that's often left over). Let it return to room temperature before using.

GRILLED PEACH CARAMEL SUNDAE

METHOD: Direct grilling
ADVANCE PREP: None
SERVES: 4 (or 8 if your peaches are really gigantic)

I'd be surprised if you haven't heard me say it before: There's nothing like grilling for bringing out a fruit's sweetness. The reason is simple: Fruits are loaded with sugar and the high, dry heat of the grill transforms these sugars into a luscious smoky caramel. To reinforce the caramel flavor, these peaches are basted with homemade caramel sauce as they grill and then are topped with toasted almonds. Served sundae style over ice cream, they're pretty hard to beat.

For the caramel sauce:

$1/2$ cup granulated sugar

1 cup heavy (whipping) cream

1 tablespoon dark rum or orange liqueur

$1/2$ teaspoon vanilla extract

For the peaches:

Vanilla or crème brûlée ice cream

4 ripe freestone peaches

$1/4$ cup slivered almonds, toasted (see page 281)

1. Make the caramel sauce: Place the sugar and $1/2$ cup of water in a deep heavy saucepan. Cover the pan, place it over high heat, and let boil for 1 minute. Uncover the pan and continue cooking the sugar mixture until it is a dark golden brown, 5 to 8 minutes. If sugar crystals splash up the side of the pan, brush them down with a natural-bristle pastry brush dipped in water.

2. Remove the pan from the heat and add the heavy cream. Stand back—the mixture will hiss and spatter. Return the pan to the heat and let simmer until the sugar is completely dissolved in the cream, whisking to mix, 2 to 4 minutes. Remove the pan from the heat and let cool to room temperature. Stir in the rum and vanilla. The caramel sauce can be made several hours ahead; it does not need to be refrigerated.

3. Scoop the ice cream into martini glasses or bowls and place them in the freezer.

4. Prepare the peaches: Cut each peach in half through the crease to the pit. Twist the halves in opposite directions; with luck they'll separate (otherwise, you'll need to cut them apart). Using a spoon, pop out and discard the pit.

5. Set up the grill

for direct grilling (see page 31) and preheat to high; use the Mississippi test to check the heat (see page 35).

6. When ready to

cook, brush and oil the grill grate. Using a basting brush, brush the peach halves all over with some of the caramel sauce. Place the peaches on the hot grate and grill until nicely browned, 2 to 4 minutes per side, basting them with a little more caramel sauce. You'll need to use about half the caramel sauce for basting.

TIP: *To toast nuts on the stove, heat a dry cast-iron skillet over medium-high heat until hot, three to five minutes. (It's essential to use a heavy skillet for toasting; do not use a nonstick one.) Add the nuts and cook them until they are fragrant and lightly browned, two to four minutes, shaking the pan or stirring the nuts to ensure even toasting. The minute the nuts are toasted, pour them into a shallow heatproof bowl and let them cool.*

To toast nuts in the oven, preheat it to 350°F. Spread the nuts out in a single layer on a rimmed baking sheet and bake them until golden brown and aromatic, five to ten minutes, stirring the nuts occasionally with a metal spatula to ensure even toasting. Once the nuts have turned golden, immediately transfer them to a heatproof bowl to cool.

7. To serve, place 2 peach halves in each ice cream–filled martini glass. Spoon the remaining caramel sauce on top, sprinkle on the almonds, and serve at once.

GRILLED FRUIT-AND-POUND-CAKE KEBABS

METHOD: Direct grilling
ADVANCE PREP: None
SERVES: 4

Here's a shish kebab you can serve for dessert. The meat and vegetables of traditional kebabs are replaced by pineapple, plums, bananas, and pound cake, while the barbecue sauce becomes a maple syrup and rum glaze. To continue the play on Middle Eastern main-course kebabs, you could serve the fruit kebabs over rice—rice pudding, that is.

For the kebabs:

2 large or 4 small ripe plums

2 bananas

Juice of 1 lemon or lime (optional)

1 small or $^1/_2$ large ripe golden pineapple, peeled, cored, and cut into 1-inch chunks

2 slices (each 1 inch thick) pound cake (see Note), cut into 1-inch cubes

1 bunch fresh mint with large leaves

$^1/_2$ cup granulated sugar

1 teaspoon ground cinnamon

$^1/_2$ teaspoon ground cardamom

For the maple rum glaze:

3 tablespoons maple syrup

3 tablespoons dark rum

3 tablespoons unsalted butter, cut into $^1/_2$-inch pieces

3 tablespoons heavy (whipping) cream

2 tablespoons dark brown sugar

You'll also need:

Eight 8-inch bamboo skewers, preferably flat or 2-pronged

1. Make the kebabs: Cut large plums in quarters or small plums in half, removing and discarding the pits. Peel the bananas and cut them crosswise into 1-inch chunks. Toss the banana chunks with the lemon juice to keep them from discoloring (it is not necessary to do this if you are planning on serving the kebabs right away). Skewer the plum wedges, banana and pineapple chunks, and pound cake cubes on the bamboo skewers, alternating ingredients and placing 3 or 4 mint leaves in between on each skewer.

2. Place the granulated sugar, cinnamon, and cardamom in a bowl and whisk to mix.

3. Make the maple rum glaze: Place the maple syrup, rum, butter, cream, and brown sugar in a heavy saucepan over high heat. Let the glaze come to a boil and cook until thick and syrupy, 3 to 4 minutes, whisking steadily. The kebabs and glaze can be prepared to this stage up to 2 hours ahead.

> **TIPS:** *The best sort of skewers for grilling these kebabs are flat bamboo skewers or small two-prong bamboo skewers, which will keep the fruit from slipping or spinning. Both are available at grill shops and online.*
>
> *Cardamom is an aromatic sweet spice popular in the Middle and Far East. If you don't have any, you can add more cinnamon.*

4. Set up the grill for direct grilling (see page 31) and preheat to high; use the Mississippi test to check the heat (see page 35).

5. When ready to cook, brush and oil the grill grate. Arrange the kebabs on a large plate or tray and lightly brush them on all sides with some of the maple rum glaze. Sprinkle the cinnamon and sugar mixture all over the kebabs. Place the kebabs on the hot grate and grill them until nicely browned on all sides, turning with tongs, 2 to 3 minutes per side, 8 to 12 minutes in all. Baste the kebabs with a little more maple rum glaze as they cook.

6. Transfer the fruit kebabs to a platter or plates. Pour any remaining glaze over them and serve at once.

Note: This is one instance where I recommend using a dense store-bought pound cake (like Sara Lee) rather than a homemade one. A homemade pound cake would tend to fall apart.

THREE RIB MENUS

So now that you've mastered the art of grilling and smoking ribs and side dishes, here are three complete menus to help take you to the next level.

MENU #1 THE SOUTHERNER

Deviled Eggs with Smoked Paprika • Chicken-Fried Pork Ribs • Smoke-Roasted Peach Crisp

SAY THE WORDS *chicken-fried* and any Southerners within earshot will perk up. Especially when it concerns ribs. Mention deviled eggs and smoke-roasted peach crisp, and they'll follow you to the ends of the earth—even north of the Mason-Dixon Line.

DEVILED EGGS
WITH SMOKED PAPRIKA

ADVANCE PREP: None
MAKES: 12 halves; serves 4

S moked cheddar and Spanish *pimentón* (smoked paprika) provide a double blast of smoke flavor in this variation on a Southern classic: deviled eggs. For even more smoke, swap the sliced olives atop the eggs with crumbled bacon.

6 *large eggs*

Ice

2 *ounces smoked cheddar cheese, cut into $^1/_2$-inch dice ($^1/_2$ cup)*

2 *tablespoons mayonnaise (preferably Hellmann's), or more if needed*

2 *teaspoons Dijon mustard*

1 *teaspoon Worcestershire sauce*

1 *teaspoon Tabasco sauce, or more to taste*

Coarse salt (kosher or sea) and freshly ground black pepper

1 *tablespoon finely minced chives*

Pimentón de la Vera (Spanish smoked paprika), for serving

6 *pitted black olives, sliced in half, for garnish*

1. Place the eggs in a large pot and add cold water to cover by 2 inches. Bring to a boil over medium heat. Let the eggs boil for exactly 11 minutes, if you are at sea level. (If you are at a higher altitude, you'll need to let the eggs boil longer.) Pour off the boiling water and fill the pot with cold water and ice.

2. When the eggs are cool enough to handle, tap each egg gently all over on a hard surface. Working under cold running water, remove the egg shells. Slice each egg in half crosswise (not lengthwise) and cut a slice off the rounded ends so the egg halves can stand upright.

3. Using a spoon, scoop out the egg yolks. Place the yolks and smoked cheddar cheese in a food processor, and process until smooth. Work in the mayonnaise, mustard, and Worcestershire and Tabasco sauces; you want a paste that is the consistency of soft ice cream. If the mixture seems too dry, add a little more mayonnaise. Season the egg yolk mixture with salt and pepper to taste; the mixture should be highly seasoned. Add the chives and pulse just to mix.

4. Using a spoon, a pastry bag fitted with a star tip, or a resealable plastic bag with a corner snipped off, fill or pipe the egg yolk mixture into the egg halves. Sprinkle each egg half with smoked paprika and garnish each with an olive slice. Serve the deviled eggs at once or cover them with plastic wrap and refrigerate until serving, up to 48 hours.

CHICKEN-FRIED PORK RIBS

ADVANCE PREP: 2 to 4 hours for smoking the ribs
SERVES: 4

Talk about decadent! Smoky barbecued ribs get dunked in a seasoned beer batter, then deep-fried to crunchy, porky awesomeness. Two icons of Southern cuisine in a single dish. Now that's barbecue!

2 racks baby back pork ribs, smoked at a previous grill
     session (see Note)
2 large eggs
$1/3$ cup beer or milk
1 cup all-purpose flour
Coarse salt (kosher or sea) and freshly ground black pepper
6 cups vegetable oil, for frying

1. Using a sharp knife, cut each rack of ribs into individual ribs.

2. Beat the eggs in a mixing bowl. Beat in the beer and pour the egg mixture into a pie plate.

3. Place the flour in a second pie plate and season it very generously with salt and pepper.

4. Dip each rib in the seasoned flour, then in the egg mixture, coating all sides. Let any excess drip off, then dredge the ribs again in the seasoned flour.

5. Heat the oil in a deep-fat fryer or a large heavy saucepan over medium-high heat until the oil reaches 350°F on a deep fry thermometer.

6. Cook the ribs 3 or 4 at a time in the hot oil, turning with tongs, until they are golden brown on all sides, 4 to 6 minutes. If not serving the ribs immediately, transfer them to a rack set on a rimmed baking sheet lined with paper towels and keep warm in an oven preheated to 250°F.

Note: Use your favorite smoked baby backs for this recipe. Some good options in this book include First-Timer's Ribs on page 54, the Maple-Glazed Ribs on page 70, or the Redeye Ribs on page 98.

SMOKE-ROASTED PEACH CRISP

METHOD: Indirect grilling
ADVANCE PREP: None
SERVES: 6 to 8

hen the guests at your barbecue think things couldn't possibly get any better, pull this bubbling peach crisp hot off the grill in all its

smoky glory. The key is to use fragrant ripe peaches—
ideally from Georgia. If the fruit is hard when you buy it,
let it ripen in a paper bag at room temperature until soft.

> **5 to 6 large ripe peaches (preferably freestone),
>   peeled and sliced**
> **$^3/_4$ cup all-purpose flour**
> **$^1/_2$ cup granulated sugar**
> **1 teaspoon grated lemon zest**
> **2 tablespoons fresh lemon juice**
> **$^1/_2$ cup coarsely crumbled sugar cookies**
> **$^1/_2$ cup firmly packed brown sugar**
> **6 tablespoons ($^3/_4$ stick) cold unsalted butter,
>   cut into 1-inch pieces**
> **Pinch of salt**
> **Peach or vanilla ice cream (optional), for serving**

You'll also need:

> **An 8- to 10-inch round cast-iron skillet; 1 cup wood chips or
>   chunks (preferably apple), soaked for 1 hour in water to
>   cover, then drained**

1. Place the peach slices in a large nonreactive
mixing bowl. Add $^1/_4$ cup of the flour and the granulated
sugar, lemon zest, and lemon juice and stir gently to mix.
Spoon the fruit mixture into the cast-iron skillet.

2. Place the cookie crumbs, brown sugar, and the
remaining $^1/_2$ cup of flour in a food processor fitted with
the metal blade and process to crumbs. Add the butter
and salt, then pulse until the mixture is coarse and crumbly.
Spoon the topping over the fruit filling. The peach crisp
can be prepared up to 4 hours ahead to this stage.

3. Set up the grill for indirect grilling (see page 33)
and preheat to medium-high (400°F). For instructions on
smoking on a gas grill, see page 36.

4. When ready to cook, if cooking on a charcoal grill,
toss half of the wood chips on each mound of coals. Place

the skillet with the peach crisp in the center of the hot grate, away from the heat, and cover the grill. Cook the peach crisp until the filling is bubbling and the topping is browned, about 40 minutes. Serve the peach crisp hot or warm, ideally à la mode.

Variation

For an outrageous twist on this crisp, replace half of the peaches with 1 pint of blueberries.

MENU #2
THE TEX-MEX

Grilled Corn Fritters with Chile-Agave Syrup • Beef Short Ribs with Mexican Mole Coloradito • Grilled Angel Food Cake with Berry Salsa and Tequila Whipped Cream

TEX-MEX: The name says it all. The rough-and-ready beef-centric culture of Texas. And the chile-and-spice-blasted grilling of our neighbor just south of the border. Put them together and you get a meal that roars with flavor, bringing together corn fritters made with grilled corn and with a chile-agave dipping syrup; smoked beef ribs with fragrant Mexican *mole coloradito*; and grilled angel food cake served with a fresh berry "salsa." You'll never think about Tex-Mex food quite the same way.

GRILLED CORN FRITTERS
WITH CHILE-AGAVE SYRUP

ADVANCE PREP: None
MAKES: About 20 fritters; serves 4 to 6

Here's a grilled twist on classic corn fritters. Grilling the corn adds a smoky caramel flavor. Mix the batter as little as possible or your fritters will be heavy. Also, fry only a few at a time so the temperature of the oil stays at a steady 350°F.

For the chile-agave syrup:
1 cup agave syrup (available in natural foods stores) or honey
Pure chile powder, such as ancho

For the fritters:
$3/4$ cup stone-ground cornmeal
$1/3$ cup all-purpose flour
1 teaspoon baking soda
$3/4$ teaspoon coarse salt (kosher or sea)
$3/4$ cup grilled corn kernels (see Note)
1 jalapeño pepper, seeded and minced
2 scallions, both white and green parts, trimmed and minced
3 tablespoons minced fresh cilantro
$1/2$ cup buttermilk or milk, or more as needed
1 large egg, beaten
About 2 cups vegetable oil, for frying

1. Make the chile-agave syrup: Divide the agave syrup among 4 small bowls. Dust the syrup with the chile powder. Set the chile-agave syrup aside until you are ready to serve the fritters.

2. Make the fritters: Place the cornmeal, flour, baking soda, and salt in a mixing bowl and whisk to mix. Stir in the corn kernels, jalapeño, scallions, and cilantro. Make a well in the center of the cornmeal mixture. Add the buttermilk and egg to the well. Starting in the center and working outward, whisk the ingredients just to mix. Do not overwhisk or the fritters will be gummy.

3. Just before serving, pour oil to a depth of at least 1 inch in a frying pan or electric skillet and heat it to 350°F on a deep fry thermometer. Working in batches so as not to crowd the pan, use 2 spoons to drop 1-inch balls of batter into the hot oil. Cook the fritters, turning them with a slotted spoon or wire skimmer, until golden brown and cooked through, 2 to 3 minutes in all. Transfer the fritters to paper towels to drain. Serve the fritters with the chile-agave syrup for dipping.

Note: This is a great use for a leftover ear or 2 of grilled corn. But if you want to grill the corn fresh, husk the corn and remove all the silk. Direct grill the corn over high heat, turning frequently with tongs, until the kernels are golden brown, 8 to 12 minutes in all. Let the corn cool slightly. Then cut the kernels off the grilled corn. The easiest way to do this is to place an ear of corn flat on a cutting board and slice the kernels off the cob using broad strokes of a chef's knife held parallel to the ear. You'll need 1 to 2 ears of corn to obtain ¾ cup.

BEEF SHORT RIBS
WITH MEXICAN MOLE COLORADITO

METHOD: Indirect grilling, followed by direct grilling
ADVANCE PREP: 2 to 4 hours for marinating the ribs (optional)
SERVES: 4 to 6

Y ou're probably familiar with *mole poblano*— Mexico's thick chocolate-chile sauce. What you may not realize is that there are many different moles in Mexico, including this fruity aromatic mole (pronounced MO-lay). The plantain is a cousin of the banana. For maximum sweetness, let it ripen at room temperature until the skin is black.

For the ribs:

3 to 4 pounds bone-in beef short ribs

4 cloves garlic, minced

4 whole bay leaves

1 tablespoon coarse salt (kosher or sea)

1 tablespoon freshly ground black pepper

1 tablespoon dried oregano (preferably Mexican)

1 to 2 tablespoons extra-virgin olive oil

For the *coloradito* sauce:

7 guajillo chiles

1 ancho chile

2 tablespoons vegetable oil

1 small onion, coarsely chopped (about $3/4$ cup)

2 cloves garlic, coarsely chopped

$1/2$ teaspoon ground cumin

1 cinnamon stick (about $2^1/2$ inches)

1 whole bay leaf

1 clove

2 tablespoons sesame seeds

1 teaspoon dried oregano

1 teaspoon coriander seeds

$1/2$ ripe plantain, peeled and diced (about $1/2$ cup)

$1/3$ cup yellow raisins

$1/4$ cup slivered almonds

$1/2$ cup crushed tomatoes with their juices

1 ounce unsweetened chocolate, coarsely chopped

2 teaspoons brown sugar, or more to taste

2 teaspoons red wine vinegar, or more to taste

1 teaspoon coarse salt (kosher or sea), or more to taste

$1/2$ to 1 cup beef broth or water

You'll also need:

3 cups wood chips or chunks (preferably oak, hickory, or apple), soaked for 1 hour in water to cover, then drained

1. Prepare the ribs: Place the ribs in a large mixing bowl and sprinkle the garlic, 4 bay leaves, 1 tablespoon of salt, pepper, and 1 tablespoon of oregano over them. Add the olive oil and turn the ribs to coat evenly. You can cook the ribs right away but they'll have even more flavor if you let them marinate, covered, in the refrigerator for 2 to 4 hours.

2. Prepare the *coloradito* sauce: Tear open the guajillo and ancho chiles and remove the stems and seeds. Place the chiles in a bowl, add 2 cups of warm water (enough water to cover the chiles), and let the chiles soak until softened, about 15 minutes.

3. Heat the vegetable oil in a large saucepan over medium-high heat. Add the onion and garlic and cook until translucent but not brown, stirring with a wooden spoon, about 3 minutes. Add the cumin and cook until fragrant, about 1 minute.

4. Drain the chiles, setting aside the soaking liquid, and add them to the onion mixture. Cook the mixture until fragrant, about 2 minutes. Add the chile soaking liquid, cinnamon stick, 1 bay leaf, clove, sesame seeds, 1 teaspoon of oregano, coriander seeds, plantain, raisins, almonds, tomatoes, chocolate, brown sugar, wine vinegar, and salt. Let the mixture simmer gently until the plantains and raisins are soft, about 20 minutes, stirring occasionally. Remove the cinnamon stick and bay leaf. Transfer the sauce to a blender and puree until smooth. Return the *coloradito* sauce to the saucepan.

5. Starting with ½ cup, add enough beef broth to obtain a thick but pourable *coloradito* sauce. Taste for seasoning, adding more salt, brown sugar, and/or vinegar as necessary; the sauce should be highly seasoned and a little sweet with just a faint hint of tartness. Keep warm. The *coloradito* sauce can be prepared several hours or even a day ahead and reheated.

6. Set up the grill for indirect grilling (see page 33) and preheat to medium-low (275° to 300°F). Place a large drip pan in the center of the grill under the grate. (For instructions on smoking on a gas grill, see page 36.)

7. When ready to cook, brush and oil the grill grate. Place the ribs bone side down in the center of the grate over the drip pan and away from the heat. If cooking on a charcoal grill, toss ¾ cup of the wood chips on each mound of coals. Cover the grill and cook the ribs until cooked through and very tender, 3 to 4 hours. When the ribs are done, the meat will have shrunk back from the ends of the bones by about ¼ inch. If using a charcoal grill, toss the remaining 1½ cups of wood chips on the coals after 1 hour and replenish the coals as needed.

8. Just before serving, generously brush the short ribs all over with some of the *mole coloradito* and move them directly over the fire. Grill until the sauce is sizzling, 1 to 2 minutes per side, turning with tongs. Transfer the ribs to a platter or plates and spoon the remaining *mole coloradito* on top.

Variation:

To cook the Beef Short Ribs with Mexican Mole Coloradito in a smoker: Set up and light the smoker according to the manufacturer's instructions (for more on smokers, see page 43) and preheat to low (250°F). Place the ribs in the smoker bone side down and smoke until cooked through, 4 to 5 hours. You'll need to replenish the wood chips or chunks after each of the first 3 hours of smoking and to replenish the coals every hour.

GRILLED ANGEL FOOD CAKE
WITH BERRY SALSA AND TEQUILA WHIPPED CREAM

METHOD: Direct grilling
ADVANCE PREP: None
SERVES: 4 to 6

I f you can cook bruschetta on the grill, why not cake? The fire adds a smoke flavor not usually associated with angel food cake. In keeping with the Tex-Mex theme, I've topped the grilled cake with a fresh berry salsa. (If you've never had jalapeño chiles for dessert, you're in for a revelation.) A tip o' the hat to Barbecue University alumna Lynn Blair, who inspired this recipe.

For the berry salsa:

4 cups mixed fresh berries, such as blueberries, raspberries, blackberries, and/or quartered strawberries

3 tablespoons thinly slivered fresh mint

1 slice ($1/4$ inch thick) candied or peeled fresh ginger, minced

1 to 2 jalapeño peppers, seeded and minced

3 tablespoons freshly squeezed lime juice, or more to taste

2 tablespoons granulated sugar, or more to taste

For the tequila whipped cream (optional):

1 cup heavy (whipping) cream

3 tablespoons confectioners' sugar or agave syrup

1 tablespoon tequila

$1/2$ teaspoon ground cinnamon

For the cake:

8 to 12 slices ($3/4$ inch thick) angel food cake

2 tablespoons butter, melted, or 2 tablespoons vegetable oil

1. Make the berry salsa: Place the berries, mint, ginger, jalapeño(s), lime juice, and granulated sugar in a mixing bowl but do not mix. The salsa can be prepared to this stage up to 2 hours ahead and refrigerated.

2. Make the tequila whipped cream, if using: Beat the cream to soft peaks in a chilled bowl, using an electric mixer or whisk. Whisk in the confectioners' sugar, tequila, and cinnamon and beat until firm. The tequila whipped cream can be prepared up to 2 hours ahead and refrigerated, covered.

3. Grill the angel food cake: Set up the grill for direct grilling (see page 31) and preheat to medium-high; use the Mississippi test to check the heat (see page 35).

4. When ready to cook, brush and oil the grill grate. Lightly brush the cake slices on both sides with the melted butter. Arrange the slices of cake on the grill, at a diagonal to the bars of the grate, and grill until lightly browned on both sides, 1 to 2 minutes per side, turning with a spatula. (If you're feeling ambitious, give each slice of cake a quarter turn halfway through to create an attractive crosshatch of grill marks.) Transfer the grilled cake slices to a platter or plates.

5. Toss the berry salsa to mix. Taste for sweetness, adding more granulated sugar and/or lime juice as necessary. Spoon the salsa over the grilled cake. Top each portion with a dollop of tequila whipped cream, if using, and serve at once. Serve any extra whipped cream on the side.

MENU #3
THE CALIFORNIAN

Grilled Artichoke Dip with Grilled Bread
• Sweet-and-Sour Wood-Grilled Country-
Style Ribs • Grilled Meyer Lemon Pie

SMOKING MAY RULE IN TEXAS and the Deep South, but
in California the grill is king: wood-grilled artichokes
from Castroville. Grilled country-style ribs (more of
a pork chop than a rib, really) with a Los Angeles
balsamic vinegar barbecue sauce. Grilled Meyer
lemon meringue pie. Well, you get the idea. So fire
it up, and if you can grill over oak logs or oak chips,
so much the better.

GRILLED ARTICHOKE DIP
WITH GRILLED BREAD

METHOD: Direct grilling
ADVANCE PREP: None
SERVES: 4

R eaders of my books will be no strangers to my love
for artichokes slow grilled over a wood fire (check
out the recipes in *Barbecue! Bible* and *BBQ USA*).
I recently discovered terrific and terrifically convenient

new ready-to-eat grilled artichokes from Monterey Farms in California. Chances are you can find it at your local supermarket or natural foods store (check www .montereyfarmsartichokes.com for a source near you). Otherwise, grill artichokes following one of the recipes in the aforementioned books.

For the artichoke dip:

1 package (6 ounces) grilled artichoke hearts, preferably Monterey Farms ArtiHearts, coarsely chopped

$1/2$ cup sour cream

$1/4$ cup mayonnaise (preferably Hellmann's)

1 teaspoon finely grated fresh lemon zest

2 teaspoons fresh lemon juice

Coarse salt (kosher or sea) and freshly ground black pepper

For the bread:

1 baguette (about 20 inches long), sliced on the diagonal into $1/2$-inch slices

$1/4$ cup best quality extra-virgin olive oil

Coarse salt (kosher or sea) and freshly ground black pepper

$1/2$ cup freshly finely grated Parmigiano-Reggiano (optional)

1. Make the artichoke dip: Place the artichoke hearts, sour cream, mayonnaise, lemon zest, and lemon juice in a mixing bowl and stir to mix. Season the artichoke mixture with salt and pepper to taste, then transfer it to a serving bowl, cover, and refrigerate until serving. The dip can be made several hours ahead.

2. Grill the bread: Just before serving, set up the grill for direct grilling (see page 31) and preheat to medium-high; use the Mississippi test to check the heat (see page 35).

3. When ready to cook, lightly brush each slice of bread on both sides with olive oil and season with salt and pepper to taste.

4. Arrange the slices of bread directly on the hot grill grate and grill, turning with tongs, until nicely browned, 2 to 4 minutes per side. Do not take your eyes off the bread for a second; grilled bread burns very easily. Just before removing the slices of bread from the grill, sprinkle them with the Parmigiano-Reggiano, if using. Transfer the grilled bread to a bread basket and serve with the artichoke dip.

SWEET-AND-SOUR WOOD-GRILLED COUNTRY-STYLE RIBS

METHOD: Direct grilling
ADVANCE PREP: None
SERVES: 4

Country-style pork ribs are not true ribs; they come from the pork shoulder in front of the baby backs. They have the genial properties of being both meaty and lean and, like pork chops, can be grilled using the direct method. The sweet-sour balsamic vinegar barbecue sauce here was inspired by my pals Jon Shook and Vinny Dotolo, the owners of Animal restaurant in Los Angeles.

For the balsamic barbecue sauce:

1 cup balsamic vinegar, or more to taste

1 cup ketchup

$1/2$ can (6 ounces) of your favorite beer

$1/4$ cup honey

3 tablespoons grainy mustard

1 tablespoon molasses

$1^1/2$ teaspoons Worcestershire sauce

1 teaspoon Tabasco sauce, or more to taste

$1/4$ cup firmly packed dark brown sugar, or more to taste

$1/2$ red onion, diced (about $3/4$ cup)

1 large clove garlic, minced

1 slice of smoky bacon, like Nueske's (optional)

Coarse salt (kosher or sea)

For the ribs:

2 pounds country-style pork ribs (see Notes)

¹/₄ cup extra-virgin olive oil

Coarse salt (kosher or sea) and cracked black pepper

You'll also need:

*1¹/₂ cups wood chips or chunks (optional; preferably oak),
soaked for 1 hour in water to cover, then drained*

1. Make the balsamic barbecue sauce: Place the
balsamic vinegar in a large heavy nonreactive saucepan
and let come to a boil over medium-high heat. Let the
vinegar boil until reduced by about one third. Add the
ketchup, beer, honey, mustard, molasses, Worcestershire
and Tabasco sauces, brown sugar, onion, garlic, bacon,
if using, and ¹/₄ cup of water. Let the mixture return to
a boil, then reduce the heat and cook the sauce at the
barest simmer until thick and richly flavored, 30 to 40
minutes. If the sauce starts to thicken too much, add a
little more water.

2. Taste the sauce for seasoning, adding more
balsamic vinegar, Tabasco sauce, and/or brown sugar as
necessary and salt to taste. The sauce should be highly
seasoned. Remove and discard the bacon. For a smoother
sauce, you can strain it before serving (I don't bother).

3. Prepare the ribs: Rub the ribs on all sides with the
olive oil and season them with salt and pepper to taste.

4. Set up the grill for direct grilling (see page 31) and
preheat to high; use the Mississippi test to check the heat
(see page 35). (For instructions on grilling with wood on a
gas grill, see Notes.)

5. When ready to cook, brush and oil the grill grate.
Toss the wood chips, if using, on the coals. Arrange the
country-style ribs on the grill, at a diagonal to the bars
of the grate, and grill until nicely browned and cooked
through, 3 to 5 minutes per side, giving each rib a quarter

turn half way through to create an attractive crosshatch of grill marks. During the last 2 minutes of grilling, generously brush the ribs on all sides with the balsamic barbecue sauce and cook until the sauce sizzles and browns. Transfer the ribs to a platter or plates and serve with the remaining balsamic barbecue sauce on the side.

Notes: Country-style ribs come bone-in and boneless. Either way you'll need about 2 pounds.

To grill with wood chips or chunks on a gas grill, place the wood chips or chunks in the smoker box, if the grill has one. Or, make a smoker pouch by wrapping the wood in heavy-duty aluminum foil, poking holes in the top of the pouch, and placing it under the grate directly over one of the burners.

GRILLED MEYER LEMON PIE

METHOD: Direct grilling, followed by indirect grilling
ADVANCE PREP: None
SERVES: 8

My wife, Barbara, is addicted to Meyer lemons, those bright canary yellow fruits with less acidity than conventional lemons and an amazing herbal-floral aroma and flavor. (Note to husbands and boyfriends everywhere—if your wife is addicted to anything, keep plenty of it on hand.) You can find Meyer lemons at specialty food markets and at a growing number of supermarkets. Yes, it's OK to use conventional lemons if you can't find Meyers. Grilling the lemons adds a subtle smoke flavor that will take you by surprise.

For the lemons:

6 Meyer lemons

$^1/_4$ cup granulated sugar in a shallow bowl

For the crust and filling:

$1^{1}/_{2}$ cups cinnamon graham cracker crumbs

$^{1}/_{3}$ cup unsalted butter, melted

$^{1}/_{4}$ cup granulated sugar

4 egg yolks

1 can (14 ounces) sweetened condensed milk

For the meringue:

4 egg whites

$^{1}/_{2}$ teaspoon cream of tartar

1 cup granulated sugar

1. Prepare the lemons: Finely grate 2 teaspoons of lemon zest from the lemons and set aside. Cut each lemon in half crosswise and remove the seeds with a fork.

2. Set up the grill for direct grilling (see page 31) and preheat to high; use the Mississippi test to check the heat (see page 35).

3. When ready to cook, brush and oil the grill grate. Dip each lemon half in the $^{1}/_{4}$ cup of sugar, shaking off the excess. Grill the lemons cut side down until golden brown, 3 to 5 minutes. Transfer the lemons to a plate and let them cool, then juice the lemons on a juicer. Set the lemon juice aside.

4. Make the crust and filling: Set up the grill for indirect grilling (see page 33) and preheat to medium (350°F).

5. Combine the graham cracker crumbs and butter in a mixing bowl and mix to form a crumbly dough. Press the mixture into an 8-inch pie pan.

6. When ready to cook the crust, place the pie pan in the center of the grate away from the heat. Cover the grill and cook the crust until lightly browned, 5 to 8 minutes. Transfer the crust to a heatproof surface; leave the fire burning.

7. Make the filling by placing the ¼ cup of sugar and the egg yolks in a mixing bowl and beating them with an electric mixer until creamy, about 5 minutes. Beat in the sweetened condensed milk, 1 teaspoon of the lemon zest, and the grilled lemon juice. Pour the lemon filling into the cooked pie crust.

8. When ready to cook the filling, place the filled crust in the center of the grate away from the heat. Cover the grill and cook until the filling is set (a toothpick inserted in the center will come out clean), 20 to 30 minutes.

9. Make the meringue: Increase the temperature of the grill to high.

10. Place the egg whites and cream of tartar in a mixing bowl and beat until soft peaks form, about 5 minutes. Gradually add the 1 cup of sugar, beating the whites until stiff, about 8 minutes (do not overbeat or the whites will collapse). Add the remaining 1 teaspoon of lemon zest and beat for 10 seconds. Spread or pipe the meringue over the pie filling.

11. When ready to cook the meringue, place the pie in the center of the grate away from the heat. Cover the grill and cook the pie until the meringue is golden brown, 5 to 10 minutes. Let the pie cool to room temperature, then cut it into wedges for serving. In the unlikely event you have leftovers, the pie can be refrigerated, covered, for up to 24 hours.

Variation
How to bake the crust and pie: Preheat the oven to 350°F. Make the crust as described in Step 5 and bake it until lightly browned, 5 to 8 minutes. Make the filling as described in Step 7, then bake it until set, 20 to 30 minutes. Increase the oven temperature to 400°F. Make the meringue as described in Step 10 and bake the pie until the meringue is golden brown, 5 to 10 minutes. Let the pie cool to room temperature before serving.

CONVERSION TABLES

Weight Conversions

U.S.	METRIC		U.S.	METRIC
1/2 oz	15 g		7 oz	200 g
1 oz	30 g		8 oz	250 g
1 1/2 oz	45 g		9 oz	275 g
2 oz	60 g		10 oz	300 g
2 1/2 oz	75 g		11 oz	325 g
3 oz	90 g		12 oz	350 g
3 1/2 oz	100 g		13 oz	375 g
4 oz	125 g		14 oz	400 g
5 oz	150 g		15 oz	450 g
6 oz	175 g		1 lb	500 g

Liquid Conversions

U.S.	IMPERIAL	METRIC
2 tbs.	1 fl oz	30 ml
3 tbs.	1 1/2 fl oz	45 ml
1/4 cup	2 fl oz	60 ml
1/3 cup	2 1/2 fl oz	75 ml
1/3 cup + 1 tbs.	3 fl oz	90 ml
1/3 cup + 2 tbs.	3 1/2 fl oz	100 ml
1/2 cup	4 fl oz	125 ml
2/3 cup	5 fl oz	150 ml
3/4 cup	6 fl oz	175 ml
3/4 cup + 2 tbs.	7 fl oz	200 ml
1 cup	8 fl oz	250 ml
1 cup + 2 tbs.	9 fl oz	275 ml
1 1/4 cups	10 fl oz	300 ml
1 1/3 cups	11 fl oz	325 ml
1 1/2 cups	12 fl oz	350 ml
1 2/3 cups	13 fl oz	375 ml
1 3/4 cups	14 fl oz	400 ml
1 3/4 cups + 2 tbs.	15 fl oz	450 ml
2 cups (1 pint)	16 fl oz	500 ml
2 1/2 cups	20 fl oz (1 pint)	600 ml
3 3/4 cups	1 1/2 pints	900 ml
4 cups	1 3/4 pints	1 liter

Oven Temperatures

F	GAS MARK	C		F	GAS MARK	C
250	1/2	120		400	6	200
275	1	140		425	7	220
300	2	150		450	8	230
325	3	160		475	9	240
350	4	180		500	10	260
375	5	190				

Note: Reduce the temperature by 20°C (68°F) for fan-assisted ovens.

Please note that all conversions are approximate but close enough to be useful when converting from one system to another.

MAIL-ORDER SOURCES

Ingredients

Arrowhead Specialty Meats
1200 Taney Street
North Kansas City, MO 64116
(816) 889-9333
www.gamemeat.com
Berkshire pork; Kobe-style
   beef ribs

Blue Ribbon Meats
3316 West 67th Place
Cleveland, OH 44102
(800) 262-0395
www.blueribbonfoodservice
   .com

British Food Centre
Kirkwood Plaza
1614 West Campbell Avenue
Campbell, CA 95008
(888) 747-5522
www.buybritish.net
D & G Old Jamaica ginger beer
   and British foods

Chaucer's Cellars
Bargetto Winery
3535 North Main Street
Soquel, CA 95073
(800) 422-7438
www.chaucerswine.com
Mead

El Mercado Latino
1514 Pike Place, Suite 6
Seattle, WA 98101
(206) 223-9374
www.LatinMerchant.com
Latin foods, including guava
   paste

Geneva Meats & Processing
   Inc.
75 East Main Street
P.O. Box 266
Geneva, MN 56035
(507) 256-7214
www.genevameats
   processinginc.com

ImportFood.com
P.O. Box 2054
Issaquah, WA 98027
(888) 618-8424
www.importfood.com
Thai foods and sauces,
   including chile garlic sauce
   and sweet garlic sauce

Jamaica Groceries & Spices
9587 SW 160th Street
Miami, FL 33157
(305) 252-1197
www.jamaica.nv.switchboard
   .com
Caribbean ingredients

Jamison Farm
171 Jamison Lane
Latrobe, PA 15650
(800) 237-5262
www.jamisonfarm.com
Artisanal lamb ribs

Jolly Grub
100 State Route 101A Unit C
Amherst, NH 03031
(866) 702-4782
www.jollygrub.com
English jams and marmalades,
   including ginger marmalade

Kalustyan's
123 Lexington Avenue
New York, NY 10016
(212) 685-3451
www.kalustyans.com
Spices and condiments from
   Asia, Africa, and the Middle
   East

koaMart.com
905 E. 8th St. #12
Los Angeles, CA 90021
www.koamart.com
Korean bean and pepper
   pastes

Lobel's
1096 Madison Avenue
New York, NY 10028
(877) 783-4512
www.lobels.com
Kurobuta pork and "true"
pork baby backs; wagyu-
style beef; veal ribs, by
special order

Merchant du Vin Corp.
18200 Olympic Avenue South
Tukwila, WA 98188
(253) 656-0320
www.merchantduvin.com
Importers of Belgian kriek
lambic beer

Mister Brisket
2156 South Taylor Road
Cleveland Heights, OH 44118
(877) 274-7538
www.misterbrisket.com
Pork, beef, and veal ribs,
including kalbi kui cut,
by special order

Pendery's
1221 Manufacturing Street
Dallas, TX 75207
(800) 533-1870
www.penderys.com
Spices and chile powders

Snake River Farms
1555 Shoreline Drive, 3rd floor
Boise, ID 83702
(877) 736-0193
www.snakeriverfarms.com
Kurobuta pork and Kobe-style
beef

Steven Raichlen's Best of
Barbecue line of grilling
tools and accessories, barbecue
rubs and sauces, plus wood chip
blends, wine barrel staves, wine
barrel chunks for smoking:
www.barbecuebible.com
www.bestofbarbecue.com

INDEX